£8.95

COMPUTER SCIENCE TEXTS

COMPUTER SCIENCE TEXTS

A First Course in Computability

V. J. RAYWARD-SMITH

MA, PhD
Senior Lecturer in Computing
University of East Anglia
Norwich NR4 7TJ, UK

BLACKWELL SCIENTIFIC PUBLICATIONS

OXFORD LONDON EDINBURGH

BOSTON PALO ALTO MELBOURNE

© 1986 by
Blackwell Scientific Publications
Editorial Offices:
Osney Mead, Oxford, OX2 0EL
8 John Street, London, WC1N 2ES
23 Ainslie Place, Edinburgh, EH3 6AJ
52 Beacon Street, Boston
    Massachusetts 02108, USA
667 Lytton Avenue, Palo Alto
    California 94301, USA
107 Barry Street, Carlton
    Victoria 3053, Australia

First published 1986

Set by Thomson Press (India) Ltd,
New Delhi, and printed and bound in
Great Britain

Distributed in North America by
Computer Science Press Inc., 1803 Research
Blvd, Rockville, Maryland 20850, USA

British Library
Cataloguing in Publication Data

Rayward-Smith, V. J.
    The first course in computability.—
    (Computer science texts)
    1 Electronic data processing
    I Title   II. Series
001.64   QA76

ISBN 0–632–01307–9

Contents

Preface

Much of computer science is centred around the design, analysis and efficient implementation of algorithms to perform various tasks. This book is designed to answer the most fundamental questions that arise from this type of activity—questions such as 'What is a computer capable of?', and given a problem, 'Is there any algorithm to solve it?', and if so, 'Is there an efficient algorithm?' These and similar questions are of such fundamental importance that they must be answered carefully and rigorously.

The rigour in this text is provided by the well-tried discipline of mathematical reasoning. Some computer scientists may find this daunting but there is really little alternative. This text has been written so that a computer scientist in his second or third year should be able to follow all of the arguments. Even a first-year student should reap considerable benefit from reading this material. The concept of solvability is a key idea in computing and the formulation of the concept of unsolvability provides an exciting insight. Once efficiency considerations are introduced the separation of solvable problems into tractable and intractable is a natural next step. The work on intractability has only been developed during the last 15 years but is nevertheless not particularly difficult.

Theoretical computer scientists tend to assume their audience are all familiar with Turing machines. These machines provide a simple computational model which enables us to discover fundamental results. They are widely used and have been widely adopted as the standard model in computability theory. This is why we have used them in this text. Many other equivalent devices would have sufficed; indeed, their use could have simplified some of the presentation. However, tradition in the subject should be respected and so long as the majority of published results are presented in terms of Turing machines, it is important that computer scientists understand their formulation.

Computability is often taught to mathematicians, and rightly so! The use of functions is central to mathematics and a full understanding of them would appear a basic requirement of any honours degree. It must be admitted, however, that many university mathematics departments relegate computability to a final year option. Maybe this book will convince university teachers that the material can be taught successfully earlier in the course and be understood by their students.

A First Course in Computability is one of three texts which together present the theoretical foundation of computing at an undergraduate level. The other two books in the series are *A First Course in Formal Language Theory* by V. J. Rayward-Smith, and *A First Course in Formal Logic and its Applications in Computer Science* by R. D. Dowsing, V. J. Rayward-Smith and C. D. Walter. All three are published by Blackwell Scientific Publications and it is hoped thereby to provide the academic computing community with a thorough presentation of computing theory. Most theory books are more suitable for advanced undergraduate and postgraduate study. It is hoped that this new series will correct this imbalance and restore theory to its rightful place, central to undergraduate computing degrees.

I would like to express my thanks to my colleagues at the University of East Anglia, Norwich, for their encouragement during the preparation of this text. In particular, I would like to thank Dr G. D. Smith for his comments on earlier drafts. I was particularly fortunate in having an able and co-operative typist, Ms Carol Bracken, without whom the manuscript would have remained an untidy pile of pencilled notes. Finally, I am grateful to Mr Hugh Prior, also of the University of East Anglia, who developed the Pascal program listed in the Appendix as a Turing Simulator.

V. J. Rayward-Smith

Introduction

A naive user of a computer can view it as a 'black box' into which he feeds his data as input and from which he receives output. He does not understand programming; someone else has programmed the machine for him. The computer, as far as this user is concerned, merely takes his input (some string of symbols, x, say) and computes some output. This output, itself a string, generally depends upon x and can thus be regarded as a function of x, $f(x)$. The exact nature of the function, f, will depend upon the program; a different program will compute a different function. (See Fig. 0.1.)

In this book, we will formulate a model for the workings of the 'black box' and its programs. Then we can study all valid programs and the functions they compute. We want our model to be simple enough for easy analysis, yet powerful enough to compute all the functions which, from experience, we expect to be computable—such functions are said to be 'effectively computable'. A formal definition of 'effectively computable' is difficult to obtain because the term is used for a conceptual class of functions, i.e. that class of functions for which a computer scientist would expect to be able to write programs. For example, the function *square*, which takes as input a representation of an integer (say in decimal notation) and delivers a representation of that same integer multiplied by itself, is effectively computable. But to what extent is *square* computable in practice? No real world computer can compute $square(x)$ for all integer representations, x. The reason is simple; any real world computer has finite store and thus cannot compute $square(x)$ if x is so large that there is not enough store. Yet, we know that given any x, we can compute $square(x)$ if only we have a large enough machine. We should not let limits on storage restrict our definition of computability. Thus we can think of an effectively computable function as any function computable on some machine with no limits on

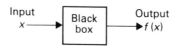

Fig. 0.1. The naive of a computer.

storage. It follows that if our model for the 'black box' is to be able to compute the effectively computable functions, then it must itself be equipped with a limitless store. Then, in any finite computation, only a finite amount of store will be used but there will be no *a priori* limit.

The model for the 'black box' that we will use is that which was proposed by one of the pioneers in this field, Alan Turing (1936). Several alternatives have been proposed, e.g. Post machines (Post, 1936), and unlimited register ideal machines (URIMs) (Shepherdson & Sturgis, 1963). *Church's thesis*, originally hypothesized in 1936 (Church, 1936a) and arising from work by Gödel (1931) and Kleene (1936), can be expressed as the statement that 'every effectively computable function is Turing comput-able, i.e. is computable on a Turing machine'. Without a rigorous and formal definition of effectively computable, this is an impossible statement to prove formally. However, all the available evidence supports the truth of this hypothesis. Firstly, no one has been able to produce an intuitively computable function that is not Turing computable. Also, other machines designed as a model for a general computing device such as Post machines and URIMs compute precisely the Turing computable functions. Finally, an attempt to produce a generating scheme for all the effectively comput-able functions defines precisely the Turing computable functions (see Chapter 5). So, whenever one comes across the phrase 'Turing computable', one can infer 'effectively computable', and vice versa.

The Turing machine (TM) is equipped with limitless store which can be viewed as a *tape* divided into a number of locations indexed $\ldots -2, -1, 0, 1, 2, \ldots$ as in Fig. 0.2. In each location, we can write a symbol from some prescribed alphabet. Initially the tape will be blank, i.e. each location will hold the blank symbol, denoted by $\wedge$. The input $x = x_1 x_2 \ldots x_n$ will then be written one symbol at a time in locations $1, 2, \ldots, n$.

The TM has a *head* which moves backwards and forwards across the tape scanning the locations and inserting and deleting symbols. The tape head can be in any one of a finite number of *states*, Q. Initially, the tape

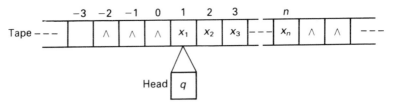

Fig. 0.2. The initial configuration of a Turing machine with input $x = x_1 x_2 \ldots x_n$.

head will be in a prescribed *initial state*, $q_0 \in Q$, and will scan location one. The machine will only halt if the tape head reaches any one of a number of *final states*.

At any time during the computation, the head will then be in some state, q_k, and will be reading some symbol on the tape (called the *current tape symbol*). The next step of the TM depends upon these values. If the machine does not halt, i.e. if q_k is not a final state, the tape head can overwrite the current tape symbol and then possibly move to the adjacent location to the left or to the right. At the same time, the state, q_k, may or may not change. If the machine halts, then its output is taken to be the symbols in locations $1, 2, \ldots, m$ where $m + 1$ is the first location greater than 0 which contains a blank symbol.

The precise action to be taken at each step of a computation is defined by the *Turing machine program*. In common with most authors, we will use the phrase 'Turing machine' not only to include the actual machine but also to include a prescribed program. Thus one Turing machine differs from another when its program differs. Any step of a TM program is given as an action depending upon the state of the head and the current tape symbol. These actions are tabulated as a list of 5-tuples of the form given in Fig. 0.3.

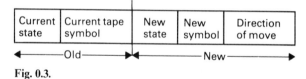

Fig. 0.3.

This list of 5-tuples is the TM program. Hopefully, for any current state which is not a final state and for any current tape symbol likely to arise when the TM is in that state, there will be just one relevant 5-tuple in the list and this will define the new state of the head, the symbol to replace the current tape symbol and the direction in which the head must move (L for left, R for right, 0 for staying put). If a TM program exhibits this uniqueness property, it is said to be *deterministic*.

As an example, let us construct a very simple Turing machine to compute the following. We assume the input is a string, x, comprising a positive number of 1s. Our TM must then result in an output of 1 if the number of 1s in x is even but otherwise it must give an output of 0. Thus this TM computes the *even* function where

$$even(x) = \begin{cases} 1 & \text{if } x \text{ contains an even number of 1s,} \\ 0 & \text{otherwise.} \end{cases}$$

We first describe an algorithm in a 'structured English' code and then we will develop the TM program from this. The essential idea is first to scan the input from left to right and remember whether an even or odd number of 1s has been scanned by using two states: q_0 for even and q_1 for odd. Eventually, we come across a blank symbol. If we are in state q_0, the number of 1s was even and if in state q_1, the number was odd. Thus, we start the TM with our input in locations $1, 2, \ldots$ and in state q_0 scanning location 1. Using $\{\ldots\}$ to enclose comments, the first stage of the algorithm is:

while current-tape-symbol $= 1$ *do*

        if state $= q_0$ *then* change to state q_1; move right

        else {state $= q_1$} change to state q_0; move right

        endif

endwhile;

{current-tape-symbol $= \wedge$} move left

We now want to delete all the 1s on the tape and write the appropriate output in location 1. To achieve this, we now move left deleting all the 1s until we meet a $\wedge$. This must be in location 0. We then move right in preparation for the third stage in which we write the output in location 1. Thus the second stage of the algorithm is:

while current-tape-symbol $= 1$ *do*

        replace symbol by $\wedge$; move left

endwhile;

        {current-tape-symbol $= \wedge$} move right

The tape head is now at location 1 and we simply write 1 if the current state is q_0 and 0 if the current state is q_1. At the same time, we change state to the halt state, q_2. Hence the final stage of the algorithm is:

{current-tape-symbol $= \wedge$}

if state $= q_0$ *then* change to state q_2; replace symbol by 1

else {state $= q_1$} change to state q_2; replace symbol by 0

endif

The first stage of the algorithm can be simply transcribed to the following list of 5-tuples;

        $(q_0, 1, q_1, 1, R)$

        $(q_1, 1, q_0, 1, R)$

        $(q_0, \wedge, q_0, \wedge, L)$

        $(q_1, \wedge, q_1, \wedge, L)$

The second stage transcribes to

$(q_0, 1, q_0, \wedge, L)$
$(q_1, 1, q_1, \wedge, L)$
$(q_0, \wedge, q_0, \wedge, R)$
$(q_1, \wedge, q_1, \wedge, R)$

and the third stage to

$(q_0, \wedge, q_2, 1, 0)$
$(q_1, \wedge, q_2, 0, 0)$

We cannot, however, simply list all the 5-tuples of the three stages if we wish our TM to be deterministic and operate as we intend. We overcome this problem by the introduction of new states. We keep q_0, q_1 for the first stage, but use q_0', q_1' for q_0, q_1 in the second stage, and q_0'', q_1'' for q_0, q_1 in the third stage. Our final program is thus

$(q_0, 1, q_1, 1, R)$
$(q_1, 1, q_0, 1, R)$
$(q_0, \wedge, q_0', \wedge, L)$
$(q_1, \wedge, q_1', \wedge, L)$
$(q_0', 1, q_0', \wedge, L)$
$(q_1', 1, q_1', \wedge, L)$
$(q_0', \wedge, q_0'', \wedge, R)$
$(q_1', \wedge, q_1'', \wedge, R)$
$(q_0'', \wedge, q_2, 1, 0)$
$(q_1'', \wedge, q_2, 0, 0)$

where q_0 is the initial state and q_2 is the only final state. We have thus shown that *even* is a Turing computable function. In Fig. 0.4, we illustrate the various configurations of the example TM as it processes as input of $x = 111$.

We can also represent a TM program diagrammatically using a labelled directed graph. We have nodes for each state q in Q. Then, for every 5-tuple (q, a, q', b, X) where q, q' are states, a, b are tape symbols, and X is one of L, R or 0, there is a directed arc from node q to node q' with (a, b, X) as a label (see Fig. 0.5).

Represented as a labelled directed graph, our example TM program is given in Fig. 0.6. The start state is indicated by an inward arrow to the corresponding node, and final states by having their corresponding nodes drawn in square boxes rather than circles. Such representations of TM

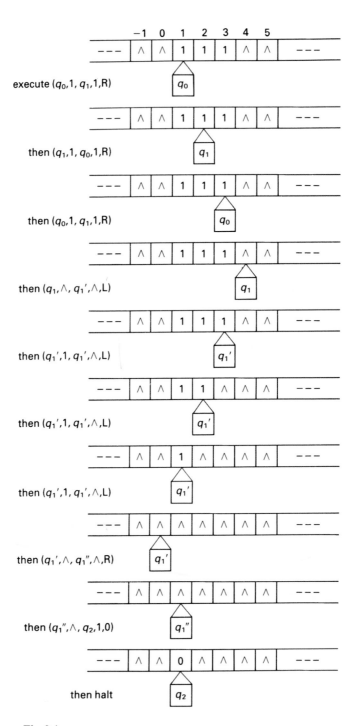

Fig. 0.4.

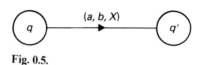

Fig. 0.5.

programs very often provide the greatest clarity. Hence, this will generally be the way that these programs are presented in this book.

We will define Turing machines rigorously in Chapter 2 and, thereafter, investigate their computing power. Firstly, however, we will need to establish our mathematical notation.

Chapter 1

Mathematical Prerequisites

But this book cannot be understood unless one first learns to
comprehend the language and interpret the characters in which it is
written. It is written in the language of mathematics...without
which it is humanly impossible to understand a single word of it.

GALILEO GALILEI

Il Saggiatore

In this chapter, we will survey the mathematics required to understand
the rest of this book. If this material is new to you, you should study it
carefully and make sure you understand all of the concepts. You might
like to supplement your reading with Chapters 1, 2 and 5 of the text,
Mathematics for Computing by McKeown & Rayward-Smith (1982). If,
on the other hand, the material is not new to you, this chapter can be
skipped through quickly, merely to ascertain the notation that we are
going to adopt.

SETS

A *set* is simply a collection of objects without repetition. Each object in
a set is called an *element* of that set. If the number of such elements is not
too large, then the set can be specified by listing its elements. For example,
if D denotes the set of days of the week, then

$$D = \{ \text{Monday, Tuesday, Wednesday, Thursday,}$$
$$\text{Friday, Saturday, Sunday} \}.$$

The elements of a set defined in this way are separated by commas and
surrounded by the special brackets { and }. Generally, there is no implied
ordering of the elements of a set, so we could equally well have defined

$$D = \{ \text{Monday, Wednesday, Friday, Thursday,}$$
$$\text{Sunday, Tuesday, Saturday} \}.$$

If an element, x, is a member of set, A, then we write $x \in A$ [read: x in
A] and if x is not an element of A, we write $x \notin A$ [read: x not in A]. Thus,

$$\text{Monday} \in D$$

1

but   Kippers$\notin D$.

Often, however, a set has a large number of elements and perhaps even an infinite number of elements. In such cases the definition of the set cannot be given by listing all its elements and some *defining property* has to be specified. An element, x, is then in the set provided that x satisfies the defining property. A suitable defining property for the set D is

'x is a day of the week'.

So, we could write

$$D = \{x | x \text{ is a day of the week}\}$$

i.e. D consists of all elements, x, that satisfy the defining property. As another example,

$$P = \{x | x \text{ is a prime number}\}$$

defines an infinite set of integers.

When defining a set in this way, care has to be taken to specify the elements under consideration as the *universe (of discourse)*. For example, if

$$X = \{x | x > 2\}$$

then the precise nature of X can only be determined given the values which x might take. For example, if x could only range over the positive integers, X would be a different set from the case where x could range over all real numbers. In the former case $2 \cdot 1 \notin X$ but in the latter $2 \cdot 1 \in X$. Every set under discussion will have all its elements contained in some specified universe, $\mathcal{U}$. Suitable universes in which X might be defined are the integers, the positive reals, etc.

A particularly important set is the *empty set*. This set contains no elements and is denoted by $\emptyset$ or $\{\,\}$.

We say a set A is a subset of a set B, written $A \subseteq B$, if every element of A is a member of the set B. If A is not a subset of B, we write $A \not\subseteq B$. Thus

$$\{1,2,4\} \subseteq \{1,2,3,4,5\}$$

but $\{2,4,6\} \not\subseteq \{1,2,3,4,5\}$.

It follows from the definition that

$$A \subseteq \mathcal{U}$$

and $\emptyset \subseteq A$ for all sets, A.

Two sets A and B are said to be *equal*, written $A = B$, provided $A \subseteq B$ and $B \subseteq A$. Thus

$$\{1,2,3,4\} = \{2,1,4,3\}$$

but $\{1,2,3,4\} \neq \{2,1,3,5\}$.

Clearly, $A = B$ iff[1] A and B contain precisely the same elements. If $A \subseteq B$ but $A \neq B$, we write $A \subset B$ and say that A is a *proper subset of B*. The set of all subsets of a set A is called the *power set* of A and is denoted by 2^A. Thus, if $A = \{1,2,3\}, 2^A = \{\varnothing, \{1\}, \{2\}, \{3\}, \{1,2\}, \{2,3\}, \{3,1\}, \{1,2,3\}\}$.

The basic operations on sets are the unary[2] operation, complement (') and the binary[3] operations union ($\cup$), intersection ($\cap$) and difference ($\backslash$). These operations are defined as follows:

If A,B are sets then

$A' = \{x|x \notin A\}$
consists of all elements in the universe which are not in A;

$A \cup B = \{x|x \in A \text{ or } x \in B\}$
consists of all elements in either A or B;

$A \cap B = \{x|x \in A \text{ and } x \in B\}$
consists of all elements in both A and B;

$A \backslash B = \{x|x \in A \text{ but } x \notin B\}$
consists of all elements in A but not in B.

For example, if $\mathscr{U} = \{0,1,2,3,4,5,6,7,8,9\}, A = \{0,1,3,5\}$ and $B = \{2,3,5\}$, then

$$A' = \{2,4,6,7,8,9\},$$
$$A \cup B = \{0,1,2,3,5\},$$
$$A \cap B = \{3,5\},$$
$$A \backslash B = \{0,1\},$$
$$B \backslash A = \{2\}.$$

[1] A standard abbreviation for 'if and only if'.
[2] Unary because the operation takes just one operand.
[3] Binary because the operation takes two operands.

Note that $\cup$ and $\cap$ are both *associative* operations, i.e.

$$(A \cup B) \cup C = A \cup (B \cup C)$$

and $(A \cap B) \cap C = A \cap (B \cap C)$, for all sets A, B and C.

Difference, however, is not associative. Similarly, $\cup$ and $\cap$ are both *commutative*, i.e.

$$A \cup B = B \cup A$$

and $A \cap B = B \cap A$, for all sets A, B,

but $\setminus$ is not. These and other properties of sets are summarized in Theorem 1.1.

Theorem 1.1 (Properties of sets)

For all sets A, B, C in the universe, $\mathcal{U}$:

(1)	Associative laws	$(A \cup B) \cup C = A \cup (B \cup C)$
		and $(A \cap B) \cap C = A \cap (B \cap C)$;
(2)	Commutative laws	$A \cup B = B \cup A$
		and $A \cap B = B \cap A$;
(3)	Complement laws	$A \cup A' = \mathcal{U}$
		and $A \cap A' = \varnothing$;
(4)	Idempotency laws	$A \cup A = A$
		and $A \cap A = A$;
(5)	Identity laws	$A \cup \varnothing = A$
		and $A \cap \mathcal{U} = A$;
(6)	Zero laws	$A \cup \mathcal{U} = \mathcal{U}$
		and $A \cap \varnothing = \varnothing$;
(7)	Involution law	$(A')' = A$;
(8)	De Morgan's laws	$(A \cup B)' = A' \cap B'$
		and $(A \cap B)' = A' \cup B'$;
(9)	Distributivity laws	$A \cup (B \cap C) = (A \cup B) \cap (A \cup C)$
		and $A \cap (B \cup C) = (A \cap B) \cup (A \cap C)$.

Since union is associative, we can write $A \cup B \cup C$ and know that however it is evaluated, the same answer will result. Extending this argument, we can write $A_1 \cup A_2 \cup ... \cup A_n$ for any sets $A_1, A_2,...,A_n$ without fear of misinterpretation. A common notation for such a union will be

$$\bigcup_{i=1}^{n} A_i.$$

Similarly we write

$$\bigcap_{i=1}^{n} A_i \quad \text{for} \quad A_1 \cap A_2 \cap \ldots \cap A_n$$

We say two sets A, B are *disjoint* if they have no elements in common. A convenient way of expressing this fact is to write $A \cap B = \emptyset$.

Let A_1, A_2 be two sets. Then the *product*, $A_1 \times A_2$, of A_1 and A_2 is a set consisting of all the pairs (a_1, a_2) where the first element, a_1, is in A_1 and the second element, a_2, is in A_2, i.e.

$$A_1 \times A_2 = \{(a_1, a_2) | a_1 \in A_1, a_2 \in A_2\}.$$

As a simple example, if $A_1 = \{0, 1\}$ and $A_2 = \{x, y, z\}$, then $A_1 \times A_2 = \{(0,x),(0,y),(0,z),(1,x),(1,y),(1,z)\}$.

The definition is extended to $A_1 \times A_2 \times A_3$, the set of all triples (a_1, a_2, a_3), $a_1 \in A_1, a_2 \in A_2$, $a_3 \in A_3$, and similarly to $A_1 \times A_2 \times \cdots \times A_n$, the set of all n-tuples $(a_1, a_2, \ldots, a_n)$ where $a_i \in A_i, i = 1, 2, \ldots, n$.

Note that $A \times B \neq B \times A$ unless $A = B$. The following distributive laws are easy to verify.

Theorem 1.2

(1) $A \times (B_1 \cup B_2) = (A \times B_1) \cup (A \times B_2)$
    and $(A_1 \cup A_2) \times B = (A_1 \times B) \cup (A_2 \times B)$;

(2) $A \times (B_1 \cap B_2) = (A \times B_1) \cap (A \times B_2)$
    and $(A_1 \cap A_2) \times B = (A_1 \times B) \cap (A_2 \times B)$;

(3) $A \times (B_1 \setminus B_2) = (A \times B_1) \setminus (A \times B_2)$
    and $(A_1 \setminus A_2) \times B = (A_1 \times B) \setminus (A_2 \times B)$.

CARDINALITY AND COUNTABILITY

If A has a finite number of elements, it is called a *finite set*, and if it has an infinite number of elements, it is called an *infinite set*.

The *cardinality* of a finite set A, denoted by $\#(A)$, is the number of elements in A. Thus, if D denotes the set of days of the week, $\#(D) = 7$. A set of cardinality one is known as a *singleton set*.

Chapter 1

For an infinite set, one useful property we would like is some technique for listing the elements, i.e. we would like a method for specifying a first element, a second element, etc. For example, if N denotes the positive integers, an obvious listing is 1,2,3,4,... and thus we safely talk about 'the ith positive integer'. It is not obvious (and, indeed, not true) that every infinite set can be so listed.

Having listed the elements of N, the next question is: Can we list the elements of Z, the set of all integers? The answer is yes. We simply alternate between positive and negative integers in increasing order of absolute value. This gives us the lising:

$$0, +1, -1, +2, -2, +3, -3,...$$

Any $z \in Z$ will eventually appear in this list.

$N \times N$ can also be listed—an ordering is given as indicated in Fig. 1.1

(m,n) comes before (m',n') in this ordering iff $m + n < m' + n'$ or if $m + n = m' + n'$ then $m < m'$.

Whenever we can find a technique for listing all the elements of a set, then we can use the term 'the ith element of the set', and in such a case we call the set *countable*. Clearly any finite set is countable, but this is not true of every infinite set. An example of an uncountably infinite set is $\mathbb{R}$—the set of all real numbers. We will show the stronger result that there is an uncountable number of real numbers ≥ 0 and < 1. We denote this set by $[0, 1)$. The proof of the result is based on a technique called *Cantor's diagonalization*. Let us assume we had some listing of all these real numbers and seek a contradiction. If we represent the numbers in this range in the usual decimal notation then, if our listing exists, we

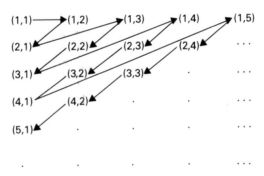

Fig. 1.1.

can write

1st real	$0 \cdot a_{11} a_{12} a_{13} ...$
2nd real	$0 \cdot a_{21} a_{22} a_{23} ...$
3rd real	$0 \cdot a_{31} a_{32} a_{33} ...$

. . .

. . .

. . .

where each a_{ij} is a simple digit. Every real number $\in [0, 1)$ must eventually occur in this listing. Now, consider the real number

$$0 \cdot a_{11} a_{22} a_{33} ...$$

made up of the 'diagonal' entries. Change each a_{ii} to b_{ii} where

$$b_{ii} = \begin{cases} a_{ii} + 1 & \text{if } a_{ii} < 9, \\ 0 & \text{if } a_{ii} = 9. \end{cases}$$

Now, $0 \cdot b_{11} b_{22} b_{33} ... \in [0, 1)$ but does not occur in the list. This is because for any i, the ith digit of $0 \cdot b_{11} b_{22} b_{33} ...$ is b_{ii} and this differs from a_{ii}, the ith digit of the ith entry of our list. This contradiction shows that $[0, 1)$ cannot be countable and hence that neither is $\mathbb{R}$.

It can be shown that for finite sets, $\#(A_1 \times A_2) = \#(A_1) \times \#(A_2)$ and by using a tableau such as in Fig. 1.1 that $A_1 \times A_2$ is countable if A_1 and A_2 are countable. This result can be generalized; for any $n > 1$, it is the case that $\#(A_1 \times A_2 \times \cdots \times A_n) = \#(A_1) \times \#(A_2) \times \cdots \times \#(A_n)$ for finite sets and that $A_1 \times A_2 \times \cdots \times A_n$ is countable if $A_1, A_2, ..., A_n$ are countable.

RELATIONS

A *relation* R is simply any subset of $A_1 \times A_2$, where A_1 is called the *domain* of R and A_2 is called the *range* of R. We will often be concerned with relations where the domain and range are the same set, A, say. We then say $R \subseteq A \times A$ is a relation *on* A. For example, if $A = \{0, 1, 2, 3\}$ then the set of ordered pairs

$$L = \{(0, 1), (0, 2), (0, 3), (1, 2), (1, 3), (2, 3)\}$$

would be the relation on A corresponding to the notion of 'strictly less than' while

$$E = \{(0,0),(1,1),(2,2),(3,3)\}$$

would be the relation on A corresponding to 'is equal to'. We will adopt the usual notation and write aRb for $(a,b){\in}R$ and $a\rlap{/}Rb$ for $(a,b){\notin}R$.

A relation R on A is said to be *reflexive* if

aRa for all $a{\in}A$.

Thus L above is not a reflexive relation on A since $(0,0){\notin}L$, but E is reflexive.

A *symmetric* relation satisfies:

aRb implies bRa.

L is not symmetric since $(0,1){\in}L$ but $(1,0){\notin}L$. However, E is symmetric.

A *transitive* relation R on A satisfies:

aRb and bRc implies aRc.

Both L and E are transitive relations.

An *antisymmetric* relation satisfies:

aRb and bRa implies $a=b$.

Both E and L are antisymmetric and so is $E{\cup}L$ but $\{(0,1),(1,0)\}$ is not.

If a relation R on A is reflexive, symmetric and transitive, then it is called an *equivalence relation*. We have shown that E is an equivalence relation on $A = \{0,1,2,3\}$ but there are others, for example,

$$V = \{(0,0),(0,2),(1,1),(1,3),(2,2),(2,0),(3,1),(3,3)\}.$$

If R is an equivalence relation on A and $a{\in}A$, then associated with a is the set of elements, $\bar{a}$, comprising all the elements related to a by R. Thus

$$\bar{a} = \{b{\in}A \,|\, aRb\}.$$

Such a set is called an *equivalence class*.

For E, there are four distinct equivalence classes, $\bar{0}=\{0\}$, $\bar{1}=\{1\}$, $\bar{2}=\{2\}$ and $\bar{3}=\{3\}$. For V, we have only two distinct equivalence classes $\bar{0}=\bar{2}=\{0,2\}$ and $\bar{1}=\bar{3}=\{1,3\}$. This illustrates the face that the equivalence classes defind by an equivalence relation R on a set A always partition A into a number of disjoint, nonempty sets (see Exercise 1.6).

If R is an arbitrary relation on A then the *reflexive* (respectively, *symmetric, transitive*) *closure* of R is the smallest reflexive (respectively, symmetric, transitive) relation on A with R as a subset. For example, if

$$R = \{(0,1),(1,1),(1,2)\}$$

is a relation on $\{0,1,2\}$, then its reflexive closure is

$$\{(0,0),(0,1),(1,1),(1,2),(2,2)\},$$

its symmetric closure is

$$\{(0,1),(1,0),(1,1),(1,2),(2,1)\}$$

and its transitive closure is

$$\{(0,1),(0,2),(1,1),(1,2)\}.$$

As a further example, the relation $<$ defined on all integers has reflexive closure, $\leq$, symmetric closure, $\neq$, and since it is already transitive, its transitive closure is the relation itself.

A relation on A is an *ordering relation* on A if it is reflexive, antisymmetric and transitive. If such an ordering exists for a nonempty set, A, then A is said to be *partially ordered* with respect to that relation. In a partially ordered, set, A with ordering relation $\subseteq$, there may exist elements a, $b \in A$ such that neither $a \subseteq b$ nor $b \subseteq a$. Such elements are said to be incomparable. A partially ordered set is said to be *totally ordered* if it has no incomparable elements. For example, Z is a totally ordered set with respect to $\leq$ but the power set of a set is partially, but not totally, ordered with respect to $\subseteq$.

For any countable set, A, we can prescribe a listing of its elements $a_1, a_2, a_3, \ldots$ and we can then define as associated total ordering: $a_i \subset a_j$ iff $i \leq j$.

If $\subseteq$ denotes an ordering on a set A, then we will use $\subset$ to denote the relation defined by $a \subset b$ iff $a \subseteq b$ and $a \neq b$. This corresponds to the use of $<$ and $\leq$ for orderings on numbers as well as $\subset$ and $\subseteq$ for set inclusion.

FUNCTIONS

A function, f, from a set, A, to a set, B, associates with each $a \in A$ a unique element of B, denoted by $f(a)$. Very often, f is defined by giving some formula or expression for $f(a)$ in terms of a.

A function $f:A \rightarrow B$ can also be viewed as the set of all pairs (a,b) where $a \in A, b \in B$ and $b = f(a)$. Thus a function $f:A \rightarrow B$ is sometimes defined as a relation in $A \times B$ with the property that if $(a,b) \in f$ and $(a,c) \in f$ then $b = c$. This last restriction simply means that $f(a)$ must be unique.

If f is a function from A to B, we write $f:A \rightarrow B$ and call A the *domain* of f and B the *codomain* of f. The set $\{ f(a):a \in A \}$ is called the *range* of f and is a subset of the codomain of f. For example, the function *twice*: $N \rightarrow N$ defined by $twice(n) = 2n$, for all $n \in N$, has as its range the set of even integers.

In general, a function $f:A \rightarrow B$ is such that $f(a)$ is defined for all $a \in A$. Such functions are often called *total functions*. Sometimes we will refer to a function $f:A \rightarrow B$ for which there are some elements $a \in A$ such that $f(a)$ is undefined. In such a case, the function is said to be a *partial function*. For example, the function *reciprocal*: $\mathbb{R} \rightarrow \mathbb{R}$ defined by *reciprocal* $(x) = 1/x$ is partial since it is not defined for $x = 0$. From any partial function, we can, of course, construct a total function by suitably specifying the domain. For example, *reciprocal* is a total function $\mathbb{R} \setminus \{0\} \rightarrow \mathbb{R}$. We will endeavour to do this so the reader can assume all functions are total unless it is specifically stated that they are partial.

The total function $f:A \rightarrow B$ is *onto* if for each $b \in B$, there exists $a \in A$ such that $f(a) = b$, and f is *one–one* if it maps unique elements of A to unique elements of B, i.e. if $f(a_1) = f(a_2)$ implies $a_1 = a_2$. In Fig. 1.2 we illustrate various functions, representing $(a,b) \in f$ by joining $a \in A$ to $b \in B$ by a directed line. If a total function $f:A \rightarrow B$ is both onto and one–one we say that f is a

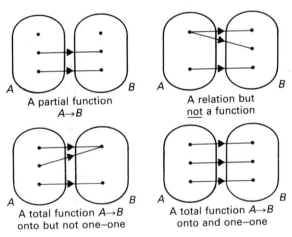

A partial function
$A \rightarrow B$

A relation but
not a function

A total function $A \rightarrow B$
onto but not one–one

A total function $A \rightarrow B$
onto and one–one

Fig. 1.2.

bijection. We could define *countability* formally as follows: a set A is countable if it is either finite or there exists a bijection $f: A \rightarrow N$. This bijection specifies the listing of the elements where the ith element of A is mapped to the positive integer, i.

If x denotes a real number then $\lceil x \rceil$ denotes the least integer greater than x and $\lfloor x \rfloor$ denotes the greatest integer less than x. The functions *roundup* and *rounddown* from $\mathbb{R}$ to Z defined by $roundup(x) = \lceil x \rceil$ and $rounddown(x) = \lfloor x \rfloor$ are thus both onto but not one–one. An example of a one–one function that is not onto is *square*:$N \rightarrow N$ defined by *square* $(n) = n^2$. Note, however, that if the domain of this function had been specified as Z then the function would not be one–one either.

Obviously, $identity(a) = a$ defines a bijection $A \rightarrow A$ for any set, A. A more interesting example of a bijection is given by *swap*:$N \rightarrow N$ where

$$swap(n) = \begin{cases} n - 1 & \text{if } n \text{ is an even number,} \\ n + 1 & \text{if } n \text{ is an odd number.} \end{cases}$$

If the codomain of a function is the set of Boolean values $\{T, F\}$, then the function is called a *predicate*. Thus *even*:$N \rightarrow \{T, F\}$ defined by

$$even(n) = \begin{cases} T & \text{if } n \text{ is an even number,} \\ F & \text{if } n \text{ is an odd number,} \end{cases}$$

is an example of a predicate defined on the natural numbers.

So far, every function that we have considered has taken a single argument, i.e. is a *unary* function. If a function, f, takes two arguments, the first from a set A_1, the second from a set A_2, and delivers a result in a set B, then we use the product notation and write $f: A_1 \times A_2 \rightarrow B$. Because f takes two arguments, it is called a *binary* function. Generalizing this notation, a function $f: A_1 \times A_2 \times \cdots \times A_n \rightarrow B$ takes n arguments and is said to be an *n-ary* function. The number of arguments taken by a function is called its *arity*.

For example, *add*:$\mathbb{R} \times \mathbb{R} \rightarrow \mathbb{R}$ is binary function defined by *add* (x, y) $x + y$. Then *tripleadd* is a 3-ary function $\mathbb{R} \times \mathbb{R} \times \mathbb{R} \rightarrow \mathbb{R}$ defined by *tripleadd* $(x, y, z) = x + y + z$.

Let $f: A \rightarrow B$ and $g: C \rightarrow D$ be two functions. If the range of f is a subset of the domain of g, then the *composition*, $g_o f$, of the two functions can be formed where $g_o f: A \rightarrow D$ is defined by $g_o f(a) = g(f(a))$ for all $a \in A$. The range of $g_o f$ is thus a subset of the range of g (see Fig. 1.3).

For example, if *succ*:$N \rightarrow N$ is defined by $succ(n) = n + 1$ then $succ_o square$:$N \rightarrow N$ is defined by $succ_o square(n) = succ(square(n)) =$

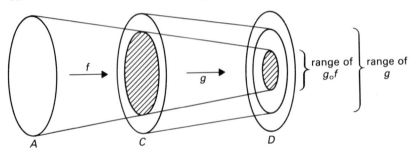

range of g_of range of g

Fig. 1.3.

$succ(n^2) = n^2 + 1$ but $square_o\ succ(n) = (n + 1)^2$. This illustrates the fact that, in general, composition is not commutative. It is, however, always associative.

If $f:A \to B$ and $f^{-1}:B \to A$ are such that $f^{-1}{}_of:A \to A$ and $f_of^{-1}:B \to B$ are both identity functions, then f^{-1} is said to be the *inverse* function of f. The inverse of a function $f:A \to B$ will only be a total function $B \to A$ when f is a bijection (see Exercise 1.12). The inverse of the identity function $identity:A \to A$ is $identity$. But this is not the only function that satisfies $f = f^{-1}$, i.e. is *self inverse*; so is $swap:N \to N$ as previously defined. functions which are not self inverse but which have inverses include those such as $addk:\mathbb{R} \to \mathbb{R}(k \neq 0)$ defined by $addk(x) = x + k$ which has inverse $subk:\mathbb{R} \to \mathbb{R}$ defined by $subk(x) = x - k$ and $multk:\mathbb{R} \to \mathbb{R}(k \neq 0,\ k \neq 1)$ defined by $multk(x) = x * k$ with inverse $divk:\mathbb{R} \to \mathbb{R}$ defined by $divk(x) = x/k$.

If $f,\ g$ are both (possibly partial) functions $A \to B$, then we say that f equals g, $f = g$, provided for every $x \in A$ either both $f(x)$ and $g(x)$ are undefined or $f(x) = g(x)$. Thus, $add2 = add1_oadd1$, $add3 = sub1_oadd4 = add1^{-1}{}_oadd4$, etc.

INDUCTION AND RECURSION

Induction is a powerful technique used whenever one wants to prove a countable number of theorems, $\{T_n|n \in N\}$. For example, we might be asked to show that $8^n - 3^n$ is divisible by 5 for $n = 1, 2, 3, \ldots$.

To prove that all the theorems hold, we proceed as follows:
(1)   We show T_1 is true;
(2)   We show that for any $k \in N$, if T_n is true for all $n < k$ then it follows that T_k is true.

Now if T_1 is true, result (2) with $k = 2$ proves that T_2 is true, then result (2) with $k = 3$ proves that T_3 is true. Continuing to apply this argument, we get $T_4, T_5, \ldots,$ are all true. The reason why induction really is a valid technique can be presented as follows. Say $\{T_n|n\in N\}$ is a countable set of theorems satisfying (a) T_1 is true and (b) for any $k\in N$, if T_n is true for all $n<k$ then T_k is true. We will show T_n is true for all $n\in N$. If this were not so, then there must exist a least $j>0$ such that T_j were false but T_n is true for all $n<j$. Now, $j\neq 1$ since this would contradict (a), but then we have a contradiction of (b) for the case $k=j$.

When giving any induction argument it is important that it is correctly presented. A suitable layout for a proof by induction that T_n is true for all $n\in N$ is described as follows.

The proof is by mathematical induction	the first line
The result holds for $n=1$ because ...	proof that T_1 is true
Assume the result holds for all $n<k$, i.e. that...	called the *induction hypothesis*
Then ... Hence the result holds for $n=k$.	proof that T_k is true follows from the induction hypothesis
Hence the result holds for all $n\in N$ by induction.	the last line

As an example we will prove that 8^n-3^n is divisible by 5 for all $n\in N$. The proof is by mathematical induction. The result holds for $n=1$ since $8^1-3^1=5$ is divisible by 5. Assume the result holds for all $n<k$, i.e. that 8^n-3^n is divisible by 5 if $n<k$.

Then $8^k-3^k=8\times 8^{k-1}-3\times 3^{k-1}$
$$=5\times 8^{k-1}+3\times(8^{k-1}-3^{k-1})$$

Now, by the induction hypothesis, $8^{k-1}-3^{k-1}$ is divisible by 5 and since $5\times 8^{k-1}$ is also clearly divisible by 5, it follows that so is 8^k-3^k. Hence the result holds for $n=k$.
Hence the result holds for all $n\in N$ by induction.

There is a close link between induction and recursion. Recursion is a method of defining a function f as an expression which itself may involve f. One of the most common examples is *fact*: $N\to N$ defined by

$$fact(n)=if\ n=1\ then\ 1$$
$$else\ n\times fact\ (n-1)$$

If we evaluate *fact*(3) say, using this definition, we find that

$$fact(3) = 3 \times fact(2)$$
$$= 3 \times 2 \times fact(1)$$
$$= 3 \times 2 \times 1.$$

If we define $n! = n \times (n-1) \times (n-2) \times \cdots \times 1$, then we can prove that $fact(n) = n!$ for all $n \in N$. Not surprisingly perhaps, the proof is by mathematical induction. Certainly $fact(1) = 1 = 1!$ So the result holds for $n = 1$. If we assume $fact(n) = n!$ for all $n < k$ then $fact(k) = k \times fact(k-1) = k \times (k-1)! = k!$ so the result holds for $n = k$. Hence the result holds for all $n \in N$ by induction.

As another example of a recursive definition consider $sum: N \times N \to N$ defined by

$$sum(m, n) = if\ m = 1\ then$$
$$if\ n = 1\ then\ 2$$
$$else\ succ(sum(m, n-1))$$
$$else\ succ(sum(m-1, n))$$

The reader should recognize that $sum(m, n) = m + n$ for all $m, n \in N$ but a formal induction proof requires some care. The problem is that there are two arguments and thus that the countable number of theorems is indexed by $N \times N$. We have defined an ordering on $N \times N$ by

$$(m, n) \subset (m', n') \quad \text{iff}$$
$$m + n < m' + n' \quad \text{or} \quad \text{if } m + n = m' + n' \text{ then } m < m'.$$

Now we can proceed by induction. The result holds for the first element in the ordering, (1,1), since $sum(1, 1) = 2 = 1 + 1$. Assume $(j, k) \neq (1, 1)$ and that the result holds for all $(m, n) \subset (j, k)$. Then

$$sum(j, k) = if\ j = 1\ then\ succ(sum(j, k-1))$$
$$else\ succ(sum(j-1, k))$$

Now both $(j, k-1) \subset (j, k)$ and $(j-1, k) \subset (j, k)$ so by the induction hypothesis $sum(j, k-1) = sum(j-1, k) = j + k - 1$. Hence, $sum(j, k) = succ(j + k - 1) = j + k$ whether or not $j = 1$. Hence the result holds for (j, k) and the result is proved by induction.

STRINGS

Whenever we use the term *string* we mean a finite sequence of symbols $a_1 a_2 \ldots a_n$ where each a_i is taken from some finite alphabet Σ; repetitions are allowed. An example of a string of symbols from the alphabet $\Sigma = \{0, 1\}$ is 001110. If a string has m symbols counted according to multiplicity, then we say the string has *length m*. Hence 001110 is a string of length six. The *empty string*, denoted by ε, is a string of no symbols and has length zero. The length of a string, x, is denoted by $|x|$. Thus, $|001110| = 6$ and $|\varepsilon| = 0$.

The mathematics of strings is really very simple. We must first specify some *alphabet*. This is the nonempty, finite set of symbols which are going to appear in our strings. If the blank symbol occurs in the strings then it must be a member of the alphabet. To avoid confusion, the blank symbol is often represented in computing texts by $\wedge$; thus $00 \wedge 11 \wedge 01$ is written for 00 11 01. Notice that the blank symbol $\wedge$ is a string of length one — it must not be confused with the empty string.

Having specified the alphabet, Σ, we will denote the set of all finite length strings over the alphabet Σ by Σ^*. Σ^* will always have a countably infinite number of elements (Exercise 1.4). For example, if $\Sigma = \{0, 1\}$, then one possible ordering of Σ^* is

$$\varepsilon, 0, 1, 00, 01, 10, 11, 000, 001, 010, \ldots$$

This ordering of the elements of $\{0, 1\}^*$ is known as the *lexicographic ordering*. Using normal set-theoretic notation, we write $x \in \Sigma^*$ if x is an element of Σ^* and $x \notin \Sigma^*$ if this is not the case. From the definition, it follows that $\varepsilon \in \Sigma^*$ for all sets, Σ.

If $x \in \Sigma^*$ is a string of length m, we can write $x = a_1 a_2 \ldots a_m$ where $a_i \in \Sigma$, $1 \leq i \leq m$. Then if $x \in \Sigma^*$ is a string of length m and $y \in \Sigma^*$ is a string of length n, the *concatenation* of x and y, denoted by xy, is defined to be the string of length $m + n$ whose first m symbols comprise a string equal to x and whose last n symbols comprise a string equal to y. Thus if $x = a_1 a_2 \ldots a_m$ and $y = b_1 b_2 \ldots b_n$ then $xy = a_1 a_2 \ldots a_m b_1 b_2 \ldots b_n$. Note that concatenation is an associative operation, i.e. $(xy)z = x(yz)$, but is obviously not commutative since, in general, $xy \neq yx$. The empty string acts as an identity with respect to concatenation since $\varepsilon x = x \varepsilon = x$ for all $x \in \Sigma^*$.

If a string $z \in \Sigma^*$ is of the form xy where $x, y \in \Sigma^*$, then x is said to be a *prefix* of z and y is said to be a *postfix* of z. For example, if $z = 00110$ then according to the definition, ε is a prefix of z and so is 0, 00, 001, 0011 and z itself. The postfixes of z are ε, 0, 10, 110, 0110 and z itself.

If $x, z \in \Sigma^*$ are such that $z = wxy$ for some $w, y \in \Sigma^*$ then x is said to be a *substring* of z. Thus, the substrings of $z = 00110$ are ε, 0, 1, 00, 01, 10, 11, 001, 011, 110, 0011, 0110 and z itself.

A (*formal*) *language* L over an alphabet Σ is simply defined as any subset of Σ^*. If L_1, L_2 are two such languages, then their (*set*) *concatenation* is the language $L_1 L_2 = \{xy|x \in L_1, y \in L_2\}$. For example, if $L_1 = \{01, 0\}$, and $L_2 = \{\varepsilon, 0, 10\}$ then $L_1 L_2 = \{01, 0, 010, 00, 0110\}$. As with concatenation, set concatenation is associative but not commutative. For any language L, $L\{\varepsilon\} = \{\varepsilon\}L = L$ and thus the singleton set $\{\varepsilon\}$ acts as an identity for set concatenation. The singleton set containing the empty string is very different from the empty set, $\varnothing$, which acts as a zero for set concatenation since $L = \varnothing L = \varnothing$ for any language, L.

If a language L is concatenated with itself, the result LL is written as L^2. This definition is generalized to $L^0 = \{\varepsilon\}$, $L^1 = L$ and $L^i = LL^{i-1} = L^{i-1}L$ for $i \geq 2$. The *Kleene closure* of L, written L^*, is then defined as

$$\bigcup_{i=0}^{\infty} L^i.$$

L^+ is defined to be

$$\bigcup_{i=1}^{\infty} L^i$$

and hence, $L^* = L^+ \cup \{\varepsilon\}$. In particular, Σ^2 denotes all the strings in Σ^* of length two, Σ^3 denotes those of length three, etc. The set of strings over Σ of length greater than or equal to one is denoted by Σ^+ and hence

$$\Sigma^+ = \bigcup_{i=1}^{\infty} \Sigma^i \quad \text{and} \quad \Sigma^* = \Sigma^* \cup \{\varepsilon\} = \bigcup_{i=0}^{\infty} \Sigma^i.$$

Much of our computation will involve functions on strings and the following functions will prove particularly useful:

$$head(x): \Sigma^* \to \Sigma^*$$

defined by

$$head(x) = \begin{cases} \varepsilon & \text{if } x = \varepsilon, \\ a & \text{if } x = ay, a \in \Sigma, \ y \in \Sigma^*, \end{cases}$$

and similarly

$$tail: \Sigma^* \to \Sigma^*$$

defined by

$$tail(x) = \begin{cases} \varepsilon & \text{if } x = \varepsilon, \\ y & \text{if } x = ay, a \in \Sigma, y \in \Sigma^*. \end{cases}$$

Thus every $x \in \Sigma^*$ can be written as the concatenation of $head(x)$ with $tail(x)$. For example, if $x = 0111$ then $head(x) = 0$ and $tail(x) = 111$. We will then write $tail^2$ for the function $tail_o \, tail$, $tail^3$ for $tail_o \, tail_o \, tail$, etc. Furthermore, we define $tail^0$ to be the identity function so $tail^0(x) = x$, for all $x \in \Sigma^*$. Formally, we define $tail^i$ ($i \geq 0$) recursively by

$$tail^i = \begin{cases} iden & \text{if } i = 0, \\ tail_o \, tail^{i-1} & \text{if } i \geq 1. \end{cases}$$

where $iden(x) = x$ for all x.

Thus, if $x = 0111$, $tail^0(x) = 0111$, $tail(x) = 111$, $tail^2(x) = 11$, $tail^3(x) = 1$, $tail^i(x) = \varepsilon$ for $i \geq 4$.

Analogously to *head* and *tail*, we define functions *foot* and *top*: $\Sigma^* \to \Sigma^*$ by

$$foot(x) = \begin{cases} \varepsilon & \text{if } x = \varepsilon, \\ a & \text{if } x = ya, a \in \Sigma, y \in \Sigma^*, \end{cases}$$

and

$$top(x) = \begin{cases} \varepsilon & \text{if } x = \varepsilon, \\ y & \text{if } x = ya, a \in \Sigma, y \in \Sigma^*. \end{cases}$$

So if $x = 0111$, $foot(x) = 1$ and $top(x) = 011$.
Then we define

$$top^i = \begin{cases} iden & \text{if } i = 0 \\ top_o \, top^{i-1} & \text{if } i \geq 1. \end{cases}$$

Concatenation can be regarded as a function $\Sigma^* \times \Sigma^* \to \Sigma^*$. We will occasionally write $concat(x, y)$ instead of simply xy when this aids clarity. Thus, for example, we might write $x = concat(head(x), tail(x))$ or $x = concat(top(x), foot(x))$.

Let Σ, Δ denote two alphabets. Then, if a function $f: \Sigma^* \to \Delta^*$ satisfies

$$f(\varepsilon) = \varepsilon$$

and $f(concat(x, y)) = concat(f(x), f(y))$ for all $x, y \in \Sigma^*$ we call f a *homomorphism*.

When defining a homomorphism $f: \Sigma^* \to \Delta^*$, it is only necessary to define $f(a)$ for all $a \in \Sigma$. The properties of a homomorphism ensure that we can then determine $f(x)$ for any $x \in \Sigma^*$. For example, consider the homomorphism $left: \{0, 1\}^* \to \{0, 1, \$\}^*$ defined by $left(0) = 0\$$, $left(1) = 1\$$. Then $left(\varepsilon) = \varepsilon$, $left(0) = 0\$$, $left(1) = 1\$$, $left(00) = 0\$0\$$, $left(01) = 0\$1\$$, $left(10) = 1\$0\$$, $left(11) = 1\$1\$$, $left(000) = 0\$0\$0\$$, etc.

In much of our work we will be interested in functions $B^n \to B$ where $B = \{0, 1\}^*$. In Chapter 5 we discuss which functions in this class of functions can be computed by a Turing machine. The functions *head*, *tail*, *foot*, *top*, *concat* as described above can all be so computed.

We can define *head* and *tail*: $B \to B$ as follows:

$head(\varepsilon) = \varepsilon$
$head(0x) = 0$
$head(1x) = 1$

and

$tail(\varepsilon) = \varepsilon$
$tail(0x) = x$
$tail(1x) = x.$

Then, when we evaluate $head(y)$, (say), we have to match y against ε, $0x$ or $1x$. If $y = \varepsilon$ then $head(\varepsilon) = \varepsilon$; if y starts with 0 so is of the form $0x$ for some $x \in B$, then $head(y) = 0$; otherwise, y is of the form $1x$ for some $x \in B$ and $head(y) = 1$.

The functions *foot* and *top* can also be defined by considering the various cases of the parameters. We could define

$foot(\varepsilon) = \varepsilon$
$foot(x0) = 0$
$foot(x1) = 1$

and

$top(\varepsilon) = \varepsilon$
$top(x0) = x$
$top(x1) = x.$

However, if we want to define *foot* and *top* using parameters ε, $0x$, $1x$, then we will need to use a recursive definition as follows.

$foot(\varepsilon) = \varepsilon$
$foot(0x) = if\ x = \varepsilon\ then\ 0\ else\ foot(x)$
$foot(1x) = if\ x = \varepsilon\ then\ 1\ else\ foot(x)$

and

$$top(\varepsilon) = \varepsilon$$
$$top(0x) = if \ x = \varepsilon \ then \ \varepsilon \ else \ concat\,(0, top(x))$$
$$top(1x) = if \ x = \varepsilon \ then \ \varepsilon \ else \ concat(1, top(x)).$$

The definition of functions by considering all possible cases of the parameters and using recursion is used extensively throughout later chapters of this book.

DIRECTED GRAPHS

A *directed graph (digraph)*, $G = (V, E)$, consists of a finite set of *vertices* (or *nodes*), V, together with a relation E on V. We can represent a digraph diagrammatically as follows: for each $v \in V$ we draw the node ⓥ on the page, and if $(v, w) \in E$ we join the node labelled v to the node labelled w by a directed line to get Fig. 1.4.

Fig. 1.4.

Figure 1.5 gives the diagram representing the digraph $G_1 = (V_1, E_1)$ where $V_1 = \{v, w, x\}$ and $E_1 = \{(v, w), (v, x), (w, x), (x, v), (x, x)\}$.

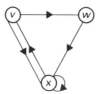

Fig. 1.5.

If, for some digraph $G = (V, E)$, $(v, w) \in E$ then we say there is an *arc* or an *edge from v to w in G*. If there is a sequence of nodes $v = v_0, v_1, \ldots v_n = w, n \geq 0$, such that $(v_i, v_{i+1}) \in E$ for $i = 0, 1, \ldots, n - 1$, then we say there is a *directed path from v to w in G of length n*. Thus the existence of a path from v to w implies that $v = w$ or we can get from the node labelled v to the node labelled w by following directed lines in our diagrammatic representation.

If $G = (V, E)$ is a digraph, then a directed *subgraph* of G is any digraph (V', E') where $V' \subseteq V$ and $E' \subseteq E$. Figure 1.6 illustrates four of the directed

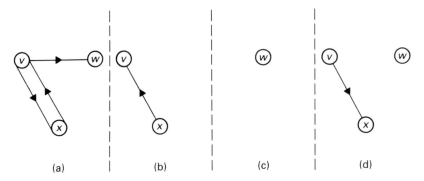

Fig. 1.6.

subgraphs of the digraph G_1 given in Fig. 1.5. Two directed subgraphs are said to be *disjoint* if they have no nodes in common. In Fig. 1.6, examples (b) and (c) are the only disjoint directed subgraphs.

If $V = \{v_1, v_2, \ldots v_n\}$ and $G = (V, E)$ is a digraph, then G can be represented using an $n \times n$ Boolean matrix, M_G, called the *adjacency matrix* where M_G is defined by

$$M_G[i,j] = \begin{cases} T & \text{if}(v_i, v_j) \in E, \\ F & \text{otherwise.} \end{cases}$$

For example, ordering the elements of V_1 alphabetically, we can represent the digraph of Fig. 1.5 by the Boolean matrix

$$\begin{bmatrix} F & T & T \\ F & F & T \\ T & F & T \end{bmatrix}$$

This is the usual way of representing digraphs and relations in a computer. Of course, if the set on which the relation is defined is large, then the matrix itself is large and storage constraints may dictate that the matrix should be stored using one of a variety of techniques available for sparse matrices (see Exercise 1.21).

If $G = (V, E)$ is a digraph and $v \in V$ then the number of arcs *from* v is denoted by *outdegree*(v) and the number of arcs *into* v is denoted by *indegree*(v). Formally, *outdegree* and *indegree* are functions $V \to Z^+$, the set of non-negative integers, defined by

$$outdegree(v) = \#\{(v, w) | (v, w) \in E\},$$
$$indegree(v) = \#\{(w, v) | (w, v) \in E\}.$$

We then define $degree: V \to Z^+$ by

$$degree(v) = outdegree(v) + indegree(v)$$

Since every arc must emanate from some vertex and must lead to some other vertex, it follows that:

Theorem 1.3

For any digraph, $G = (V, E)$,

(1) $\sum\limits_{v \in V} outdegree(v) = \sum\limits_{v \in V} indegree(v) = \#(E)$;

(2) $\sum\limits_{v \in V} degree(v) = 2\#(E)$.

For the example digraph, G_1, the *outdegree, indegree* and *degree* functions can be tabulated as follows:

	outdegree	indegree	degree
v	2	1	3
w	1	1	2
x	2	3	5

In many applications, it is desirable to associate with each arc in a digraph some label selected from a set of labels, L. We thus formally define a *labelled digraph* to be a digraph, $G = (V, E)$, together with a labelling function $l: E \to L$. As with unlabelled digraphs, we will usually represent a labelled digraph diagrammatically by simply writing the label $l(e)$ alongside the directed line representing the arc e. For example, we might label the example digraph G_1 using the labelling function $l: E \to Z^+$ defined by

$$l((v, w)) = outdegree(v) + indegree(w) \text{ for all } (v, w) \in E,$$

and then the resulting labelled digraph can be represented diagrammatically as in Fig. 1.7.

Now, consider the labelled digraph $G = (V, E)$ which has been labelled using $l: E \to L$. To represent this in a computer, we will generally use a

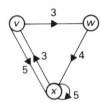

Fig. 1.7.

labelling matrix. We first define an order on the elements of V, $v_1, v_2 \ldots, v_n$, say. The i, j^{th} entry of the labelling matrix, M_G^l will then specify the label on the arc (v_i, v_j), if it exists, and will otherwise use some special symbol $\omega \notin L$ to denote the absence of an edge. Formally, the labelling matrix M_G^l is defined as an $n \times n$ matrix whose entries are elements of $L \cup \{\omega\}$ defined by

$$M_G^l[i,j] = \begin{cases} \omega & \text{if } (v_i, v_j) \notin E, \\ l((v_i, v_j)) & \text{otherwise.} \end{cases}$$

Thus to represent the labelled digraph described in Fig. 1.7 we might use $\omega = -1$ and order the vertices alphabetically. Then the labelling matrix is the integer matrix

$$\begin{bmatrix} -1 & 3 & 5 \\ -1 & -1 & 4 \\ 3 & -1 & 5 \end{bmatrix}$$

GRAPHS

With directed graphs, every arc has an associated direction and we say the arc, (v, w), goes from v to w. Also, since the arcs are defined as a subset of $V \times V$, there can be at most one arc from any $v \in V$ to any other $w \in V$. These restrictions, although often useful, are sometimes too limiting.

We thus define a *graph*, $G = (V, E)$, to be a structure comprising a finite set of *vertices*, V, and a set of *arcs* or *edges*, E; each edge $e \in E$ is *incident* to two elements which are called the endpoints of e. We represent a graph diagrammatically in the obvious way. For example, if Fig. 1.8 we represent a graph with four vertices, A, B, C and D, and six edges $e_1, e_2, \ldots e_6$. Note that in this graph there are two edges incident to A, B (e_1 and e_2) and one edge with identical endpoints (e_6). If an edge e has endpoints v_1, v_2, we sometimes represent this edge by $v_1 \overset{e}{-} v_2$ (or $v_2 \overset{e}{-} v_1$). An edge with

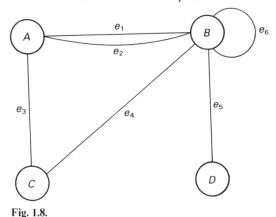

Fig. 1.8.

identical endpoints is called a *self-loop*. Two edges incident to the same two elements are said to be *parallel*. Thus the example has one pair of parallel edges and one self-loop.

The degree of vertex, $v \in V$, *degree(v)* is the number of times v is used as an endpoint of the edges. In our example, $degree(A) = 3$, $degree(B) = 6$, $degree(C) = 2$, $degree(D) = 1$. Any vertex $v \in V$ for which $degree(v) = 0$ is called *isolated*. Clearly, each edge contributes once towards the degree of each of its endpoints. Hence, corresponding to Theorem 1.3, we have the result that for any graph $G = (V, E)$,

$$\sum_{v \in V} degree(v) = 2\#(E).$$

A *complete graph* on V has exactly one edge between each pair of distinct vertices $v, w \in V$. Thus, if K_n is a complete graph on n vertices, then each vertex has degree $n - 1$ and the graph has a total of $n(n-1)/2$ edges. K_n has no self-loops and no parallel edges.

A *path* in a graph G is a sequence of edges $e_1, e_2, \ldots$ such that (i) e_i and e_{i+1} have a common endpoint and (ii) if e_i is not the first or last edge in the sequence, then it shares one of its endpoints with e_{i-1} and the other with e_{i+1}. In our example, $e_1 e_2 e_3$ is a path, so is $e_1 e_6 e_2 e_3$ but $e_5 e_3 e_4$ is not.

If $e_1 e_2 \ldots e_l$ is a path where l is finite then we say the path has *length* l. We could describe such a path and the associated vertices as $v_0 \overset{e_1}{-} v_1 \overset{e_2}{-} v_2 - \cdots v_{l-1} \overset{e_l}{-} v_l$. We would then say the path *starts* at v_0 and *ends*

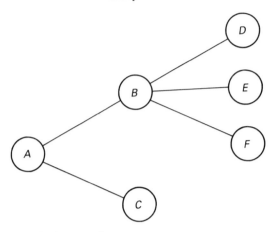

Fig. 1.9. An example tree.

at v_l; it is a path *connecting* v_0 and v_l. In our example, $e_1e_2e_3$ is a path connecting A and C.

A *circuit* is a path whose start and end vertices are the same. A path is called *simple* if no vertex appears on it more than once. A circuit is called simple if no vertex other than the start/end vertex appears more than once and the start/end vertex only appears at the start and at the end; however, the trivial circuit comprising $v_i \overset{e}{-} v_j \overset{e}{-} v_i$ which occurs between any two vertices v_i, v_j connected by an edge is not a simple circuit. In our example, $e_3e_1e_5$ and e_4e_5 are simple paths connecting C and D, $e_4e_2e_1e_5$ and $e_3e_2e_6e_5$ are not; $e_4e_2e_3$ is a simple circuit, $e_3e_1e_2e_3$ is not. If a graph has no simple circuits it is called *circuit-free*.

A graph G is *connected* if for any two vertices u, v there exists a path in G connecting u and v. A connected graph G which is circuit free is called a *tree*. For example, the graph described in Fig. 1.9 is a tree.

Theorem 1.4

If $G = (V, E)$ is a graph then the following conditions are equivalent:
(1) G is a tree;
(2) G is circuit-free but if any new edge is added to G a circuit is formed;
(3) G contains no self-loops and for every distinct $v, w \in V$, there is a unique path connecting v and w;
(4) G is connected but if any edge were to be deleted from G then this would no longer be the case;

(5)   *G* is circuit-free and has $\#(V) - 1$ edges;
(6)   *G* is connected and has $\#(V) - 1$ edges.

Proof. (1)⇒(2):$G = (V,E)$ is connected and circuit-free. Say $e \notin E$ connecting $v, w \in V$ is added to *G*. If $v = w$ we would have a self-loop so assume $v \neq w$. Now *G* was connected so in *G* we already had a path with endpoints v and w. By introducing e we must thus form a circuit.

(2)⇒(3): Since *G* is circuit-free it can contain no self-loops. Now consider $v, w \in V$, $v \neq w$. If there is more than one path connecting v, w then there must be a circuit. If there is no path connecting v,w then we have a contradiction since we know that the addition of the edge $v-w$ must create a circuit. Hence there must be a unique path connecting v,w.

(3)⇒(4): Since for every distinct $v,w \in V$ there is a path from v to w, *G* must be connected. Say an edge $v-w$ is deleted from *G*. Then there can be no path left in *G* connecting v,w since that edge compromised the unique path between v and w. Hence with the deletion of any edge, *G* would no longer be connected.

(4)⇒(1): We have to show *G* is circuit-free. This is true since if *G* had a circuit, then we could delete any edge in this circuit and still keep *G* connected.

Having established the equivalence of conditions (1), (2), (3), (4), we can use these results to show the remaining two conditions are also equivalent and that either hold iff *G* is a tree by induction on $\#(V)$. We first show that any tree, $G = (V,E)$, must have $\#(V) - 1$ edges. This result is trivially true for $\#(V) = 1$ so we assume $\#(V) \geq 2$. Consider the case where $\#(V) = n$ and the result has been shown to hold for all trees with number of vertices $< n$. Now, if *G* is a tree, we know it must be circuit-free and connected. If we delete an edge from *G*, then *G* must be split into two connected components, $G_1 = (V_1 E_1)$ and $G_2 = (V_2,E_2)$, both of which are circuit-free. Thus G_1 and G_2 must both be trees and thus by the induction hypothesis, must contain $\#(V_1) - 1$ edges and $\#(V_2) - 1$ edges respectively. Thus, *G* must contain $(\#(V_1) - 1) + (\#(V_2) - 1) + 1$ edges = $\#(V_1 \cup V_2) - 1 = \#(V) - 1$ edges and the proof by induction is completed. Hence, it follows that (1)⇒(5) and (1)⇒(6).

For the next step in the proof of the theorem, we need to show that if *G* is connected and has $\#(V) - 1$ edges it must be circuit-free and similarly, that if *G* is circuit-free and has $\#(V) - 1$ edges it must be connected. These results are both trivial if $\#(V) = 1$ so assume $\#(V) \geq 2$.

Now, let us assume that G is connected and has $\#(V) - 1 \geq 1$ edges. If G contains circuits then we can eliminate edges but maintain connectivity. When no more edges can be so eliminated we have a connected graph with no circuits, i.e. a tree. But we have shown that a tree must have $\#(V) - 1$ edges. Hence no edges of G can be eliminated whilst maintaining connectivity, i.e. G must be circuit-free.

On the other hand, let us assume G is circuit-free and has $\#(V) - 1 \geq 1$ edges. Take any edge $e \in E$ and extend this edge into a path by adding new edges to its ends as often as possible. The process must terminate since G has no circuits and the endpoints must then be distinct and both have degree 1. Say we removed from G one of these vertices and the single edge leading to it. The resulting graph $G^1 = (V^1, E^1)$ has $\#(V^1) = \#(V) - 1$ and $\#(E^1) = \#(E) - 1$. It must be circuit-free and we can use an induction argument to deduce that it must be connected. Hence G must also be connected. Hence we have shown $(5) \Leftrightarrow (6)$.

The proof of the theorem is completed by observing that (5) and $(6) \Rightarrow (1)$ by definition.

A graph $G^1 = (V^1, E^1)$ is a *subgraph* of a graph $G = (V, E)$ if $V^1 \subseteq V$ and $E^1 \subseteq E$. If G^1 contains all the vertices of G it is called a *spanning subgraph* of G. If, additionally, G^1 is a tree, it is called a *spanning tree* of G.

Say we have a graph $G = (V, E)$ and a cost function $c: E \to \mathbb{R}^+$ which associates a positive real number with each edge in G. We will represent this situation diagrammatically by labelling each edge in the diagram with its associated cost. An example is given in Fig. 1.10. We define the cost of such a graph to be $c(G) = \sum_{e \in E} c(e)$. So the cost of our example is 27. A common problem is to find a connected spanning subgraph G^1 of such a graph so that $c(G^1)$ is minimized. Clearly G^1 will be circuit-free since otherwise we could remove an edge and thus reduce the cost of the subgraph and yet keep it connected. Hence G^1 must be a tree and is thus called the *minimal*

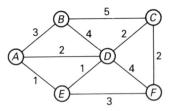

Fig. 1.10.

spanning tree (MST) of G. There are various well known algorithms to construct MTSs. The following is due to Kruskal (1956).

Let $G = (V, E)$ be the given graph. We can assume there are no parallel edges, for all but the cheapest of such can be removed. Then, the algorithm which selects the edges in the MST proceeds as follows:

begin $F \leftarrow \varnothing$;

while $\#F < \#(V) - 1$ *do*

        select $e \in E \backslash F$ *such that*

                (i) *e* does not form a circuit with edges already in *F*,

        and   (ii) subject to (i), $c(e)$ is as small as possible;

        $F := F \cup \{e\}$

endwhile

output (F)

end

For the example of Fig. 1.10, Kruskal's algorithm selects edges A–E, E–D, D–C, C–F and A–B. By theorem 1.4, Kruskal's algorithm must result in a spanning tree. To prove that the algorithm constructs a spanning tree of minimal cost is not difficult. Say, Kruskal's algorithm selects $e_1, e_2, \ldots, e_{n-1}$ where $n = \#(V)$ and $c(e_1) \le c(e_2) \le \cdots \le c(e_{n-1})$. Say T is the cheapest possible spanning tree and T has edges E. Let us assume $E \ne \{e_1, e_2, \ldots, e_{n-1}\}$, so there must exist a least k such that $e_k \notin E$. Say $E = \{e_1, e_2, \ldots, e_{k-1}, f_k, f_{k+1}, \ldots, f_{n-1}\}$, then by the construction of Kruskal's algorithm, $c(e_k) \le \min \{c(f_j) | k \le j < n\}$. $E \cup \{e_k\}$ must contain a circuit of which e_k must be an edge. This circuit must also contain at least one f_j for $k \le j < n$. For any such f_j, consider $(E \backslash \{f_j\}) \cup \{e_k\}$. This set of edges must form a tree but its cost is $\le c(T)$. Since $c(T)$ was minimal the cost must be exactly $c(T)$ and this shows that $c(f_j) = c(e_k)$. We can continue this argument and replace each of $f_k, f_{k+1}, \ldots, f_{n-1}$ one at a time by elements of $e_k, e_{k+1}, \ldots, e_{n-1}$ and hence deduce that

$$c(T) = \sum_{i=1}^{n-1} c(e_i).$$

Kruskal's algorithm for minimal spanning trees is just one example of a large number of elegant algorithms concerning graphs. A good overview of such algorithms is found in the texts *Graphs Algorithms* (Even, 1979), or *The Design and Analysis of Computer Algorithms* (Aho et al., 1974).

In many applications, we are not particularly concerned with the names of the vertices appearing in our graphs. We would wish to distinguish between graphs (a), (b) and (b), (c) in Fig. 1.11 but not between (a), (b). After all, if in (a), we relabelled vertices A,B,C,D as D,B,C,A respectively, both graphs would be identical. When two graphs only differ by the naming of their vertices, we say that they are *isomorphic*. Formally, two graphs $G_1 = (V_1, E_1)$ and $G_2 = (V_2, E_2)$ are isomorphic iff there exist bijections $f:V_1 \rightarrow V_2$ and $g:E_1 \rightarrow E_2$ such that for every edge $u \overset{e}{-} v$ in G_1, there exists an edge $f(u) \overset{g(e)}{-} f(v)$ in G_2. Isomorphism is an equivalence relation on the set of all graphs.

Finding whether or not two given graphs are isomorphic may not be an easy task. Certainly for two graphs to be isomorphic, they must each have the same number of vertices and edges. Moreover, any bijection $f:V_1 \rightarrow V_2$ used in establishing the isomorphism must satisfy $degree\,(v) = degree\,(f(v))$ for all $v \in V$. There are other similar properties that can be exploited to restrict the number of bijections $V_1 \rightarrow V_2$ which might have to be considered. At worst, however, if V_1 and V_2 both have n nodes then it appears that we might have to check through all $n!$ possible bijections $V_1 \rightarrow V_2$ to see if any can be used to prove the isomorphism we seek. Unfortunately despite considerable research effort, there is currently no known algorithm for testing isomorphism which does not perform very slowly on some graphs.

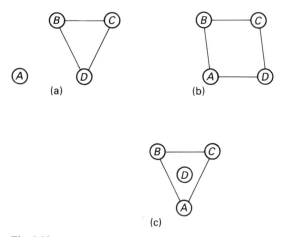

Fig. 1.11.

GÖDEL NUMBERING

For any countable set, A, we can exhibit a one–one function from A to the set of natural numbers, N. Thus we know that each $x \in A$ can be encoded as a unique integer, $g(x)$. Now, we might have designed some encoding g where the range of g may not be the whole of N. In such a case, for each $i \in N$ we will want some procedure for determining whether i is in the range of g and, if so, of determining $g^{-1}(i)$. We can define an ordering of the elements of A by saying $x \in A$ precedes $y \in A$ iff $g(x) < g(y)$. Then, if we wish to obtain the first n elements of A in this listing of A, we use the following algorithm.

$i := 1; j := 1;$
while $j \leq n$ *do if* i is in the range of g *then output* $(g^{-1}(i))$; $j := j + 1$ *endif*;

$i := i + 1$
endwhile

For example, we might encode $A = \{0,1\}^*$ as follows. For each $x \in \{0,1\}^*$, we define the integer $g(x)$ by

$$g(x) = \begin{cases} 1 & \text{iff } x = \varepsilon, \\ p_1^{a_1} \times p_2^{a_2} \times \cdots \times p_n^{a_n} & \text{if } x = b_1 b_2 ... b_n, b_i \in \{0, 1\} \end{cases}$$

for $1 \leq i \leq n$, where p_i denotes the ith prime number and $a_i = b_i + 1$.

Thus, if x is the string 1100, then $g(x) = 2^2 \times 3^2 \times 5 \times 7 = 1260$.

The function, g, is an example of a Gödel numbering of the set $\{0,1\}^*$. A *Gödel numbering* of a set is an assignment of natural numbers to elements of the set which must satisfy the following conditions:

(1) different Gödel numbers are assigned to different elements (i.e. g is one–one);
(2) there is an algorithm to calculate the Gödel number of any element (i.e. we can effectively calculate g);
(3) given any natural number, there is an algorithm to test whether that number is a Gödel number of some element in the set and, if so, to determine the corresponding element (i.e. we can effectively calculate g^{-1}).

The Gödel numberings we use in this text will always have the property that if $m < n$ and $g(x)$ is divisible by p_n then $g(x)$ is also divisible by p_m. The algorithm to decode a Gödel number is then particularly straightforward.

In the example above, the function, g, is clearly one–one since any integer has a unique factorization into prime factors. The range of g comprises the number one together with those integers whose prime factorization is of the form $p_1^{a_1} \times p_2^{a_2} \times \cdots \times p_n^{a_n}$ for some n and $a_i \in \{1,2\}$ for $1 \leq i \leq n$. The integers ≤ 30 in the range of g are thus $1,2,4,6,12,18,30$ corresponding to strings $\varepsilon,0,1,00,10,01,000$. Note the ordering obtained from this Gödel numbering is not the lexicographic ordering met before.

Such Gödel numbering is a useful encoding technique. As a further example, consider, Γ, the set of all graphs with unnamed vertices. Figure 1.12(a) gives an example of an element of Γ with four vertices and five edges. Γ has exactly one graph representing each equivalence class under graph isomorphism. We can prove Γ is countably infinite by assigning to each $G \in \Gamma$ a Gödel number, $g(G)$. Firstly, we could name the vertices of G by $p_1, p_2, \ldots, p_n$ and then a possible numbering is given by

$$p_1^{k_1} \times p_2^{k_2} \times \cdots \times p_n^{k_n}$$

where for each $i, 1 \leq n, k_i$ is computed according to the following algorithm.

$k_i := 1$;
for j from 1 to n do

        $e := $ number of edges connecting p_i to p_j;
        $k_i := k_i \times p_j^e$.

endfor

Thus $k_i = 1$ iff the vertex labelled p_i is isolated.

So if the graph of Fig. 1.12(a) is labelled as in Fig. 1.12(b), the number associated with it is

$$2^{3^2 \cdot 5} \times 3^{2^2 \cdot 3 \cdot 5} \times 5^{2 \cdot 3} \times 7 = 2^{45} \times 3^{60} \times 5^6 \times 7.$$

Although there is only one graph (up to isomorphism) having a given number according to our construction, any given graph with n nodes has

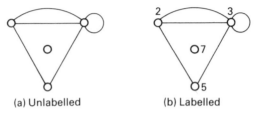

(a) Unlabelled   (b) Labelled

Fig. 1.12.

$n!$ different numberings according to the way in which we assign the labelling $p_1,p_2,...,p_n$ to the vertices of G. Since we wish to make the Gödel numbering unique, we must define $g(G)$ to be the smallest of these $n!$ possible numberings. It is then easy to check that such a g is one–one.

Gödel numbering is a powerful encoding technique which enables us to represent various discrete structures such as graphs with an integer encoding. For this reason, we concentrate our attention throughout much of this book on functions which are defined over the natural numbers. Also, since each such number can be represented in binary notation as a string in $\{0,1\}^*$, we will also be investigating computable functions over the set $B = \{0,1\}^*$.

EXERCISES

1 If the universe is taken as the set of positive integers less than 20, then list the elements of the following sets.

  (a) $\{x|x + 2 < 10\} \cup \{x|x \text{ is prime}\}$,

  (b) $\{x|x = x^2\}$,

  (c) $\{x|2x = 1\}$,

  (d) $\{x|3x < 20\}' \setminus \{x|x \text{ is even}\}$.

2 Let A be a finite set. Show that $\#(2^A) = 2^{\#(A)}$.
3 Show that Q, the set of all rational numbers, is countably infinite.
4 Show that if Σ is a finite alphabet, then Σ^* is countably infinite.
5 If $R \subseteq A \times B$ is a relation then its *inverse*, R^{-1}, is a relation in $B \times A$ defined by

$$R^{-1} = \{(b,a)|(a,b)\in R\}.$$

  (a) Show that $(R^{-1})^{-1} = R$;
  (b) What conditions must be imposed on R if R^{-1} is a total function? If $A = B$ so that R is a relation on A, show
  (c) R is reflexive iff R^{-1} is reflexive;
  (d) R is symmetric iff R^{-1} is symmetric;
  (e) R is transitive iff R^{-1} is transitive.
6 Show that the equivalence classes defined by an equivalence relation R on a set A partition A into a number of disjoint, nonempty sets. [Hint: $\bar{a}$ is nonempty since $a\in\bar{a}$; consider $\bar{a},\bar{b}$ and show that if $\bar{a}\cap\bar{b}\neq\varnothing$ then $\bar{a} = \bar{b}$.]

7 Show that if R_1, R_2 are two relations on A then
(a) R_1 is reflexive implies $R_1 \cup R_2$ is reflexive;
(b) R_1 and R_2 are reflexive implies $R_1 \cap R_2$ is reflexive.
Do these results remain true if every occurrence of 'reflexive' is replaced by 'symmetric'? What about replacing them by 'transitive'? What about 'antisymmetric'?

8 Let R be a relation in $A \times B$ and S a relation in $B \times C$. The *composition* of these two relations, $S_o R$, is defined to be the relation in $A \times C$ such that

$$S_o R = \{(a,c)| \text{ there exists } b \in B \text{ such that } (a,b) \in R \text{ and } (b,c) \in S\}.$$

(a) Show that composition is an associative operation.
(b) If R and S are total functions which are both onto, show that $S_o R$ is also a total function A onto C.

9 Explain how a relation $R \subseteq \mathbb{R} \times \mathbb{R}$ can be represented as a set of points in the Cartesian plane. If the line joining (x_1, y_1) and (x_2, y_2) is a subset of R for all $(x_1, y_1) \in R$ and $(x_2, y_2) \in R$, then R is said to be a *convex set*. Represent each of the following on the Cartesian plane and state which are convex sets.
(a) $R = \{(x,y)| x + y \geq 2, x \geq 0, y \geq 0\}$;
(b) $S = \{(x,y)| y \leq 2x + 4, y \leq 4 - 2x, x^2 + y^2 \geq 4, y \geq 0\}$.

10 Which of the following functions $\mathbb{R} \to \mathbb{R}$ are onto and which are one–one? Hence, determine which are bijections.
(a) *cube* $(x) = x^3$;
(b) *mod* $(x) = \begin{cases} x & \text{if } x \geq 0, \\ -x & \text{if } x < 0; \end{cases}$
(c) *sin* (x);
(d) *exp* $(x) = e^x$;
(e) *rec* $(x) = \begin{cases} 1 & \text{if } x = 0, \\ 1/x & \text{if } x \neq 0. \end{cases}$

11 Using the definitions given in question 10, define as simply as possible $exp_o \ rec$ and $rec_o \ cube_o \ mod$.

12 Show that $f: A \to B$ must be onto for $f^{-1}: B \to A$ to be total and that if f is not one–one then f^{-1} is not a function. Prove that f is a bijection if and only if f^{-1} is total function.
Find the inverses for all the bijections in question 10.

13 Prove by induction that 7 divides $3^{2n+1} + 4^{2n+1}$ for all $n \in N$.

14 Prove by induction that $S_n = 1^2 + 2^2 + \cdots + n^2$ is equal to $n(n + 1)(2n + 1)/6$ for all $n \in N$.

Let $C_n = 1^3 + 2^3 + \cdots + n^3$. Evaluate C_1, C_2, C_3 and postulate a formula for C_n. Prove its correctness by induction. [Hint: see if you can see a connection between C_n and $1 + 2 + \cdots + n = n(n+1)/2$.]

15 Consider the following recursive definitions of functions. For each one, postulate a simple formula for its definition and prove your answer correct by induction.

(a) $sq:N \to N$ where
$sq(x) = if\ x = 1\ then\ 1$
    $else\ sq(x-1) + 2x - 1$

(b) $mult:N \times N \to N$ where

$mult(x,y) = if\ x = 1\ then\ y$
    $else\ mult(x-1, y) + y$

(c) $power:N \times N \to where$

$power(x,y) = if\ x = 1\ then\ 1$
    $else\ mult(power(x, y-1), x)$

16 Show that the number of distinct partial functions $N \to N$ is uncountable.

17 If Z^+ denotes the non-negative integers, show that $length: \Sigma^* \to Z^+$ defined by

$$length(x) = \begin{cases} 0 & if\ x = \varepsilon \\ 1 + length(y) & if\ x = ay, a \in \Sigma, y \in \Sigma^*, \end{cases}$$

satisfies $length(x) = |x|$.

Use this recursive definition of length to show $length(xy) = length(x) + length(y)$ for all $x, y \in \Sigma^*$.

18 Give a recursive definition of $rev:\Sigma^* \to \Sigma^*$ such that if $x = a_1 a_2 \ldots a_n (a_i \in \Sigma, i = 1, \ldots, n)$ then $rev(x) = a_n \ldots a_2 a_1$.
Using the recursive definitions of length and reversal, show that $length(rev(x)) = length(x)$ for all $x \in \Sigma^*$.

19 If $L_1 = \{a, bc, ba\}$ and $L_2 = \{\varepsilon, bcc, a\}$, evaluate $L_1^2 L_2 \backslash L_2^2 L_1$.

20 Using the definition of length given in question 17, show that $tail^i(x) = \varepsilon$ iff $top^i(x) = \varepsilon$ iff $length(x) \le i$.

21 A *sparse matrix* M is one where the majority of entries are the same. If this is the case, we can represent M as a list of triples corresponding to the minority of differing elements. For each such element, the triple consists of its two indices and its value. Assuming, M is an integer $m \times n$ matrix, show that this saves space providing $3k < mn$ *where k is the number* of elements which differ from the majority. What is the corresponding result if M is a real matrix? [Remember a real requires two words of store for its representation.] If M_G is an adjacency matrix for a digraph with n nodes and m edges, how could it be efficiently stored if m was considerably less than n?

22   A vertex, v, in a graph $G = (V,E)$ whose degree is 1 is called a *leaf*. Show that if $\#(V) > 1$ and G is a tree then there are at least two leaves in V.

23   An *Euler path* of a graph $G = (V,E)$ is a path which includes every edge in E exactly once. Show that G has an Euler circuit iff either

(a) no vertices have odd degree, or

(b) just two vertices have odd degree.

24   Consider a tree $T = (V,E)$ where $V = \{1,2,\dots,n\}$. The following procedure then constructs from T a string $w_T \in V^{n-2}$.

begin $i := 1;$
while $i \le n - 2$ *do begin let* $j \in V$ be the smallest integer such that j is a leaf;
                          eliminate j and its incident edge, e, from T;
                          set the ith letter of the w_T string to be
                                        the other endpoint of e;
              $i := i + 1$
      end

Find the string $\in \{1,2,3,4,5,6\}^4$ constructed by this procedure from the tree given in Fig. 1.13. Describe a procedure which given a string $w \in \{1,2,\dots,n\}^{n-2}$ will produce a tree, T, such that $w = w_T$. Illustrate

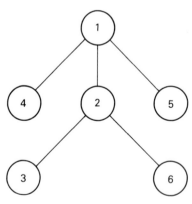

Fig. 1.13.

the working of your procedure by applying it to the string 1123.

Deduce that there is a one–one correspondence between trees with vertices $V = \{1,2,\ldots,n\}$ and strings in V^{n-2}. Hence, prove Cayley's theorem, viz. the number of distinct spanning trees constructable from n distinct vertices is n^{n-2}.

25 Prove that the function $g:\Gamma \to N$ defined in the text as a Gödel numbering is indeed one–one. Compute $g\,G)$ for the graph of Fig. 1.13. What property of a Gödel number of a graph ensures that the graph is a tree?

Chapter 2

Turing Machines

Tempt me no more; for I
Have known the lightning's hour,
The poet's inward pride,
The certainty of power.

CECIL DAY LEWIS
Tempt me no more

THE FORMAL DEFINITION

From our discussion in the introduction, we can now formally define a *Turing machine* (TM) as a 6-tuple, $M = (Q, \Sigma, T, P, q_0, F)$ where

(1) Q is a finite set of *states*,

(2) Σ is a finite set of *symbols* which can appear on the tape, one of which is denoted by $\wedge$ and is called the *blank symbol*,

(3) $T \subseteq \Sigma \setminus \{\wedge\}$ is the set of *input symbols*,

(4) P is a *program* which is a partial function

$$(Q \setminus F) \times \Sigma \to Q \times \Sigma \times \{L, R, 0\},$$

(5) $q_0 \in Q$ is the *initial state*,

(6) $F \subseteq Q$ is a set of *final states*.

Note that we allow symbols to appear on the tape which are neither blank nor in the input alphabet. Such symbols are called *auxiliary symbols* and the *auxiliary alphabet* is defined to be $\Sigma \setminus T \setminus \{\wedge\}$.

Since P is a partial function, $P(q, a)$, $q \in Q \setminus F$, $a \in \Sigma$, is either undefined or a unique element of $Q \times \Sigma \times \{L, R, 0\}$. $P(q, a) = (q', a', X)$ for some $q' \in Q$, $a' \in \Sigma$, $X \in \{L, R, 0\}$ iff the 5-tuple (q, a, q', a', X) appears in the program listing (as used in the Introduction). We have defined P as a partial function to ensure that the program is deterministic, i.e. that given any $q \in Q$, $a \in \Sigma$, there is at most one possible move for the TM when in state q and scanning symbol a.

As mentioned in the Introduction, we will generally be representing Turing machines by labelled digraphs. If $M = (Q, \Sigma, T, P, q_0, F)$ is a TM then we represent it by a labelled digraph $G_M = (Q, E)$ where $E = \{(q_i, q_j) |$ for some $a, a' \in \Sigma$ and $X \in \{L, R, 0\}$, $P(q_i, a) = (q_i, a', X)\}$. The arc from

36

a vertex q_i to a vertex q_j will then be labelled with all the triples (a, a', X) such that $P(q_i, a) = (q_j, a', X)$. Formally, the labelling is given by the function $l: E \to 2^{\Sigma \times \Sigma \times \{L,R,0\}}$ defined by

$$l((q_i, q_j)) = \{(a, a', X) | P(q_i, a) = (q_j, a', X)\}.$$

In our diagrammatic representation of such labelled diagraphs the labels will not appear as sets, however. We will simply list the triples in the corresponding set, i.e. we will be omitting the surrounding $\{\ldots\}$ and the commas separating the triples, both of which are formally required according to the definition (see, for example, Figs. 2.4 and 2.6b).

Now, we need to formalize the computation performed by a TM. Say at some stage the tape head is in state q and scanning the symbol a in location i. Let λ denote the leftmost location on the tape which holds a nonblank symbol and let ρ denote the corresponding rightmost location. Since the tape head is scanning location i, the string to the left of the tape head, α, is defined by

$$\alpha = \begin{cases} \varepsilon & \text{if } i \leq \lambda, \\ \text{string in locations } \lambda \text{ through } i-1 & \text{otherwise.} \end{cases}$$

Similarly, β, the string to the right of the tape head is defined by

$$\beta = \begin{cases} \varepsilon & \text{if } i \geq \rho, \\ \text{string in locations } i+1 \text{ through } \rho & \text{otherwise.} \end{cases}$$

The *configuration* of a TM is then defined to be the 5-tuple (q, i, α, a, β) as illustrated in Fig. 2.1.

The *initial configuration*, C_0, depends upon the input $x \in T^*$ and the start state $q_0 \in Q$. If $x = \varepsilon$, then $C_0 = (q_0, 1, \varepsilon, \wedge, \varepsilon)$. Otherwise $x = ay$ $a \in T$, $y \in T^*$ and $C_0 = (q_0, 1, \varepsilon, a, y)$. Thus, in either case, the initial configuration is

$$C_0 = (q_0, 1, \varepsilon, \text{if } x = \varepsilon \text{ then } \wedge \text{ else } head(x), tail(x))$$

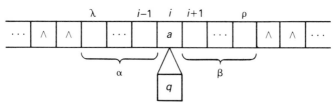

Fig. 2.1.

The configuration of a TM, M, then keeps changing as dictated by its program. We denote this sequence of configurations by $C_0, C_1, C_2, \ldots$ and call this sequence the *computation sequence* for M with input x. If $M = (Q, \Sigma, T, P, q_0, F)$ is in configuration $C_n = (q, i, \alpha, a, \beta)$ then the next configuration, C_{n+1}, is only defined if $q \notin F$ and $P(q, a)$ is defined. In that case

$$C_{n+1} = \begin{cases} (q', i-1, top(\alpha), if\ \alpha = \varepsilon\ then \wedge else\ foot(\alpha), b\beta) \\ \qquad\qquad\qquad\qquad if\ P(q, a) = (q', b, L), \\ (q', i+1, \alpha b, if\ \beta = \varepsilon\ then \wedge else\ head(\beta), tail(\beta)) \\ \qquad\qquad\qquad\qquad if\ P(q, a) = (q', b, R), \\ (q', i, \alpha, b, \beta) \qquad\qquad if\ P(q, a) = (q', b, 0). \end{cases}$$

These moves are illustrated in Fig. 2.2. If the next configuration is not defined because $q \in F$ then we say that the TM, M, *halts and succeeds*. In the case where no move is possible but $q \notin F$, we say that the TM *halts and fails*. In the second case, no output is defined but, in the first case, we will define the resulting output to be the string in $(\Sigma \setminus \{\wedge\})^*$ found in locations 1 though $k-1$ where $k \geq 1$ is the leftmost such location to contain a blank symbol. Say C_m is the configuration in which M halts

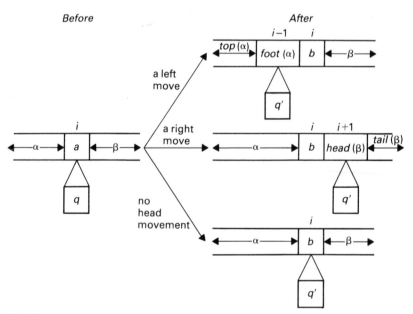

Fig. 2.2.

and succeeds. Before we can formally define $output(C_m)$, we need to define the function $front: \Sigma^* \rightarrow (\Sigma \backslash \{\wedge\})^*$ as follows

$$front(x) = \begin{cases} \varepsilon & \text{if } head(x) = \wedge \text{ or } x = \varepsilon, \\ concat(head(x), front(tail(x))) & \text{otherwise.} \end{cases}$$

The function *front* takes a string $x = a_1 a_2 \ldots a_n$ in Σ^* as an argument and delivers either ε (in the cases where $x = \varepsilon$ or $a_1 = \wedge$) or $a_1 a_2 \ldots a_{k-1}$ (where a_k is the first blank symbol in x). If no blank symbol occurs in x, $front(x) = x$. Thus, for example, $front(011 \wedge 0 \wedge 100)$ delivers 011 and $front(0001) = 0001$.

Now, we can formally define $output(C_m)$. If $C_m = (q, i, \alpha, a, \beta)$ then

$$output(C_m) = \begin{cases} front(tail^{-i}(\beta)) & \text{if } i \leq 0, \\ front(tail^{|\alpha|-i+1}(\alpha)a\beta) & \text{if } |\alpha| + 1 \geq i \geq 1, \\ \varepsilon & \text{otherwise} \end{cases}$$

These three possible situations are illustrated in Fig. 2.3.

Say the TM, $M = (Q, \Sigma, T, P, q_0, F)$, is given an input $x \in T^*$ and this

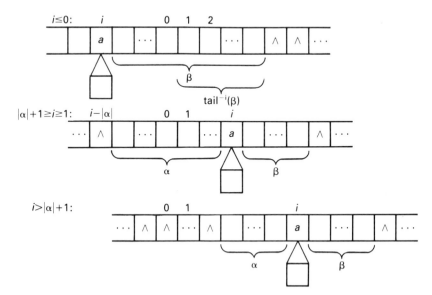

Fig. 2.3.

results in a finite computation sequence $C_0, C_1, C_2, \ldots, C_m$. If M halts and succeeds in C_m then this is a *successful computation sequence of length* m and the TM, M, is said to evaluate *output*(C_m). Thus, in this case, the TM, M, has computed a result given input x and this result is denoted by $f_M(x)$. Since M is deterministic, $x = y$ implies $f_M(x) = f_M(y)$. However, for some $x \in T^*$, it may be that f_M is not defined. This can arise either because the machine halts and fails or because it never halts at all. Thus, in general, f_M is a partial function from T^* to Σ^*. The function f_M is called the *function computed* by M. We then say that a function $f : T^* \to \Sigma^*$ is *(Turing) computable* iff there is a TM, M, such that $f = f_M$.

EXAMPLES

The following are Turing-computable:
(a) The partial function *undef* which is undefined for all $x \in \{0, 1\}^*$;
(b) the total function *cons0*: $\{0, 1\}^* \to \{0, 1\}^*$ defined by

$$cons0(x) = 0x \text{ for all } x \in \{0, 1\}.$$

(c) the total functions *head*: $\{0, 1\}^* \to \{0, 1\}$ and *tail*: $\{0, 1\}^* \to \{0, 1\}^*$.
   The corresponding TMs are given in Fig. 2.4(a), (b) and (c). As in the introduction, they are represented as labelled digraphs. The reader should study each of them carefully to verify that they are correct. Note that it does not matter how the states are named provided distinct states have distinct names. For this reason, we do not generally give names to states in our diagrams. The start state is indicated by an inward arrow and final states are represented by squares rather than circles.
   Two TMs, $M_1 = (Q_1, \Sigma_1, T, P_1, q_{01}, F_1)$ and $M_2 = (Q_2, \Sigma_2, T, P_2, q_{02}, F_2)$, both with the same input alphabet, T, are said to be *equivalent* iff $f_{M_1}(x) = f_{M_2}(x)$ for all $x \in T^*$.
   A TM, $M = (Q, \Sigma, T, P, q_0, F)$ can only halt and fail if there exists some $q \in Q$ and $a \in \Sigma$ such that $P(q, a)$ is not defined. This situation can always be avoided by constructing an equivalent TM, $M' = (Q \cup \{q_d\}, \Sigma, T, P', q_0, F)$ where $q_d \notin Q$ is a 'dead-end' state. If $q \in Q \backslash F$ and $a \in T$ then $P'(q, a) = P(q, a)$ provided $P(q, a)$ is defined but otherwise $P'(q, a) = (q_d, a, 0)$. Once in the dead-end state, M' remains there since $P'(q_d, a) = (q_d, a, 0)$ for all $a \in \Sigma$. Clearly M and M' are equivalent but where M will halt and fail, M' will enter the dead-end state and there loop forever. We have thus proved the following result.

Theorem 2.1

If f is a partial function which is Turing-computable then there exists a
TM, M, such that $f_M = f$ and M only halts in a final state, i.e. all halts
are successes.

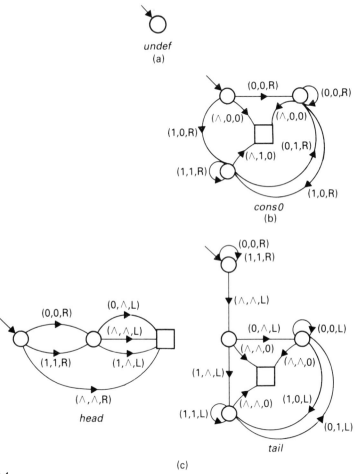

Fig. 2.4.

FURTHER TURING COMPUTABLE FUNCTIONS

In this section, we are briefly going to investigate some computable
functions defined over the natural numbers, N. We first need to decide

how we will represent such integers in our programs. To keep the TMs simple, we do not want to have too many symbols in the tape alphabet. We are thus inclined to restrict our input alphabet as much as possible.

One way of representing $x \in N$ is to use a *unary representation* which simply represents x as a string of x 1s. Thus 1 is represented by 1, 2 by 11, 3 by 111, etc. An alternative method familiar to all computer scientists is the *binary representation* where 1 is represented by 1, 2 by 10, 3 by 11, etc. Unary representation has the advantage of ultimate simplicity but binary representation is very familiar and more succinct. The string to represent $x \in N$ using unary representation is of length x but in binary representation it is only of length $\lfloor \log_2 x \rfloor + 1$. Both methods of representation can be formally defined using recursive functions.

unaryrep: $N \to \{1\}^*$ is defined by

$$unaryrep(x) = \begin{cases} 1 & \text{if } x = 1, \\ concat(1, unaryrep(x-1)) & \text{otherwise.} \end{cases}$$

and *binaryrep*: $N \to \{0, 1\}^*$ is defined by

$$binaryrep(x) = \begin{cases} 1 & \text{if } x = 1, \\ concat(binaryrep(x'/'2), 0) & \text{if } x > 1 \text{ is even,} \\ concat(binaryrep(x'/'2), 1) & \text{if } x > 1 \text{ is odd.} \end{cases}$$

where '/' denotes integer division.

We will be showing that whichever method of representation is used, the class of Turing computable functions over N is not affected. For the time being, we will opt for unary representation and consider the simple arithmetic operations of addition and multiplication.

Say we wish to compute $x + y$ for $x, y \in N$. We will encode our input as a string of x ones followed by the $+$ symbol, followed by a string of y ones. We want to construct a TM, which given such an input, computes as output the unary representation of $x + y$. This is easy; all we need to do is to remove the $+$ from our input and close up the two strings in $\{1\}^*$ by moving the whole representation of y one place to the left. Equivalently, we can replace $+$ by 1 and then delete the rightmost 1 in the resulting string. Using this second method, our unary adder can be as described in Fig. 2.5.

Multiplication of two numbers $x, y \in N$ is a little more complex. Again, we assume input is a unary encoding of x, followed by the operator (in this case, $\times$), followed by a unary encoding of y. Our TM must result in a unary encoding of the product of x and y. The first stage in our program

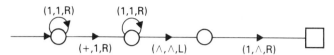

Fig. 2.5. A unary adder.

is a move of the input so that instead of occupying locations $1, 2, \ldots, k$ ($k = x + y + 1$), it occupies locations $-k, -k+1, \ldots, 1$. This enables us to use the positive part of the tape as work space without having the original input overwritten. We construct the output string as follows. Initially it is empty but then, for every distinct 1 in the unary encoding of y, we make a fresh copy of the encoding of x and append it to the output string. This technique is illustrated in Fig. 2.6(a) and the complete TM is given as a labelled diagram in Fig. 2.6(b). Note that we are using 0 and = as auxiliary symbols in this program. The = symbol is used to mark location 0.

The reader should make sure that he understands the working of this unary multiplier—it illustrates some important general techniques (viz. marking particular locations and using auxiliary symbols in copying). We will be giving further illustrative examples of TMs later in this chapter

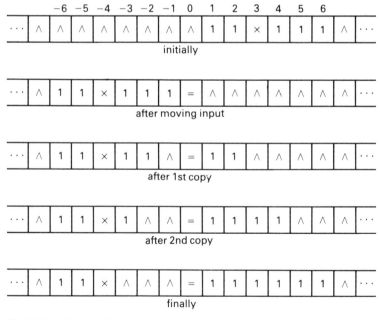

Fig. 2.6(a). Computation of 2×3.

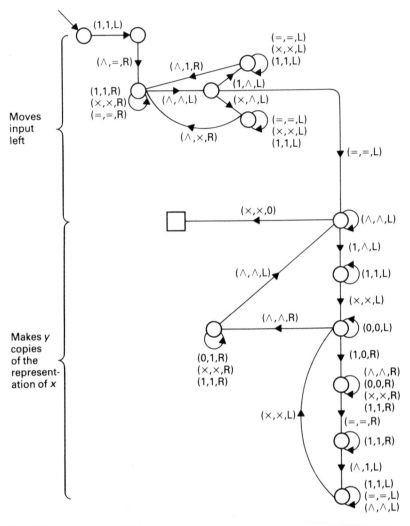

Moves input left {

Makes y copies of the representation of x {

Fig. 2.6(b). A unary multiplier.

and these techniques will be widely used. The reader will also need them if he is to construct the TMs requested in Exercises 2.1–2.4. Also, in the Appendix to this book, we give a Turing machine simulator written in Pascal together with details of its use. By using this simulator, the reader can check whether a particular TM in which he is interested performs as expected on any prescribed input.

We have shown that TMs are capable of computing addition and multiplication. By repeatedly copying the input and using the unary adder and multiplier, any polynomial function $N \to N$ defined by $p(x) = a_0 + a_1 x + a_2 x^2 + \cdots + a_n x^n$ can be shown to be Turing computable. In Exercise 2.3, the reader is asked to show that subtraction and integer division are also computable.

However, we have so far assumed a unary representation. It is now time to consider other representations. It does not matter which representation of numbers we use. Providing representations are well defined by some formal rule, Church's thesis tells us that there exists a Turing machine to compute them. Thus given x in a given representation, there must be a TM to compute x in some alternative representation. Similarly, there must be a TM to reverse this process, i.e. given an input of x in the alternative representation, there must be a TM to compute the equivalent original representation of x. We represent this diagrammatically in Fig. 2.7. Now, let f denote a function defined over the integers and T_f be a TM which computes f assuming input and output in the original representation. Then, we can construct a TM, T'_f, which also computes f but assumes input and output in the alternative representation. T'_f simply applies DECODE to each of its parameters, then runs T_f and then applies CODE to the output.

To illustrate our argument, we will construct the CODE and DECODE machines for the unary/binary representation. Let us first discuss the DECODE machine. This machine will take as input a binary representation of a natural number and compute its equivalent unary representation. Necessarily, the leftmost input symbol is 1. We then set the output also to be 1. The input is then processed from left to right character by character. If the next character is 0, we must double the length of the output; if it is 1, we must not only double it but also add an additional 1. In Fig. 2.8, we illustrate the workings of the DECODE machine assuming the input has already been copied from locations $1, 2, \ldots, n$ to locations

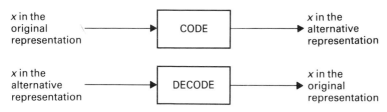

Fig. 2.7.

...	-4	-3	-2	-1	0	1	2	3	4	5	6	...
...	∧	1	0	1	=	∧	∧	∧	∧	∧	∧	...

...	∧	∧	0	1	=	1	∧	∧	∧	∧	∧	...

...	∧	∧	∧	1	=	1	1	∧	∧	∧	∧	...

...	∧	∧	∧	∧	=	1	1	1	1	1	∧	...

Fig. 2.8. Converting the representation of five.

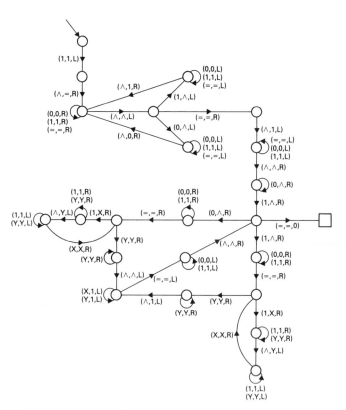

Fig. 2.9. Binary to unary converter.

$-n, \ldots, -2, -1$ and that location 0 has been marked with the auxiliary symbol, $=$. The detailed code for the complete machine is given in Fig. 2.9.

Now, let us consider the construction of a unary to binary converter. Our input will comprise a string of $k > 0$ ones. If $k = 1$, our output will also be 1, otherwise, we will need to find if k is odd or even. If k is even, our output should be a binary representation of $k'/2$ followed by 0 else we need a binary representation of $k'/2$ followed by 1. To achieve this, we simply scan the input string from left to right replacing the first 1 and then every alternate 1 by the auxiliary symbol X. If this process is completed by replacing a 1 by an X, the original string must have had an odd number of 1s and otherwise it had an even number. In the first case the rightmost symbol of the corresponding binary string is 1 and in the second case it is 0. Moreover, the number of ones left in the string is, in either case, precisely $k'/2$. Hence, we can apply this process repeatedly each time determining the next rightmost symbol in the binary representation. For example, consider the unary representation of eleven; the process constructs the binary representation as follows

	input string	output string
input	11111111111	ε
after 1st iteration	X1X1X1X1X1X	1
after 2nd iteration	XXX1XXX1XXX	11
after 3rd iteration	XXXXXXX1XXX	011
after last iteration	XXXXXXXXXXX	1011

The TM to convert unary representation into equivalent binary representation is given in Fig. 2.10. The input is in locations $1, \ldots, k$. The zero location is marked with the auxiliary symbol, $=$, and the output is constructed one symbol at a time in locations $-1, -2, \ldots$. After the penultimate iteration, there can only be one 1 left in the input string. This is replaced by an X in the final iteration, a 1 is then placed in location 1 and the remainder of the binary representation is copied from the negative part of the tape to locations $2, 3, \ldots$.

A NON-COMPUTABLE FUNCTION

Let $f: N \rightarrow N$ be a Turing-computable, partial function. Then we can assume that there exists a Turing machine $T_f = (Q, \Sigma, \{1\}, P, q_0, F)$ which

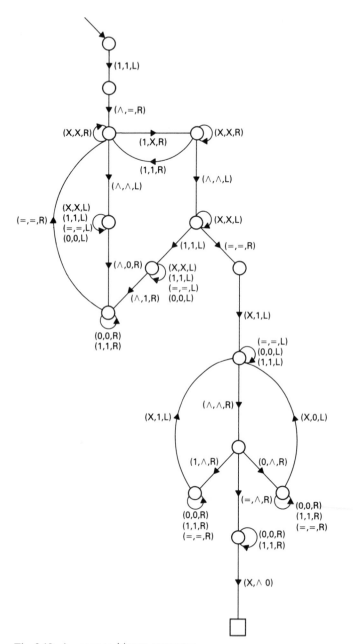

Fig. 2.10. A unary to binary converter.

computes f using unary representation. Without loss of generality, we can assume that the states of Q are labelled $q_0, q_1, q_2, \ldots$ and that the symbols in Σ are $1 = s_0, \wedge = s_1, s_2, s_3, \ldots$. Thus Q is a finite subset of the countable set $\bar{Q} = \{q_i | i \geq 0\}$ and Σ is a finite subset of the countable set $\bar{\Sigma} = \{s_i | i \geq 0\}$. To specify, T_f, we need simply to list its program as a set of 5-tuples and state which states are final states. Each 5-tuple in the program is then of the form $t = (q_i, s_j, q_k, s_l, X)$ where i, j, k and l are non-negative integers and $X \in \{L, R, 0\}$. A 5-tuple, t, can be encoded as the integer, $g(t)$, using a Gödel numbering technique,

$$g(t) = 2^{i+1} 3^{j+1} 5^{k+1} 7^{l+1} 11^{m+1}$$

where $m = 0$ if $X = L$, $m = 1$ if $X = R$ and $m = 2$ if $X = 0$. A finite sequence of 5-tuples, $\underline{t} = (t_1, t_2, \ldots, t_n)$, can then be encoded as the integer

$$g(\underline{t}) = 2^{g(t_1)} 3^{g(t_2)} \cdots p_n^{g(t_n)}$$

where p_n is the nth prime number. Then, if the TM, T_f, has a program determined by the 5-tuples $(t_1, t_2, \ldots, t_n)$ and final states $q_{\lambda 1}, q_{\lambda 2}, \ldots, q_{\lambda r}$, $\lambda 1 < \lambda 2 < \cdots < \lambda r$, we can encode T_f as

$$g(T_f) = 2^{g(L)} 3^{\lambda 1 + 1} 5^{\lambda 2 + 1} \cdots p_{r+1}^{\lambda r + 1}.$$

Having established this Gödel numbering, we can deduce the following.

Theorem 2.2

The set $\{T_f | T_f$ is a TM of the type described above which computes a partial function $f: N \to N\}$ is countably infinite.

Now, since this set is countable, its elements can be listed, $T_{f_1}, T_{f_2}, \ldots$ where T_{f_i} computes $f_i: N \to N$. Any $f_i: N \to N$ which is computable has at least one corresponding T_{f_i} which occurs in this listing. Using a technique similar to that of Cantor's diagonalization described in Chapter 1, we can construct a function $g: N \to N$ which does not have a corresponding T_g in this list. We simply define

$$g(n) = \begin{cases} f_n(n) + 1 & \text{if } f_n(n) \text{ is defined,} \\ 1 & \text{if } f_n(n) \text{ is undefined.} \end{cases}$$

Now, say g has a corresponding Turing machine which occurs in our list. Then g must be computed by T_{f_k} for some k. But T_{f_k} computes f_k and from the definition of g, $g(k) \neq f_k(k)$ so $g \neq f_k$. Hence we have a contradiction. This shows that g is not computable. We have proved

Theorem 2.3

There are noncomputable functions $N \to N$.

Actually, the situation is even worse than this theorem suggests. In Exercise 16 of Chapter 1, the reader was asked to show that there are an uncountable number of partial functions $N \to N$. We have shown that only a countable number are Turing-computable, so there must be an uncountable number of noncomputable functions. This may seem a rather depressing result. But, remember, it is not an indictment of Turing machines. All the research effort in computability has indicated that *Church's thesis* is correct, i.e. that every effectively computable function is Turing-computable. We now know, however, that the majority of functions are not likely to be effectively computable and hence, although theoretically of importance, they are not going to have any practical significance.

MULTITAPE TURING MACHINES

If we accept *Church's thesis* to be true (and we do!), Turing machines have the potential for computing any function which can be computed on any other machine. In particular, if we embellish Turing machines with additional facilities, we should not expect the new machines to have greater computing power. In this section we illustrate this claim by considering Turing machines with more than one tape. In Chapter 4, a further illustration is given when we consider nondeterministic Turing machines. Yet another is given in Exercise 2.10.

A multitape Turing machine consists of $n(> 1)$ infinite tapes over which n tape heads move. The n heads are connected to a control, as in Fig. 2.11. The control can be in any of a finite number of states, Q. The program specifies the next move which depends upon the state, q, of the control and the symbols scanned by each of the tape heads. Depending upon these values, the machine can change state, write a new symbol at each location being scanned, and move any or all of the tape heads independently to the left or to the right.

Tape 1 is going to be used for input and output so that the remaining

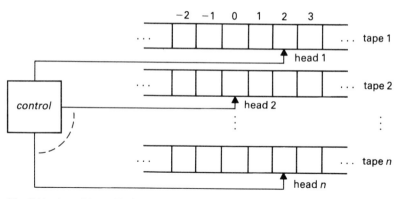

Fig. 2.11. A multitape Turing machine.

tapes provide extra workspace. Initially, an input $x \in T^*$ is written in locations $1, 2, \ldots, |x|$ of the first tape with all other locations on this and other tapes blank. All tape heads start by scanning location 1 of their respective tapes. The machine eventually halts if the control enters one of a set of final states, $F \subseteq Q$. The output will be written on tape 1. If location 1 of that tape contains a blank symbol then the output is ε; otherwise, the output will be the string of symbols found in locations $1, \ldots, k-1$ of tape 1 where k is the leftmost location > 0 which contains a blank. As with (one-tape) Turing machines, we allow auxiliary symbols to be written on the tapes and thus, in general, the output is an element of Σ^* where $T \subseteq \Sigma$.

Rather than formulate a rigorous definition of a multitape TM we will continue with an informal presentation. From this, the reader should be able to produce a formal argument if he so wishes. We can now outline the proof of the following expected result.

Theorem 2.4

A function $f: T^* \to \Sigma^*$ is TM-computable iff it is computable on a multitape Turing machine.

Proof.
$\Rightarrow$: This is obvious. The multitape TM simply performs all its calculations on the first tape according to the (one-tape) TM program which computes f.
$\Leftarrow$: We will outline the proof for the case where f is computed by a 2-tape TM, M. Even in outline the proof is quite involved and can be

omitted at a first reading. Generalizing the argument to the case where M has n-tapes is, however, a fairly straightforward exercise and is left to the reader.

From M, we will construct a (one-tape) TM, M', which also computes f. Let Σ denote the tape alphabet of M. Then, the tape alphabet of M' comprises 3-tuples of the form (X, B_1, B_2) where the first component, X, is either 0 or 1 and the other two components, B_1, B_2, are elements of Σ (but possibly superscripted by 1). We will be simulating a configuration of M by a configuration of M'. Firstly, consider any location k. Say the symbol on tape 1 in this location is A_1 and on tape 2 it is A_2. Location k of M' will then contain (X, B_1, B_2). $X = 1$ or 0 according to whether $k = 1$ or not, and for $i = 1, 2, B_i = A_i^1$ if head i is scanning location k of tape i and $B_i = A_i$, otherwise. If $x = a_1 a_2 \ldots a_n (n > 0)$ is input to machine, M', the first step of M' is a scan of this input replacing the contents of locations $1, 2, \ldots, n$ by $(1, a_1^1, \wedge^1), (0, a_2, \wedge), \ldots .(0, a_n, \wedge)$ respectively. If $n = 0$ we simply set location 1 to contain $(1, \wedge^1, \wedge^1)$. We assume that the blank symbol for machine M is the triple $(0, \wedge, \wedge)$ and that all other locations contain this symbol. The content of the tape of M' then represents the initial contents of the tapes of M.

We now need to describe the part of the TM, M', which simulates the action of M. Say Q denotes the set of states of M, then M' will have states $Q \times \Sigma^2 \times 2^{\{1,2\}} \times \{\langle, =, \rangle\} \times \{L, 0, R\}^2$. M' will be in state $(q, (A_1, A_2), S, X, (Y_1, Y_2))$ iff in the corresponding configuration of M, (i) M is in state q, and (ii) head$_1$ is scanning A_1 and head$_2$ is scanning A_2.

Any location of the TM, M', which has one or more components superscripted by 1 is called an *active location*. There will be at most two active locations, the first with its second component superscripted and the second with its third component superscripted. The first component of the state of M' is used to locate active locations. If the tape head of M' is scanning location k then for $i = 1, 2, i \in S$ iff the ith active location is to the left of location k. The symbol X is used to denote whether $k < 1, k = 1$ or $k > 1$ respectively. The symbols (Y_1, Y_2) are used in the simulation of a single move of M by M'. Figure 2.12 illustrates the construction we have described.

Having set the input as described above, M moves its head back to location 1 (marked by having its first component equal to 1) and enters state $(q_0, (a_1, \wedge), \phi, = , (0, 0))$. The simulation of M' can now begin.

To simulate a move of M, M' proceeds in two phases. In the first phase, M' computes from its current state, (i) the next state of the control of M,(ii) the symbols which must be written by each tape head of M and

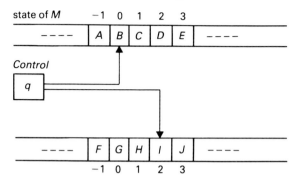

a corresponding
state of M'

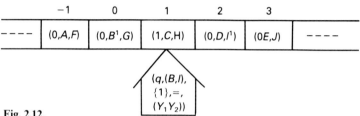

Fig. 2.12.

(iii) the direction of move of each of the tape heads. This information
is stored in the first, second and fifth components, respectively, of the state
of M'. The second phase is then entered. The tape head must visit each
of the two active locations in turn. As M' traverses the tape, the third
and fourth components of its state must be updated. The information in
the third component enables M' to know in which direction it will find
the next active location it seeks. When M' finds the ith ($i = 1,2$) active
location, the $(i + 1)$th component of the triple stored there will be
superscripted by 1. This symbol must be replaced by the ith component
of the second component of the state of M'. The superscript 1 is then attached
to the $(i + 1)$th component of the triple being scanned, or of the triple in
the location to the left, or that in the location to the right, according to
whether the ith component of the fifth component of M' is 0, L or R,
respectively. The second phase of the simulation of a move is only
completed when both active locations have been visited and their
corresponding entries updated. During this visiting process, the second
component of the state of M' can also be updated so that it contains the
new pair of symbols scanned by M.

Having completed phase two, the simulation of a move of M by M'

is achieved. This simulation process is then repeated as many times as
necessary thereby allowing M' to simulate the computation performed
by M. If M enters a final state, M' will then use its fourth component to
locate location 1. Once location 1 has been found, the required output is
achieved by scanning right and replacing each triple found in a location
by the second component of that triple. However, as soon as a triple with
second component $\wedge$ or $\wedge^1$ is found the blank symbol $(0, \wedge, \wedge)$ is written
and M enters its final state. This ensures that the output defined by
executing M given input x is exactly $f(x)$, as required.

RESTRICTED TURING MACHINES

Our basic TM model, although simple and relatively easy to use,
nevertheless provides us with the power to compute any effectively
computable function. In this section we consider some restrictions on our
model which do not limit this power. For example, one restriction that we
can make is to limit the tape so that it is not infinite in both directions
but only in one. Thus, instead of being indexed $\ldots -2, -1, 0, 1, 2, \ldots$, the
tape is simply indexed $1, 2, \ldots$. The TM program is executed in the normal
way except that if a left move is attempted while the tape head is scanning
location 1 then the machine halts and fails. We call such a restricted TM,
a *one-way infinite tape Turing machine*, whilst our usual model could be
called a two-way infinite tape Turing machine.

Theorem 2.5

If $f: T^* \rightarrow \Sigma^*$ is a TM-computable partial function, then it is computable
on a one-way infinite tape Turing machine.

Proof. As in the previous section, we will just outline the necessary
construction and leave the formalization to the reader. Since f
is TM-computable there exists a two-way infinite tape TM, $M =
(Q, T, \Sigma, P, q_0, F)$, such that $f = f_M$. We will show how to construct from M a
one-way infinite tape TM, M', such that $f_{M'} = f_M$.

   The key to this proof is the representation of the contents of a two-way
infinite tape on a one-way infinite tape by using a similar technique to
that used in Chapter 1 to show that Z was countable. We map the contents
of the locations of the two-way tape onto the locations of the one-way
tape as shown in Fig. 2.13. Locations 1 and 2 of the one-way infinite tape
both contain the special symbol $* \notin \Sigma$, the purpose of which will soon

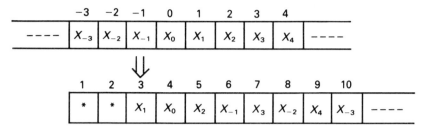

Fig. 2.13.

become apparent. The contents of location $i \geq 1$ of M is to be found in location $2i + 1$ of M', whilst the contents of location $i \leq 0$ of M is to be found in location $4 - 2i$ of M'.

Now, suppose the tape head for M is scanning location $i > 1$, then at the equivalent point in the calculation using M', we require that its tape head must be scanning location $2i + 1$. If the move for M is to replace the scanned symbol by X and move right, for M' it must also be to replace the scanned symbol by X but then move two places to the right. Similarly, in such a position, a left move for M is replaced by a move two places to the left for M'. We thus construct from P, the program for M, P'_R, a program which only differs from P in that each right move is replaced by two right moves and each left move by two left moves. We will also assume that the states used in P'_R are identical to those of P except that they all have an additional R subscript. We can then use P'_R to mimic the action of P on the positive part of M's tape.

On the other hand, if M is scanning a location $i < 0$, the corresponding location on M' is $4 - 2i$. In such a situation a left move for M corresponds to two right moves for M' and a right move for M similarly corresponds to two left moves for M'. Thus, we construct P'_L identical to P except for using L as a subscript for all the states and replacing each right move by two left moves and each left move by two rights.

Having constructed P'_R and P'_L we are well on the way to constructing P'. The first thing P' does is to move its input two places to the right and write the special symbol, $*$, in locations 1 and 2. Then the tape head is moved to location 3 and it starts to execute P'_R. If at any stage, a double left move causes it to scan $*$ it must then be scanning location 1. If M' is currently in state q_R then the equivalent configuration of M is to be in state q scanning the symbol in location 0. Thus, we define $P'(q_R, *)$ so that it results in a move three places to the right to scan location 4 of M' and at the same time enters the corresponding state, q_L, of P'_L. Execution of

P'_L will then proceed. During this execution, if at any stage a double left move results in the machine scanning $*$ again, we must necessarily be scanning location 2. M' must then move right once to scan location 3 and change from some $q_L \in P'_L$ to the corresponding $q_R \in P'_R$.

In this way, the symbol $*$ is used to change from the execution of P'_R to that of P'_L and vice versa. Thus we enable P' to mimic the execution of P. One final modification is then required to ensure the correct output. When P enters a final state, P' must adjust its tape content by moving the contents of locations $3,5,7,\ldots$ to locations $1,2,3,\ldots$ up to and including the first blank symbol. This completes the construction of P.

In general, we will keep to our two-way infinite tape model for Turing machines since this avoids having to consider the special case of halting and failing when attempting a left move from location 0. However, on occasions, the use of the one-way infinite tape model is justified since it can simplify proofs.

There are other restrictions that can be made to our TM model without effecting the computing power. A good survey of such restrictions is to be found in Fischer (1965). For example, we can view the TM as a 2-tape device, the first tape being used for input/output only and the second tape as a work tape. We can then insist that the alphabet used on the work tape comprises just one symbol other than the blank. To prove this result is fairly easy. Say $M = (Q, \Sigma, T, P, q_0, F)$ is an example of our usual model of a TM with n possible nonblank tape symbols. We can encode the ith of these symbols by $1^i \wedge^{n-i}$ and the blank symbol by $\wedge^n$. Thus each symbol in Σ is represented uniquely in precisely n tape locations. The 2-tape TM constructed from M first encodes the input from its first tape onto its second tape using this encoding. Then, on its second tape it can simulate the action of M but working with the encoded symbols. If this simulation halts, the output can be deduced by decoding the information from the work tape back to the output tape.

Another similar result which we will be requiring later and which is based on a binary encoding, is the following.

Theorem 2.6

Every TM-computable function $\{0,1\}^* \to \{0,1\}^*$ can be computed by a one-tape TM which uses only $\{0, 1, \wedge\}$ as its tape alphabet.

Proof (outline). Say $M = (Q, \Sigma, \{0,1\}, P, q_0, F)$ computes $f : \{0,1\}^* \to \{0,1\}^*$ and that the nonblank symbols of Σ are $0, 1, s_1, s_2, \ldots, s_n$ for some $n \geq 1$. We can encode each of these symbols as a string in $\{0,1\}^*$ of length $k = \lceil \log_2(n+2) \rceil$ using a binary encoding. For example, if $n = 5$, we find $k = 3$ and encode 0 as 000, 1 as 001, s_1 as 010, s_2 as 011, s_3 as 100, s_4 as 010 and s_5 as 110. In this case, 111 is not used. We construct a TM, M', from M as follows. M' first encodes the input $\in \{0,1\}^*$ using the binary encoding we have outlined. M' can then simulate the action of M, and if this simulation halts, can decode the information on its tape to obtain the required output. During this decoding any encoding of s_i on the tape can be decoded as $\wedge$ without affecting the final output since the output cannot involve any symbols not in $\{0,1\}$. Providing each encoding of 0 and 1 are decoded correctly, the correct output is ensured. It is thus assured that M' never has symbols other than $0, 1$ and $\wedge$ occurring on its tape.

EXERCISES

1   Construct a TM to compute $length : \{0,1\}^+ \to N$ assuming the output is to be represented in unary notation. Hence, or otherwise, construct the TM which compute $length$ assuming the output is to be represented in binary notation.

2   Construct a TM to compute $rev : \{0,1\}^* \to \{0,1\}^*$ (as defined in Exercise 18 of Chapter 1).

3   Consider the function $palindrome : \{0,1\}^* \to \{0,1\}$ defined by

$$palindrome(x) = \begin{cases} 1 & \text{if } x = rev(x), \\ 0 & \text{otherwise.} \end{cases}$$

Show that $palindrome(x) = 1$ iff either $length(x) \leq 1$ or else x is of the form $0y0$ or $1y1$ and $palindrome(y) = 1$. Hence, construct a TM to compute $palindrome$. Is this method more or less efficient that constructing $rev(x)$ directly and checking whether x equals $rev(x)$?

4   Construct a TM to compute the partial functions sub and div: $N \times N \to N$ defined by

$$sub(x,y) = \begin{cases} x - y & \text{if } x > y, \\ \text{undefined} & \text{otherwise.} \end{cases}$$

and

$$div(x,y) = \begin{cases} k & \text{if } x = ky \text{ for some } k \in N, \\ \text{undefined} & \text{otherwise.} \end{cases}$$

In both cases, assume that the input comprises a unary representation of *x* followed by an operator symbol (− or ÷ as appropriate) followed by a unary representation of *y*.

5 Adjust your answers to question 4 so that the TMs will never halt and fail given an input in {−,÷,1}*.

6 Test that your answers to questions 1,2 and 3 are correct by running the programs on the TM simulator given in the Appendix. In each case, make sure you choose a range of inputs that fully tests your program.

7 Code the TM programs of question 4 as 5-tuples and input them to the TM simulator. Describe the inputs which you would use to test the correctness (or otherwise!) of your programs. (You can similarly use the TM simulator to test all your TM programs.)

8 Define a function {0,1}* → {0,1}* which is *not* Turing-computable.

9 If the input to the unary adder is *m* ones followed by +, followed by *n* ones, what is the length of the resulting successful computation? What is the corresponding result for the unary multiplier? How could the average case efficiency of these programs be improved?

10 Consider extending the tape of a TM to two dimensions where the tape head's position is given by coordinates $(i,j), i,j \in Z$. Depending on the state and symbol scanned, the *two-dimensional Turing machine* can change its state and move its tape head one unit in any of four directions (left, right, up and down). At any time, only a finite number of locations can have a nonblank symbol written in them. Input and output is obtained from locations $(1,1),(1,2),(1,3),\ldots$ in the obvious way. Show that any function computable by a two-dimensional Turing machine is also computable by a (one-dimensional) TM.

Chapter 3

Solvability and Unsolvability

The troubles of our proud and angry dust
Are from eternity, and shall not fail.
Bear them we can, and if we can we must.
Shoulder the sky, my lad, and drink your ale.

A. E. HOUSMAN
Last Poems

A UNIVERSAL TURING MACHINE

In the Appendix to this book, we describe a computer program for a Turing machine simulator. The input to this simulation program must comprise a description of a Turing machine, $M = (Q, \Sigma, T, P, q_0, F)$, together with a string, $x \in T^*$. The TM description must satisfy a particular format which is also specified in the Appendix. For the time being, let us denote an *encoding* of the TM, M, by $e(M)$. Then, given an input of $e(M)$ and x, the simulation program (which we assume has sufficient storage allocation) will simulate the action of M with input x. If M would halt and succeed with this input and thus compute $f_M(x)$, the simulator will also result in an output of $f_M(x)$. If M would halt and fail given input x, then the simulator will output a message to this effect. However, if M would loop forever, then so will the simulator and thus no message will be obtained. Unfortunately, as we shall be proving in this chapter, this problem with looping is unavoidable. There is no way that our simulator can always detect when an arbitrary TM, M, is stuck in a loop and thus there is no possibility of the simulator always being able to inform us of such a situation.

Church's thesis tells us that any function computable by a Pascal program is also computable by some Turing machine. Thus there must be a TM which performs the actions of our simulator. Moreover, unlike our Pascal program, such a TM need not suffer from a restricted amount of store. From this we can deduce that there is a TM, U, which will take as input on its tape $e(M)$, an encoding of a TM, $M = (Q, \Sigma, T, P, q_0, F)$, followed by a separator symbol, $*$, say, followed by a string $x \in T^*$. Then, given

59

Input

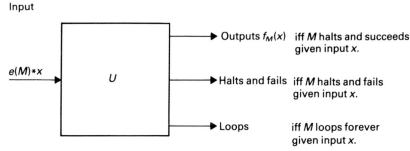

Fig. 3.1. A universal TM.

this input, $e(M)*x$, U halts and succeeds iff M halts and succeeds given input x. Moreover, in such a situation, the output of U is the same as that of M, viz. $f_M(x)$. Also, U halts and fails given input $e(M)*x$ iff M halts and fails with input x and, finally, U loops forever given input $e(M)*x$ iff M loops forever given input x.

We summarize the situation in Fig. 3.1. A Turing machine of this form is called a *universal Turing machine*. The precise nature of a universal TM will depend upon the exact encoding used for its input. We are assuming that any encoding of the TM, M, is 'sensible'. By this we mean that (i) there is some effective procedure for computing $e(M)$ from M, (ii) that given $e(M)$ this uniquely determines M and that one can effectively decode the encoding, and (iii) that the encoding does not contain an unnecessary amount of spurious padding symbols. One possible sensible encoding might be obtained from a Gödel numbering of the TM (see Chapter 2).

The problem with a universal TM is that it simulates too well! If the machine M loops forever given input x, then a universal TM will loop forever given input $e(M)*x$. No output will then result. How can we tell when to switch off the universal TM? It may be in a loop or it may still be in the middle of some computation which will eventually halt. It would be so much more satisfactory if we could adjust our universal TM so that given an input $e(M)*x$ it either computes $f_M(x)$ or it tells us that $f_M(x)$ is undefined. This would require U to be able to recognize when M was stuck in a loop.

THE HALTING PROBLEM

An algorithm is a procedure which always yields an answer. More formally, we can define an *algorithm* to be a Turing machine which always

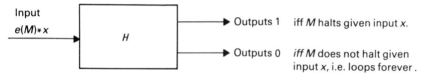

Fig. 3.2. An impossible TM.

halts. If an algorithm exists which solves a given problem, we say that problem is *solvable*; otherwise, it is *unsolvable*. For example, we have shown in chapter two that addition and multiplication of integers is a solvable problem. We are now asking whether there is an algorithm to solve the *halting problem for Turing machines*. This is the problem: 'Given a TM, $M = (Q, \Sigma, T, P, q_0, F)$, and an input $x \in T^*$, will M eventually halt?' Thus, we seek a TM, H, which behaves as in Fig. 3.2. We are going to show that such a TM cannot possibly exist! This will be established in the following theorem. Not only is this one of the most important theorems in this book, but also it has one of the most attractive and subtle proofs.

Theorem 3.1

The halting problem for Turing machines is unsolvable.

Proof. We will assume the TM, H, does exist and then obtain a contradiction. Assuming H does exist, construct another TM, H', as follows. H' takes as input $e(M)$, an encoding of a Turing machine, M, and copies it to obtain the string $e(M)*e(M)$. H' then runs H with this input except that where H would output 1, H' instead loops forever. Figure 3.3 describes the action of H'.

Now, what happens if we input $e(H')$ to H'? From the above construction, we see that H' loops iff it halts and halts iff it loops! This

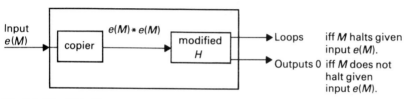

Fig. 3.3. The TM, H'.

clear contradiction establishes the non-existence of the TM, H', and hence
of H.

The unsolvability of the halting problem for Turing machines is quite a
remarkable result which has serious repercussions throughout computing.
Since we can simulate a TM using a conventional computer program with
unlimited storage, it follows that there is no algorithm which can take an
arbitrary such program and an arbitrary input to that program and tell
you whether or not the program will halt. It may be that for some particular
program you can show that it will always halt, but this theorem says that
there is no general strategy that can be applied.

Generally, a computer programmer will be given some *specification*
defining exactly what his program should achieve. For example, a simple
programming task may be to write a program in Pascal, say, which meets
the following specification:

INPUT: three integers a, b, c

OUTPUT: two roots of the equation $ax^2 + bx + c = 0$ (provided they
exist).

As is so often the case with specifications in practice, this specification is
incomplete—a complete specification would state what output should be
provided when the roots do not exist, or when both roots are equal, or
when $a = 0$, etc. When all this has been decided the programmer then has
the task of writing a program, P, to meet some complete specification, S.
He must ensure that the program does indeed achieve this objective;
ideally, he should show that for all inputs for which the specification, S,
is defined, his program, P, terminates and yields the output defined by S
on that input. The program is then said to be *totally correct*.

Now, if we have a programming language that enables us to simulate
the action of Turing machines, then we know that there is no general
algorithm available for proving whether an arbitrary program with
unlimited storage halts or not. Even if (as usual) the storage is finite, the
problem, although theoretically solvable, remains impossible to solve in
practice. There are so many possible configurations of a machine of any
reasonable size that it is impractical to test to see if any one of these
possible configurations is repeated. This appears to be a very serious
problem to the computer scientist (as indeed it is!).

There are two ways by which we may overcome this problem. One
possibility is to restrict our programming language to such an extent that

we can find an algorithm which can tell whether an arbitrary program in that language does or does not halt on some given input. Clearly, the restrictions on the language would have to ensure that we could not simulate the simple operations of a TM. A better approach is probably to develop some general techniques which can be applied to particular programs written in the given language. If these techniques are applied intelligently they will usually produce a proof of termination for a correct program. We cannot guarantee their success, but the expectation is that a competent programmer should generally be able to formulate such a proof for his program. The precise techniques will depend upon the programming language under consideration. For example, in Pascal, one possible cause of infinite looping is the failure to exit from a while statement. A while statement has the form

> *while B do S*

where B is a Boolean expression and S some statement. The Boolean expression, B, is evaluated and, if it is true, S is executed and the while statement re-entered. Only when B evaluates to false can this process stop and the statement be completed. Thus, the above while statement is equivalent to

if B then begin
> *S; while B do S*
> *end*

Say the Boolean expression is of the form $x \subseteq c$ where $\subseteq$ is some total ordering relation, x a variable and c a constant. The programmer may be able to prove his program does not loop forever because of this while statement providing he can show that if $x = x_i$(say) before execution of S then after execution of $S, x = x_{i+1}$ where $x_i \subset x_{i+1}$. Thus the value of x 'increases' at each iteration of the while statement but the while statement will only be executed whilst the value of x remains 'less than' c. Providing the set of values which x can take contains c and is countable, termination is assured.

Techniques for proving programs correct are usually based upon mathematical logic. This material is covered in Dowsing, Rayward–Smith & Walter (1985). In that text, simple rules are established which enable a programmer to obtain a *partial verification* of a correct program, i.e. to show that if the program terminates then it satisfies its specification. It should be admitted, however, that most programs which are written are never formally shown even to be partially correct let alone totally correct.

In this way, programming bugs are allowed to remain in code with perhaps drastic consequences (misfunction of weaponry, collapsing bridges, financial mismanagement, etc.). The responsibility of a programmer is to produce correct code, and no code can be deemed correct until it has been proved correct. It is because such proofs are difficult, especially for large programs, that many programmers have decided that testing their program with a wide range of test data is sufficient. In the absence of a widely applicable and well-developed methodology with suitable software tools, this practice will no doubt continue.

The halting problem for TMs is not the only unsolvable problem—in fact there is a significant number of them which arise in various branches of mathematics and computing. The proof of many of these results relies upon the unsolvability of the halting problem. The main part of such a proof is in showing that if the given problem were solvable then so would be the halting problem. We will be giving some examples of such proofs in this and the subsequent chapter. Firstly, however, we need some formal notation to simplify our discussion.

For many problems there is a corresponding problem with a yes/no solution. For example, the problem of addition of two integers x, y can be expressed as 'Given integers x, y and z, does $z = x + y$?' Problems with yes/no solutions are called *decision problems* and, in common with most books and research on computability, we will be spending much of our time discussing such problems. Whenever we have such a decision problem, we will present it in a standard format. This format includes a title (with possible abbreviation) for the problem, a description of instances of the problem and a statement of the question being asked. Thus the addition example might be written as follows:

Addition of integers (ADD)
INSTANCE: Three integers, x, y and z.
QUESTION: Does $z = x + y$?

Another decision problem we have met is

Halting problem (HP)
INSTANCE A Turing machine, $M = (Q, \Sigma, T, P, q_0, F)$, and a string $x \in T^*$.
QUESTION: Does M halt given x as input?

In general, if Π is a decision problem, then there is a set, D_Π, the *domain* of Π, comprising all *instances* of the problem. For some of these instances the answer is yes and for others the answer is no. Thus D_Π is divided into two disjoint subsets, Y_Π, the *yes instances*, and N_Π, the *no instances*. We then say that Π is *solvable* iff there exists a Turing machine, M_Π, which, given a (sensible) encoding $e(I)$ of any instance $I \in D_\Pi$, always halts successfully and with an output which determines whether or not $I \in Y_\Pi$. Without loss of generality, we will assume an output of 1 if $I \in Y_\Pi$ and an output of 0 otherwise. If no such Turing machine exists, the decision problem is *unsolvable*. ADD is an example of a solvable decision problem, and much of the work done in chapter two can be related to such problems. Now, however, we have an example of an unsolvable problem (HP) and we will soon be discovering others.

Consider two decision problems Π and Π'. We say that Π *reduces to* Π' (written $\Pi \rightarrow \Pi'$) if an algorithm to solve Π' can be directly used to solve Π. More formally, $\Pi \rightarrow \Pi'$ iff there is a TM that will take as input, $e(I)$, an encoding of any instance of Π, and yield as output, $e'(I')$, some encoding of an instance I' of Π', such that $I \in Y_\Pi$ iff $I' \in Y_{\Pi'}$. Whenever we use the word encoding in this book, we mean a sensible encoding and, under this assumption, it is easy to show that $\rightarrow$ is transitive (Exercise 3.4).

We can also deduce the following important results.

Theorem 3.2

(1) If $\Pi \rightarrow \Pi'$ and Π' is solvable then so is Π.
(2) If $\Pi \rightarrow \Pi'$ and Π is unsolvable then so is Π'.

Proof. (1) From the definition of $\rightarrow$, $I \in Y_\Pi$ iff $I' \in Y_{\Pi'}$ where there exists a TM which given input $e(I)$ for any $I \in D_\Pi$ will output $e'(I')$. Now, since Π' is solvable, there exists another TM which can take $e'(I')$ as input and determine whether or not $I' \in Y_{\Pi'}$. Thus combining these two TMs as in Fig. 3.4 gives an algorithm to solve Π.

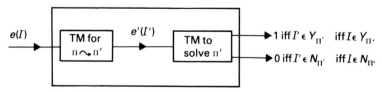

Fig. 3.4. A TM to solve Π.

(2) If Π' were solvable then from (1) we could deduce that Π is also solvable and hence get a contradiction.

From this result and that of theorem 3.1, we can deduce that, if a decision problem Π is such that $HP \rightsquigarrow \Pi$, then Π must also be unsolvable. We will now use this observation to prove that the following are unsolvable.

Empty word halting problem (εHP)

INSTANCE: A TM, $M = (Q, \Sigma, T, P, q_0, F)$.

QUESTION: Does M halt given input, ε?

Uniform halting problem (UHP)

INSTANCE: A TM, $M = (Q, \Sigma, T, P, q_0, F)$.

QUESTION: Does M halt for every input $x \in T^*$?

$HP \rightarrow \varepsilon HP$ is given by the following reduction. From an instance I of HP comprising a TM, $M = (Q, \Sigma, T, P, q_0, F)$, and a string $x \in T^*$, we construct an instance I' of εHP comprising a TM, M', as follows. M' is constructed so that it first writes x onto its tape and then simulates the action of M. Clearly, M halts for input $x \in T^*$ iff M' halts for input ε. Thus $I \in Y_{HP}$ iff $I' \in Y_{\varepsilon HP}$.

$HP \rightarrow UHP$ is given by a similar but slightly more cunning reduction. Given an instance I of HP comprising a TM, $M = (Q, \Sigma, T, P, q_0, F)$, and a string $x \in T^*$, we construct an instance I'' of UHP comprising a TM, M'', as follows. M'' is constructed so that it first clears its input tape, then it writes x onto the tape and finally it simulates the action of M. Thus, M halts for input $x \in T^*$ iff M'' halts for all inputs $\in T^*$. So $I \in Y_{HP}$ iff $I'' \in Y_{UHP}$.

These two reductions prove the following.

Theorem 3.3

(1)   The empty word halting problem (εHP) is unsolvable.
(2)   The uniform halting problem (UHP) is unsolvable.

Associated with the problem of proving computer programs correct is that of proving programs equivalent, i.e. showing that two programs perform exactly the same task. In terms of Turing machines, we have already defined a TM, $M_1 = (Q_1, \Sigma_1, T, P_1, q_{01}, F_1)$, to be *equivalent* to a

TM, $M_2 = (Q_2, \Sigma_2, T, P_2, q_{02}, F_2)$ iff $f_{M_1} = f_{M_2}$. We can then define the

Equivalence problem for Turing machines (ETM)
INSTANCE: Two TMs, $M_1 = (Q_1, \Sigma_1, T, P_1, q_{01}, F_1)$, $M_2 = (Q_2, \Sigma_2, T, P_2, q_{02}, F_2)$, with the same input alphabet, T.
QUESTION: Is M_1 equivalent to M_2?

The following result should come as no surprise to the reader.

Theorem 3.4

The equivalence problem for Turing machines is unsolvable.

Proof. We show UHP $\rightsquigarrow$ ETM. Let an instance, I, of UHP be defined by a TM, $M = (Q, \Sigma, T, P, q_0, F)$. From M, we can construct a two tape TM, M', which copies its input onto its second tape and there simulates M. If and only if M halts, M' clears its first tape, writes 1 in the first location and halts itself. Thus M' computes

$$f_{M'}(x) = \begin{cases} 1 & \text{if } M \text{ halts given input } x \in T^*, \\ \text{undefined} & \text{otherwise.} \end{cases}$$

Let M'' be the one tape TM constructed from M' according to theorem 2.4. Then $f_{M''} = f_{M'}$. Thus, $I \in Y_{\text{UHP}}$ iff $f_{M''}(x) = 1$ for all $x \in T^*$. We can easily construct a TM, M_1, which computes $f_{M_1}(x) = 1$ for all $x \in T^*$. We simply define $M_1 = (\{q_0, q_1, q_2\}, T \cup \{\wedge\}, T, P, q_0, \{q_2\})$ where

$$P(q_0, a) = (q_0, 1, R) \text{ for all } a \in T \cup \{\wedge\},$$

and $P(q_1, a) = (q_2, \wedge, 0)$ for all $a \in T \cup \{\wedge\}$,

The instance I' of ETM is then defined by M'' and M_1 constructed as above. $I \in Y_{\text{UHP}}$ iff $f_{M''} = f_{M_1}$ iff $I' \in Y_{\text{ETM}}$. Since there is an effective construction of I' from I, it follows that UHP $\rightsquigarrow$ ETM and since UHP is unsolvable the theorem is established.

POST'S CORRESPONDENCE PROBLEM

Post's correspondence problem (PCP) is yet another unsolvable problem. Although the proof that HP $\rightsquigarrow$ PCP is quite tricky, it is nevertheless well worth studying. The unsolvability of PCP is an important result; it is used extensively to prove the unsolvability of problems in formal language theory. We will be using the result for this purpose in Chapter 4.

PCP is a decision problem described in the standard format by

Post's correspondence problem (PCP)

INSTANCE: A finite alphabet, T, and two n-tuples ($n > 0$) of strings in T^+, $x = (x_1, x_2, \ldots, x_n)$ and $y = (y_1, y_2, \ldots, y_n)$.

QUESTION: Is there a sequence of integers, $i_1, i_2, \ldots, i_m$ ($m \geq 1$) such that $x_{i_1} x_{i_2} \ldots x_{i_m} = y_{i_1} y_{i_2} \ldots y_{i_m}$?

For example, the instance of PCP with $T = \{0, 1\}$, $x = (011, 11)$, $y = (0, 111)$ is in Y_{PCP} since there is a yes solution, $x_1 x_2 x_3 = y_1 y_2 y_3 = 0111111$. An example of an instance which can be shown to be in N_{PCP} is given by $T = \{0, 1\}$, $x = (01, 100, 010)$, $y = (010, 00, 100)$; see Exercise 3.6. Just because one can produce *ad hoc* arguments to show a particular instance of PCP is or is not in Y_{PCP} does not mean that PCP is solvable. In fact, as stated above, PCP is not solvable. Remember, the claim is that there is no algorithm which can be used to test whether an *arbitrary* $I \in D_{PCP}$ is or is not in Y_{PCP}.

A modified version of PCP is going to prove particularly important to us. This is described as follows.

Modified Post's correspondence problem (MPCP)

INSTANCE: A finite alphabet, T, and two n-tuples ($n > 0$) of strings in T^+, $x = (x, x_2, \ldots, x_n)$ and $y = (y_1, y_2, \ldots, y_n)$.

QUESTION: Is there a sequence of integers, $i_1, i_2, \ldots, i_m$ ($m \geq 1$) such that $i_1 = 1$ and $x_{i_1} x_{i_2} \ldots x_{i_m} = y_{i_1} y_{i_2} \ldots y_{i_m}$?

The only difference between MPCP and PCP is that, in the former, the first string selected from each n-tuple must be indexed by 1. We show that if MPCP is unsolvable then so is PCP by establishing the following result.

Theorem 3.5

MPCP $\rightarrowtail$ PCP.

Proof. Let $I \in D_{MPCP}$ be defined by an alphabet, T, and n-tuples $x = (x_1, x_2, \ldots, x_n)$, $y = (y_1, y_2, \ldots, y_n)$. Without loss of generality, we can assume that there are no symbols in T which do not occur in at least one of the strings in x or in y. Let £, \$ be two symbols not in T and set $T' = T \cup \{£,\$\}$. Define two homomorphisms, *left*: $T^+ \to (T')^+$ and *right*: $T^+ \to (T')^+$ by $left(a) = \$a$ and $right(a) = a\$$ for all $a \in T$. Thus *left* inserts a \$ to the left of each and every symbol in a string and similarly *right* inserts one to the right.

Now, define $x' = (x'_1, x'_2, \ldots, x'_n, £)$ and $y' = (y'_1, y'_2, \ldots, y'_n, \$£)$ as follows:

$$x'_1 = concat(\$, right(x_1)),$$

$$x'_i = right(x_i) \quad \text{for } 1 < i \leq n,$$

and $\quad y'_i = left(y_i) \quad \text{for } 1 < i \leq n.$

Let I' denote the instance of PCP defined by T', x' and y'. It is not difficult to show that $1, i_2, \ldots, i_m$ is a solution to I implies $1, i_2, \ldots, i_m, n+1$ is a solution to I'. But say $i_1, i_2, \ldots, i_{m'}$ is a solution to I'. Then, necessarily $i_1 = 1$ (since all strings in y' start with \$ and only x_1 in x starts with \$) and $i_{m'} = n+1$ (since all strings in x except x'_{n+1} end with \$ and no string in y' ends with \$). With these observations, it then follows that $1, i_2, \ldots, i_{m'-1}$ must be a solution to I. Combining these arguments, we have $I' \in Y_{PCP}$ iff $I \in Y_{MPCP}$. Since the construction I' from I is clearly effectively computable, the theorem is established.

Theorem 3.6

HP $\to$ MPCP.

Proof. Let I be an instance of HP comprising a TM, $M = (Q, \Sigma, T, P, q_0, F)$, and a string $x \in T^*$. We will show how to construct effectively an instance, I', of MPCP such that $I \in Y_H$ iff $I' \in Y_{MPCP}$.

From theorem 2.5, we can assume that M has a one-way infinite tape and, from an obvious minor modification of theorem 2.1, that this M never halts and fails. We can represent a configuration $C = (q, i, \alpha, a, \beta)$ of the TM, M, by a single string $\bar{C} \in (Q \cup \Sigma)^*$ as follows. C is represented by $\bar{C} = \alpha_1 q \alpha_2$ where $|\alpha_1| = i - 1$ and α_1 is the string of symbols to the left of the tape head and $\alpha_2 = a\beta$ is the string of symbols in locations $i, i+1, i+2, \ldots$ up to the rightmost nonblank symbol (see Fig. 3.5). Note that α_1 is not necessarily equal to α since it may have some leading blank symbols.

The initial configuration is thus represented by $q_0 x$. Say subsequent configurations are $\alpha_1 q_1 \beta_1, \alpha_2 q_2 \beta_2, \ldots, \alpha_m q_m \beta_m$ where $q_m \in F$, then we will construct an instance of MPCP which will have a solution with prefix

Chapter 3

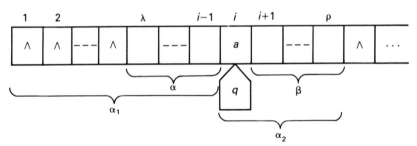

Fig. 3.5.

$q_0x\$\alpha_1q_1\beta_1\$\ldots\$\alpha_mq_m\beta_m\$$. The symbol $\$\notin Q\cup\Sigma$ is a new symbol specially introduced. If M does not halt on x then the instance of MPCP which we construct will not have a solution.

The instance, I', of MPCP is constructed as follows. I' is defined with alphabet $Q\cup\Sigma\cup\{\$\}$, $x_1 = \$$ and $y_1 = \$q_0x\$$ are the first pair and subsequent corresponding pairs are constructed according to the following rules:

(1)   for each $X\in\Sigma$, X occurs in x and in y;

(2) $\$$ occurs in both x and y;

(3)   for each $q\in Q\backslash F$, $q'\in Q$ and $X,Y,Z\in\Sigma$,

    (a)ZqX occurs in x and $q'ZY$ in y if $P(q,X)=(q',Y,L)$,

    (b)qX occurs in x and $q'Y$ in y if $P(q,X)=(q',Y,0)$,

    (c)qX occurs in x and Yq' in y if $P(q,X)=(q',Y,R)$,

    (d)$Zq\$$ occurs in x and $q'ZY\$$in y if $P(q,\wedge)=(q',Y,L)$,

    (e)$q\$$ occurs in x and $q'Y\$$ in y if $P(q,\wedge)=(q',Y,0)$,

    (f)$q\$$ occurs in x and $Yq'\$$ in y if $P(q,\wedge)=(q',Y,R)$;

(4)   for each $q\in F$, $X,Y\in\Sigma$,

    (a)XqY occurs in x and q occurs in y,

    (b)$Xq\$$ occurs in x and $q\$$ occurs in y,

    (c)$\$qY$ occurs in x and $\$q$ occurs in y;

(5)   for each $q\in F$

    $q\$\$$ occurs in x and $\$$ occurs in y;

(6)   no other elements occur in x,y other than these.

Now, suppose that from the initial configuration of M there is a valid sequence of configurations represented by $q_0x,\alpha_1q_1\beta_1,\alpha_2q_2\beta_2,\ldots,\alpha_kq_k\beta_k$ where none of $q_0,q_1,,\ldots,q_{k-1}$ are final states. We claim that we can find elements of y which concatenated together form the string $\$q_0x\$\alpha_1q_1\beta_1\$\ldots\$\alpha_kq_k\beta_k\$$. Moreover, the corresponding elements of x concatenated together form the string $\$q_0x\$\alpha_1q_1\beta_1\$\ldots\$\alpha_{k-1}q_{k-1}\beta_{k-1}\$$.

We can prove this claim by induction on k. It clearly holds for $k = 0$ since we must choose the pair $(\$, \$q_0 x\$)$ first. Suppose the claim is true for all $i < k$ and, in particular, for $i = k - 1$. So we can find elements of y which when concatenated together form $\$q_0 x \$ \alpha_1 q_1 \beta_1 \$ \ldots \$ \alpha_{k-1} q_{k-1} \beta_{k-1} \$$ and such that the corresponding elements of x concatenated together form $\$q_0 x \$ \alpha_1 q_1 \beta_1 \$ \ldots \$ \alpha_{k-2} q_{k-2} \beta_{k-2} \$$. Now, we want to append the string $\alpha_{k-1} q_{k-1} \beta_{k-1} \$$ to x. Except for q_{k-1} we could obtain all the symbols in this string using the pairs constructed in rules (1) and (2). However, since $q_{k-1} \notin F$, the q_{k-1} can only be obtained from a pair constructed in rule (3). That pair represents a move of the TM and thus, corresponding to the elements of x which concatenated together form $\alpha_{k-1} q_{k-1} \beta_{k-1} \$$, we have precisely those elements of y which concatenated together form $\alpha_k q_k \beta_k \$$. The result is thus established for $i = k$ and the induction argument complete. In fact, we have shown a slightly stronger result, viz. that any matching process starting with $(\$, \$q_0 x\$)$ must proceed by generating strings of the form we have described.

Now, say we eventually reach a situation where we have constructed a string $\$q_0 x \$ \alpha_1 q_1 \beta_1 \$ \ldots \$ \alpha_{m-1} q_{m-1} \beta_{m-1} \$$ from the symbols of x and a string $\$q_0 x \$ \alpha_1 q_1 \beta_1 \$ \ldots \$ \alpha_m q_m \beta_m \$$ from the corresponding symbols of y and that $q_m \in F$. Using the pairs of symbols constructed by rules (4) and (5) a solution to MPCP can now easily be obtained which has the string $\$q_0 x \$ \alpha_1 q_1 \beta_1 \$ \ldots \$ \alpha_m q_m \beta_m \$$ as a prefix. Thus, if M with input x reaches a final state, then the instance, I' of MPCP has a solution. However, if M does not reach a final state, the string of symbols from y will always be longer than that of corresponding symbols from x and there can be no solution to this instance of MPCP. Hence, we have shown that $I \in Y_{HP}$ iff $I' \in Y_{MPCP}$ and since the construction of I' from I is clearly effectively computable the theorem is established.

An immediate corollary to this theorem and its predecessor is:

Theorem 3.7

PCP is an unsolvable problem.

FURTHER UNSOLVABLE PROBLEMS

There are unsolvable problems in many branches of mathematics. We describe here just three examples; for many readers, this section will have to be omitted since they will not have sufficient mathematical background. We do not use these results later in the text; they are included here merely for those interested. In the next chapter, we will also provide further examples of unsolvable problems which all readers should be able to understand.

Our first example is known as *Hilbert's tenth problem.* Consider a polynomial $p(x_1,x_2,\ldots,x_n)$ with variables $x_1,x_2,\ldots,x_n$ and integer coefficients. Then the equation

$$p(x_1,x_2,\ldots,x_n) = 0$$

for which integer solutions are required is called a *diophantine equation.* Such equations do not always have solutions of course, e.g. $x^2 - 2 = 0$ has no integer solutions. In 1900, in a famous lecture, Hilbert set a number of problems on which he believed mathematicians should work during the 20th century. His tenth problem was to find whether or not there was an effective procedure to determine whether a given diophantine equation has a solution. It was not until 1972 that Matijacevič finally established that determining the existence of solutions to diophantine equations was yet another unsolvable problem. Matijacevič's work completed pioneering work on this problem by M. Davis, J. Robinson and H. Putman. For complete details, the reader is referred to Bell & Machover (1977).

Mathematical logic is a source of a number of unsolvable problems. Without doubt, the most fundamental, which is expounded upon in any book on the subject, is that of validity in the first-order predicate calculus. One is able to produce an axiom scheme for the predicate calculus and to show that any statement is provable using this axiom scheme iff it is *valid*, i.e. true in all possible interpretations. In Church (1936b), it is proved that provability (and hence validity) in the predicate calculus is unsolvable. This is perhaps the most fundamental unsolvability result for the whole of mathematics. For the computer scientist it means that any attempt at automatic theorem proving can only be partially successful. We discuss this further in the companion text by Dowsing, Rayward-Smith & Walter (1985). Problems with automatic theorem proving have theoretical consequences for the computer scientist who wishes to use logic as a programming language (see Kowalski, 1979).

Our final example is taken from group theory. Suppose that G is a group with identity e and elements $x_1,x_2,\ldots$. A *word* in G is any string constructed from these elements using the group operation, $*$, and inverses. For example, $x_1*x_1*x_2^{-1}*x_3*x_1^{-1}*x_4$ is a word in G. Since G is closed under $*$

and inverses, each such word represents some element of G. The following problem is unsolvable.

Word problem for groups (WPG)

INSTANCE: A group G and a word w in G.
QUESTION: Is w = e, the identity element of G?

However, if this problem is restricted to finite groups only, the problem becomes solvable.

EXERCISES

1   Explain how a TM can be sensibly encoded as a string in $\{0,1\}^*$. State clearly any assumptions that you are making.
2   (a) Design a TM, M, which computes 1 for all inputs $\in\{0,1\}^*\{00\}$ but which computes 0 for all other inputs in $\{0,1\}^*$.

(b) Define the decision problem *Integer division by four* using the standard notation. Use your answer to part (a) to show that this problem is solvable.
3   If Π is a decision problem then the *complement* of Π, Π^c, is defined to be the same as Π except that the question is negated. Show that $\Pi^c \rightarrow \Pi$ and hence that Π is solvable iff Π^c is solvable.
4   Show that $\rightarrow$ is reflexive and transitive but not symmetric.
5   Show that the following problem is unsolvable.
Sometimes halts (SH)
INSTANCE: A TM, $M = (Q, \Sigma, T, P, q_0, F)$.
QUESTION: Does there exist $x \in T^*$ such that M halts given x as input?
6   Show that $T = \{0,1\}, x = (01,100,010), y = (010,00,100)$ is an instance of PCP which must lie in N_{PCP}.
7   Is PCP solvable where the alphabet is constrained to have just one symbol? What about two symbols?
8   Construct the instance of MPCP corresponding to the instance of HP with the TM which computes the function *head* and the input 011 (see Fig. 2.4c).
9   Use your answer to question 8 to construct the instance of PCP corresponding to the given instance of HP.

Chapter 4

Formal Languages

...an important subarea of computer science.

J. E. HOPCROFT & J. D. ULLMAN
Formal Languages and their Relation to Automata

TURING MACHINES AS RECOGNIZERS

A TM which solves a decision problem, Π, essentially acts as a recognizer; it recognizes whether or not a given input, $e(I)$, is or is not in some language, $L_{\Pi,e} = \{e(I) | I \in Y_\Pi\}$. In this chapter, we will be concerned with investigating the languages recognizable by TMs and discovering properties thereof.

A language $L \subseteq T^*$ is called *recursive* iff there exists a Turing machine with input alphabet T which computes the *characteristic function* of L,

$$\chi_L(x) = \begin{cases} 1 & \text{if } x \in L, \\ 0 & \text{if } x \in T^* \backslash L. \end{cases}$$

Note that we do not allow the TM in this definition to give an undefined output for any input $x \in T^*$. Thus this TM must always halt and succeed. Hence, for any $x \in T^*$, the TM can decide whether or not $x \in L$.

An alternative but equivalent characterization or recursive languages can be obtained as follows. We say a string $x \in T^*$ is *accepted* by a TM, $M = (Q, \Sigma, T, P, q_0, F)$, iff M halts and succeeds given input x. A string $x \in T^*$ is *rejected* by the TM iff M halts and fails given input x. If M loops forever given input x we can say neither that M accepts x nor that it rejects x.

Theorem 4.1

$L \subseteq T^*$ is recursive iff there exists a TM, $M = (Q, \Sigma, T, P, q_0, F)$ such that M accepts all $x \in L$ and rejects all $x \in T^* \backslash L$.

Proof. $\Rightarrow$: L is recursive so we can assume there exists a TM, M', which computes χ_L. From theorem 2.5, we can assume that M' is a one-way

TM. Since χ_L is total, M' cannot halt and fail. From M' we can construct M, also a one-way TM. M simulates the action of M' but marks location 1 so that if during a computation of M', location 1 holds a symbol $X \in \Sigma$, M will instead have a pair $(X, *)$ in location 1. The $*$ is a new symbol and does not affect the computation; it merely marks location 1. When M' would halt, M uses this marker to allow it to move its tape head (if necessary) leftwards until it reaches location 1. If it finds $(1, *)$ in location 1, it enters its unique final state, q_f; otherwise it will find $(0, *)$ there and no next move is defined.

$\Leftarrow$: Again, we use theorem 2.5 and assume, without loss of generality, that M is a one-way TM. Then we further assume $M = (Q, \Sigma, T, P, q_0, F)$ is amended by the addition of a new state, q_d, such that if $P(q, a)$ were undefined it is now set to be $(q_d, a, 0)$. So, the only way the amended can reject a string is when it is in state q_d. The one-way TM, M', to compute χ_L is now easily constructed. M' simulates the action of the amended M but marks location 1. Then if this simulation of the amended M results in the machine entering state q_d, M' then moves its tape head to the marked location 1 and writes 0 followed by a $\wedge$ in location 2. It then halts. Otherwise, the simulation of the amended M must result in the machine entering a state in F. In such a case, M' again moves its tape head to location 1 but this time writes 1 followed by a $\wedge$ in location 2 before it halts.

Unfortunately, TMs may loop forever given certain inputs. In chapter 3, we have shown that the halting problem is unsolvable so that given an arbitrary TM, M, there is no way of determining whether or not it will halt for an arbitrary $x \in T^*$. Our definition of recursive does not allow the TM to loop and thus does not really characterize the most general languages which can be recognised by TMs. Thus, we define the *recursively enumerable(r.e.) languages* in T^* to be those languages $L \subseteq T^*$ for which there exists a TM which computes the *partial characteristic function* of L,

$$\chi'_L(x) = \begin{cases} 1 & \text{if } x \in L, \\ \text{undefined} & \text{if } x \in T^* \backslash L. \end{cases}$$

Hence for any $x \in L$, the TM will be able to confirm that x is in L. However, if it is given an arbitrary $x \in T^*$, we may get not output at all. It is easy then to prove the following.

Theorem 4.2

Every recursive language is recursively enumerable.

Proof. Simply amend the TM, M, which computes χ_L so that instead of halting with output 0, it loops forever.

The converse of this theorem is not true, however; after the discussion of the previous chapter, this result is perhaps not surprising. It nevertheless is an important result because it shows that a machine looping indefinitely is not only, in general, undetectable but, worse, it is, in some sense, unavoidable. In order to establish the fact that there are r.e. languages which are not recursive, we will first establish some properties of the languages we have defined.

Theorem 4.3

(1)   Recursive languages are closed under union, intersection and set concatenation, i.e. if $L_1, L_2 \subseteq T^*$ are recursive, so are $L_1 \cup L_2$, $L_1 \cap L_2$ and $L_1 L_2$.
(2)   Recursively enumerable languages are closed under union, intersection and set concatenation.

Proof. We will sketch a proof that recursive languages are closed under union. The other proofs follow very similar arguments.
    Say χ_{L_1}, χ_{L_2} are computed by TMs, M_1, M_2, respectively. Then, consider a 3-tape TM, M, constructed as follows. For any $x \in T^*$ input on the first tape, M proceeds by copying this onto tape 2 and tape 3. On tape 2, M simulates the action of M_1 and on tape 3 the action of M_2. If the simulations confirm that both $x \in L_1$ and $x \in L_2$, M clears its input tape except for location 1 in which it writes 1. Otherwise, M clears its input tape except for location 1 in which it writes 0.

Theorem 4.4

Recursive languages are closed under complementation, i.e. if $L \subseteq T^*$ is recursive then so is $\bar{L} = T^* \backslash L$.

Proof. If M recognizes L then $\bar{M}$ will recognize $\bar{L}$ where $\bar{M}$ is constructed from M by ensuring that an output 1 is replaced by an output of 0 and vice versa.

Now, we can enumerate all the strings in T^* so that x_i denotes the ith string (Exercise 4 of Chapter 1). Also, we can enumerate a set of TMs which recognize r.e. languages in T^* such that every r.e. language in T^* is recognized by at least one of these machines (Exercise 4.1). Say L_i denotes the ith such language which is recognized by the TM, M_i. So, $x_i \in L_i$ iff $f_{M_i}(x_i) = 1$. Now consider the language

$$L_d = \{x_i \,|\, x_i \in L_i\}.$$

Theorem 4.5

L_d is an r.e. language but $\bar{L}_d$ is not.

Proof (outline). L_d is recognized by M_d which operates as follows. Given as input $x \in T^*$, M_d first starts the enumeration of T^*, $x_1, x_2, \ldots$ to discover what index i is such that $x_i = x$. M_d then generates M_i and transfers control to a universal TM that simulates M_i with input x_i. Thus, $x = x_i$ is such that $f_{M_i}(x_i) = 1$ iff $f_{M_d}(x) = 1$. Hence $f_{M_d} = \chi'(L_d)$ so L_d is r.e.
   Now, if $\bar{L}_d = T^* \setminus L_d$ is r.e. then it must be recognized by some TM, $\bar{M}_d$, with input alphabet T. So, in the enumeration of such TMs, $\bar{M}_d = M_k$ for some k. Thus $x_k \in \bar{L}_d$ iff x_k is recognized by M_k. But, from the definition of $\bar{L}_d$, $x_k \in \bar{L}_d$ iff x_k is not recognized by M_k. This contradiction proves that $\bar{L}_d$ cannot be r.e.

We have thus shown that recursive languages are closed under complementation but that r.e. languages are not. Thus, we have proved:

Theorem 4.6

Not every r.e. language is recursive.

NONDETERMINISTIC TURING MACHINES

When defining Turing machines in Chapter 2, we defined the program to be a partial function from $(Q \setminus F) \times \Sigma \to Q \times \Sigma \times \{L, R, 0\}$. By insisting that the program was a function we ensured that $P(q, a)$, $q \in Q \setminus F$, $a \in \Sigma$, could have at most one value. However, this constraint can be relaxed and if we allow the machine to have several choices for its next move we say that it is nondeterministic. A *nondeterministic Turing machine* (NDTM) is formally defined as for a deterministic Turing machine except that the program becomes a function $(Q \backslash F) \times \Sigma \to 2^{Q \times \Sigma \times \{L,R,0\}}$. Thus given $q \in Q \backslash F$, $a \in \Sigma$, $P(q, a)$ is a set of possible next moves (which may be empty).

We say a string $x \in T^*$ is *accepted* by a NDTM, $M = (Q, \Sigma, T, P, q_0, F)$ iff there is some sequence of choices of move which leads M, given x as input, to enter a final state. The set of all such strings is denoted by $T(M)$, the *language accepted* by M. One can view a deterministic TM as a NDTM such that for $q \in Q \backslash F$, $a \in \Sigma$, $P(q, a)$ is either empty or a singleton set. Then, using arguments similar to those used in the proof of theorem 4.1, it is not difficult to prove the following result.

Theorem 4.7

L is accepted by a deterministic TM iff L is r.e.

Given that deterministic TMs are capable of computing any effectively computable function, the r.e. languages represent the 'effectively recogniz-able' languages. Thus, one might not expect the addition of nondeterminism to enable TMs to accept languages that are not r.e. Indeed this is the case; nondeterminism is really only significant when one considers matters such as speed of computation (see Chapter 6).

Theorem 4.8

L is accepted by a nondeterministic TM iff L is r.e.

Proof. $\Leftarrow$: this is an immediate corollary of theorem 4.7 since we can regard a deterministic TM to be a restricted NDTM.

$\Rightarrow$: we need to show that if L is accepted by a NDTM then L is accepted by a deterministic TM. Say $M = (Q, \Sigma, T, P, q_0, F)$ is the nondeterministic machine such that $L = T(M)$ then we will outline the construction of a deterministic TM, M', such that $L = T(M')$. Consider the sets $P(q, a)$, $q \in Q$, $a \in \Sigma$, and let m be the maximum cardinality of any of these sets. If $m = 1$ then M is deterministic and we have nothing to prove. So, we assume $m > 1$. Any finite sequence of choices of move for M can be encoded as a finite sequence of the digits 1 through m. Not all such digit sequences will represent possible sequences of moves since $\#P(q, a)$ may be less than m for some $q \in Q$, $a \in \Sigma$.

M' is a three tape TM. On the first tape we write the input $x \in T^*$. On the second tape M' will generate all the sequences of digits 1 through m one at a time and in a *lexicographic* way, i.e. shortest sequences first and for sequences of the same length, in numerically increasing order. For each such sequence generated, the input is copied to tape 3 and M' there simulates M using the sequence on tape 2 to select between possible alternative moves. If for some digit in the sequence there is no corresponding choice of move, M' stops simulating M, clears tape 3, generates the next sequence on tape 2, and restarts the simulation of M with a fresh copy of x on tape 3. If there is a sequence of choices of move which would lead M to accept x, this sequence will eventually be found on tape 2 of M'. When M' reaches that sequence and simulates M it too will accept x. If no such sequence exists, M' will continue trying potentially longer and longer sequences of choice and thus loop forever.

PHRASE STRUCTURE GRAMMARS

Phrase structure grammars provide a finite set of derivation rules (known as productions) which enable one to generate strings. These strings will be over some terminal alphabet, T, say. In addition to this terminal alphabet, the grammar will also use a nonterminal alphabet, N, say, where the two alphabets N and T have no elements in common. Each derivation rule is of the form $\alpha \to \beta$ where $\alpha \in (N \cup T)^+$ and $\beta \in (N \cup T)^*$. Starting with a prescribed start symbol in N, usually denoted by S, the derivation of a string in T^* proceeds by repeatedly replacing substrings which match a left hand side of a derivation rule by the corresponding right hand side.

For example, a simple grammar may have $N = \{S, A, B\}$, $T = \{a, b\}$ and derivation rules

$$S \to A$$
$$S \to B$$
$$A \to aA$$
$$A \to a$$
$$B \to bB$$
$$B \to b$$

From S we can derive either A or B. If we derive A then we can derive from A in one step the string a, or in two steps the string aa (by deriving aA from A and then replacing the A in aA by a) or in k steps a string of k as which we will denote by a^k. Similarly we can derive from B any string b^k for $k \geq 1$ in k steps.

If a string, β, can be derived from a string, α, by applying one of the derivation rules of the grammar, we write $\alpha \Rightarrow \beta$. If $\alpha_1 \Rightarrow \alpha_2$, $\alpha_2 \Rightarrow \alpha_3, \ldots$ $\alpha_{n-1} \Rightarrow \alpha_n$ $(n \geq 1)$, we abbreviate this to $\alpha_1 \Rightarrow \alpha_2 \Rightarrow \ldots \Rightarrow \alpha_n$ or even more briefly as $\alpha_1 \stackrel{*}{\Rightarrow} \alpha_n$. Thus, using the above grammar,

$$S \Rightarrow A \Rightarrow aA \Rightarrow aaA \Rightarrow aaa$$

is a valid derivation of a^3 from S. We can also represent this derivation using a *derivation tree* as in Fig. 4.1.

We now need to formalize these concepts.

A *phrase structure grammar* (PSG) is a 4-tuple, $G = (N, T, P, S)$, where
(1) N is a finite set of *nonterminals*. Conventionally elements of N are represented by upper case letters (possibly subscripted);
(2) T is a finite set of *terminals* such that $N \cap T = \emptyset$. Conventionally, the elements of T are represented by lower case letters (possibly subscripted and usually towards the beginning of the alphabet);
(3) P is a finite set of *productions* of the form $\alpha \rightarrow \beta$ where α, the string on the left hand side of the production, is such that $\alpha \in (N \cup T)^+$ and β, the string on the right hand side of the production, is such that $\beta \in (N \cup T)^*$;
(4) $S \in N$ is a symbol designated as the *start symbol* of the grammar.

So formally, our example PSG is the four tuple, $G_1 = (\{S, A, B\},$

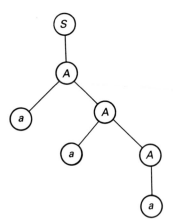

Fig. 4.1.

$\{a, b\}, P, S)$, where P is the set of productions

$$\{S \to A, S \to B, A \to aA, A \to a, B \to bB, B \to b\}.$$

We will generally not use such formal set theoretic notation, but simply write out the productions as a list, using | for 'or'. Thus the above productions can be written

$S \to A|B$
$A \to aA|a$
$B \to bB|b$

As you may have noticed, once we have adopted our conventions of upper and lower case letters for nonterminals and terminals, it is only necessary to specify the productions and the start symbol to specify the grammar. If, as is usual, the start symbol is S, we will not have to specify that either.

Now, consider the PSG, G_2, with productions

$S \to asBC|aBC$
$CB \to BC$
$aB \to ab$
$bB \to bb$
$bC \to bc$
$cC \to cc$

This is an example where the left hand side of the productions are not all single nonterminals. It can be shown that we can derive from S any string of the form $a^n b^n c^n, n \geq 1$. For example

$S \Rightarrow aSBC$
$\Rightarrow aaBCBC$ (using $S \to aBC$)
$\Rightarrow aabCBC$ (using $aB \to ab$)
$\Rightarrow aabBCC$ (using $CB \to BC$)
$\Rightarrow aabbCC$ (using $bB \to bb$)
$\Rightarrow aabbcC$ (using $bC \to bc$)
$\Rightarrow aabbcc$ (using $cC \to cc$)

is a valid derivation of $a^2b^2c^2$.

By now you should have a good intuitive notion of what is meant by a 'derivation'. We will now use our formal definition of a grammar to state precisely what it means for a string to be derivable in a grammar. Let $G = (N, T, P, S)$ be any PSG and let $\gamma_1 \alpha \gamma_2 \in (N \cup T)^+$ be a string of terminals and nonterminals of length ≥ 1. If $\alpha \to \beta$ is a production in P

then α in $\gamma_1\alpha\gamma_2$ can be replaced by β to yield $\gamma_1\beta\gamma_2$. In that case we write

$$\gamma_1\alpha\gamma_2 \underset{G}{\Rightarrow} \gamma_1\beta\gamma_2$$

[read: $\gamma_1\alpha\gamma_2$ *generates* $\gamma_1\beta\gamma_2$ or $\gamma_1\beta\gamma_2$ *is derived from* $\gamma_1\alpha\gamma_2$].

If $\alpha_1, \alpha_2, \ldots, \alpha_n \in (N \cup T)^*$ and $\alpha_1 \underset{G}{\Rightarrow} \alpha_2, \alpha_2 \underset{G}{\Rightarrow} \alpha_3, \ldots, \alpha_{n-1} \underset{G}{\Rightarrow} \alpha_n$, we write $\alpha_1 \underset{G}{\Rightarrow} \alpha_2 \underset{G}{\Rightarrow} \alpha_3 \ldots \underset{G}{\Rightarrow} \alpha_{n-1} \underset{G}{\Rightarrow} \alpha_n$ or in a more abbreviated form, $\alpha_1 \underset{G}{\overset{+}{\Rightarrow}} \alpha_n$ [read: α_1 generates α_n in one or more steps]. Thus $\underset{G}{\overset{+}{\Rightarrow}}$ is the transitive closure of the relation $\underset{G}{\Rightarrow}$. The reflexive closure of $\underset{G}{\overset{+}{\Rightarrow}}$ is denoted by $\underset{G}{\overset{*}{\Rightarrow}}$ and thus $\alpha_1 \underset{G}{\overset{*}{\Rightarrow}} \alpha_n$ iff $\alpha_1 = \alpha_n$ or $\alpha_1 \underset{G}{\overset{+}{\Rightarrow}} \alpha_n$.

If $\alpha \in (N \cup T)^*$ is such that $S \underset{G}{\overset{*}{\Rightarrow}} \alpha$ then α is said to be a *sentential form* of G. A *sentence* of G is then any sentential form in T^*, i.e. a terminal string which can be derived from S. The *language generated by* G, $L(G)$, is then defined to be the set of all sentences of G. Thus

$$L(G) = \{x \in T^* | S \underset{G}{\overset{*}{\Rightarrow}} x\}.$$

In many examples, the grammar G to which we are referring is clear from context. In such cases we can drop the subscript, G, from $\underset{G}{\Rightarrow}, \underset{G}{\overset{+}{\Rightarrow}}$ or $\underset{G}{\overset{*}{\Rightarrow}}$ and simply write $\Rightarrow, \overset{+}{\Rightarrow}$ or $\overset{*}{\Rightarrow}$.

Using the examples G_1, G_2 above, the reader should check that

$$L(G_1) = \{a^n | n \geq 1\} \cup \{b^n | n \geq 1\}$$

and

$$L(G_2) = \{a^n b^n c^n | n \geq 1\}.$$

Sometimes, it may be that two different grammars G and G' generate the same language $L(G) = L(G')$. In that case the grammars are said to be *equivalent*. An example of a grammar equivalent to G_1 is G_3 with productions

$$S \rightarrow aA|bB|a|b$$
$$A \rightarrow aA|a$$
$$B \rightarrow bB|b$$

Phrase structure grammars provide a very general mechanism for generating languages, and TMs the most power in recognising them, so perhaps the following result is not all that surprising. It certainly provides support for the claims of *Church's thesis.*

Theorem 4.9

$L \subseteq T^*$ is generated by a PSG, $G = (N, T, P, S)$, iff L is r.e.

Proof. $\Rightarrow$: We outline a nondeterministic TM, M, such that $L = T(M)$. The tape alphabet of M contains $N \cup T$ as well as $\wedge$ which we assume $\notin N \cup T$ and a special introduced symbol $\$ \notin N \cup T \cup \{\wedge\}$. Initially, M has $x \in T^*$ written on its tape. It then copies x into locations $-|x|, \ldots, -1$, marks location 0 with the $\$$ symbol and writes S in location 1. M will now nondeterministically simulate a derivation in G in the positive part of its tape. Say at some stage the string $A_1 A_2 \ldots A_k \wedge$, $A_i \in N \cup T$, $i = 1, \ldots, k$, is found in locations $1, 2, \ldots k, k + 1$. M nondeterministically chooses locations $i > 0$ and $j \geq i$. If either i or j contain a $\wedge$ another choice is made. Then, M examines the substring $A_i A_{i+1} \ldots A_j$ and if it is the left hand side of a production in P it is replaced by the corresponding right hand side. M may have to shift $A_{j+1}, \ldots, A_k$ either to the left or to the right to make room or to fill up the space. This process is repeated until the simulation of the derivation finally can stop, i.e. when there are no nonterminal symbols on the tape. The tape will then contain the string $x\$y$ for some $x, y \in T^*$. The TM then halts if $x = y$ but otherwise clears y, replaces it by S and restarts its simulation of a derivation.

$\Leftarrow$: We can assume that L is accepted by a deterministic one-way TM, $M = (Q, \Sigma, T, P, q_0, F)$. Furthermore (Exercise 4.4), we can assume that M never prints a blank symbol on its tape. We will construct a PSG, G, which will generate L. Essentially G generates two copies of a string $x \in T^*$ and simulates the action of M on the second of them. If M accepts the string, G converts the first copy to a terminal string. If not, no terminal string is derived.

Formally, we define the nonterminals of G to be $([T \cup \{\varepsilon\}] \times \Sigma) \cup Q \cup \{S_1, S_2, S_3\}$ where $S_1, S_2, S_3 \notin Q$ and S_1 to be the start symbol. The productions are then defined as follows.

Initialization productions

$$S_1 \rightarrow q_0 S_2$$
$$S_2 \rightarrow [a, a] S_2 \quad \text{for each } a \in T$$
$$S_2 \rightarrow S_3$$
$$S_3 \rightarrow [\varepsilon, \wedge] S_3$$
$$S_3 \rightarrow \varepsilon$$

Simulation productions

$[b,Z]q[a,X] \rightarrow q'[b,Z][a,Y]$ for each $a,b \in T \cup \{\varepsilon\}$, $Z \in \Sigma$ and for each $q,q' \in Q$, $X,Y \in \Sigma$ such that $P(q,X) = (q',Y,L)$,

$q[a,X] \rightarrow [a,Y]q'$ for each $a \in T \cup \{\varepsilon\}$ and for each $q,q' \in Q$, $X,Y \in \Sigma$ such that $P(q,X) = (q',Y,R)$,

$q[a,X] \rightarrow q'[a,Y]$ for each $a \in T \cup \{\varepsilon\}$ and for each $q,q' \in Q$, $X,Y \in \Sigma$ such that $P(q,X) = (q',Y,0)$.

Final productions

$$\left.\begin{array}{c} [a,X]q \rightarrow qaq \\ q[a,X] \rightarrow qaq \\ q \rightarrow \varepsilon \end{array}\right\} \quad \text{for each } a \in T \cup \{\varepsilon\}, X \in \Sigma \text{ and } q \in F.$$

Now, $S_1 \stackrel{*}{\Rightarrow} q_0[a_1,a_1][a_2,a_2]...[a_n,a_n]S_2$ for any $a_i \in T$, $i = 1,2,...,n$. Say M accepts $a_1 a_2 ... a_n \in T^*$ then for some $k \geq n$, M must used only locations $1,...,k$. We can generate from S_1 the string $q_0[a_1,a_1][a_2,a_2]... [a_n,a_n][\varepsilon,\wedge]^m$ where $m = k - n$ using just the initialization productions. Then, using the simulation productions we simulate the action of M on the second components of the ordered pairs in this string. An induction argument on the number of steps in the derivation can be used to show that $q_0[a_1,a_1][a_2,a_2]...[a_n,a_n][\varepsilon,\wedge]^m \stackrel{*}{\Rightarrow} [a_1,X_1][a_2,X_2]...[a_{r-1},X_{r-1}]$ $q[a_r,X_r]...[a_{n+m},X_{n+m}]$ iff the TM, M, given input $a_1 a_2 ... a_n$, can reach a configuration $(q,r,X_1 X_2 ... X_{r-1}, X_r, front(X_{r+1} ... X_{n+m}))$. Then, if and only if the TM reaches a halt state, $q \in F$, the final 'productions of the grammar can be used to generate $a_1 a_2 ... a_n$. Thus we prove $S_1 \stackrel{*}{\Rightarrow} a_1 a_2 .... a_n$ iff $a_1 a_2 ... a_n \in T(M)$. So G generates $L = T(M)$.

Associated with PSGs are two important decision problems.

Membership problem for PSGs (MPSG)
INSTANCE: A PSG, $G = (N,T,P,S)$, and a string $x \in T^*$
QUESTION: Is $x \in L(G)$?

and the

Emptiness problem for PSGs (EPSG)
INSTANCE: A PSG, $G = (N,T,P,S)$.
QUESTION: Is $L(G) = \varnothing$?

As a consequence of theorem 4.9, both of these problems are easily shown to be unsolvable. MPSG is essentially the same as halting problem. EPSG is unsolvable since it can be shown MPSG $\rightsquigarrow$ EPSG as follows. Given $G = (N, T, P, S)$ and $x \in T^*$ we can construct G' which generates $L(G) \cap \{x\}$—by theorems 4.3(2) and (4.9). Then $x \in L(G)$ iff $L(G') \neq \emptyset$. Some other unsolvable decision problems concerning PSGs are given in Exercise 4.5.

CONTEXT-SENSITIVE GRAMMARS

PSGs were introduced by Noam Chomsky in his classic 1956 paper (Chomsky, 1956), and properties thereof were proved in a second paper (Chomsky, 1959). From these pioneering papers a whole theory of formal languages has developed. The general PSGs which we have defined are usually called *type 0 grammars*. They are the most general type of grammar and generate the most general class of language, viz. r.e. languages. In this section and the next two, we discuss restrictions which we can place on the grammar and how such restrictions affect the class of language generated. We get a hierarchy of languages called the *Chomsky hierarchy*. This hierarchy is discussed in great detail in the classic and scholarly text, *Formal languages and their relation to automata* (Hopcroft & Ullman, 1969).

If we restrict each production, $\alpha \rightarrow \beta$, of a PSG, $G = (N, T, P, S)$, so that $|\alpha| \leq |\beta|$ then the grammar is called a *context-sensitive grammar* (CSG) or *type 1 grammar*. The language generated by such a grammar is similarly called a *context-sensitive* or *type 1 language*. Of course, one implication of this definition is that the empty string, ε, is not in any context-sensitive language since any string derivable from the start symbol, S, must have length ≥ 1. It is, however, common to allow ε to be in context-sensitive languages by extending the definition of CSGs to permit the production $S \rightarrow \varepsilon$ providing S does not appear as a substring in the right hand side of any production. We will follow this convention. Then, if L is a CSL generated by $G = (N, T, P, S)$ and $\varepsilon \notin L$ we can easily construct the CSG,

$$G' = (N \cup \{S'\}, T, P \cup \{S' \rightarrow S, S' \rightarrow \varepsilon\}, S'), S' \notin N \cup T,$$

which generates $L \cup \{\varepsilon\}$.

The following result is important since it shows that the *membership problem for CSGs* is solvable.

Theorem 4.10

If $G = (N, T, P, S)$ is a CSG then $L(G)$ is a recursive language.

Proof. One can determine by inspection of G whether or not $\varepsilon \in L(G)$. So consider $x \in T^+$ such that $|x| = n$. We need an algorithm to check whether or not $x \in L(G)$. Let $T_m^n = \{\alpha | \alpha \in (N \cup T)^+, |\alpha| \leq n$ and $S \overset{*}{\Rightarrow} \alpha$ by a derivation of at most m steps$\}$. Then $T_0^n = \{S\}$ and we can calculate T_m^n from T_{m-1}^n using $T_m^n = T_{m-1}^n \cup \{\alpha |$ for some $\beta \in T_{m-1}^n, \beta \Rightarrow \alpha$ and $|\alpha| \leq n\}$. If $S \overset{*}{\Rightarrow} \alpha$ and $|\alpha| \leq n$ then α will be in T_m^n for some m; if S does not derive α or $|\alpha| > n$ then α will not be in T_m^n for any m.

The TM to check whether or not $x \in L(G)$ will construct $T_0^n, T_1^n, T_2^n, \ldots$ where $n = |x|$. Clearly $T_i^n \subseteq T_{i+1}^n$ from the definition. Also, if $T_i^n = T_{i+1}^n$ then $T_{i+1}^n = T_{i+2}^n = \cdots$. Thus we are constructing a *chain* $T_0^n \subset T_1^n \subset T_2^n \ldots \subset T_i^n = T_{i+1}^n = \cdots$. Now, $\#(T_i^n) \leq k^n$ where $k = \#(N \cup T)$ so the chain must eventually reach an i such that $T_i^n = T_{i+1}^n$. The algorithm to check whether or not $x \in L(G)$ can thus halt when it reaches such a stage. Then $x \in L(G)$ iff $x \in T_i^n$.

Unfortunately, the converse of this theorem is not true, i.e. there exist recursive languages that are not context sensitive. The proof is not difficult. In Exercise 4.7, the reader is asked to show that there are a countably infinite number of phrase structure grammars with $N \subset \{A_i | i \geq 0\}, S = A_0$ and $T = \{0, 1\}$. We can further show that the set of CSGs in this set of grammars is also countably infinite and thus list them as $G_1, G_2, G_3, \ldots$. Now, we have also shown that we can enumerate the strings in $\{0, 1\}^*$ as $x_1, x_2, x_3, \ldots$. Hence we can define the language $L = \{x_i | x_i \notin L(G_i)\}$. L is clearly recursive since given $x \in \{0, 1\}^*$ one can determine for which $i, x = x_i$, then generate G_i and then, by theorem 4.10, test whether or not $x_i \in L(G_i)$. However, L is not a context-sensitive language. If it were then $L = L(G_j)$ for some j. Now, consider x_j. If $x_j \in L$ then $x_j \in L(G_j)$ and, so by the definition of L, $x_j \notin L$. If $x_j \notin L$ then $x_j \notin L(G_j)$ so, again by the definition of L, $x_j \in L$. In either case we have a contradiction and this establishes the following result.

Theorem 4.11

There are recursive languages that are not context sensitive.

Since, in a CSG, G, every production $\alpha \to \beta$ (with the exception of the special case production, $S \to \varepsilon$) satisfies $|\alpha| \leq |\beta|$, it is apparent that if

$\gamma_1 \alpha \gamma_2 \Rightarrow \gamma_1 \beta \gamma_2$ then $|\gamma_1 \alpha \gamma_2| \leq |\gamma_1 \beta \gamma_2|$. So, during the derivation of a string of $x \in T^+$, every sentential form has length ≥ 1 and $\leq |x|$. Now, consider the nondeterministic TM constructed in the proof of the first part of theorem 4.9. If G is a CSG then, because of the constraint on the length of the sentential form used to derive x, the TM will accept any $x \in L(G)$ using only the locations $-|x|-1, -|x|, -|x|+1,\ldots,|x|,|x|+1$. The locations $-|x|-1$ and $|x|+1$ will always hold a special symbol which acts as an end marker. If a sentential form cannot be fitted in locations $1,2,\ldots,|x|$, we know that it cannot be used in the derivation of x. As soon as we attempt to use location $|x|+1$ to store some symbol in a sentential form we know that we should then abandon this derivation. The positive part of the tape can be cleared and simulation restarted with S in location 1.

A nondeterministic TM which for all inputs x, will only use $k_1|x| + k_2$ locations for some fixed integers k_1, k_2 is called a *linear-bounded automaton* (LBA). We have shown that any context-sensitive language, L, can be accepted by a linear-bounded automaton since the TM we have described need never use more than $2|x|+2$ locations to accept $x \in L$. The reverse of this result is also true, i.e. that any language accpeted by a LBA is necessarily context-sensitive. An effective construction to prove this result is given in Kuroda (1964). As a consequence of this result we can prove the following.

Theorem 4.12

The emptiness problem for context-sensitive grammars (ECSG) is unsolvable.

Proof. We show PCP $\rightsquigarrow$ ECSG. Let $\underline{x} = (x_1, x_2,\ldots, x_n)$, $\underline{y} = (y_1, y_2,\ldots, y_n)$ be two n-tuples of strings in T^+ which define an instance, I, of PCP. We can construct an LBA, M, which given an input string $z \in T^+$, generates nondeterministically sequences of integers $i_1, i_2,\ldots, i_m (1 \leq m \leq |z|$ and $1 \leq i_j \leq n$, for all j). M then tests such a sequence to see whether or not $z = x_{i_1} x_{i_2}\ldots x_{i_m} = y_{i_1} y_{i_2}\ldots y_{i_m}$. If so, M accepts z. Now, z is accepted by this LBA iff z provides a solution to I. We know that there must exist some CSG, G, such that $L(G)$ is the language accepted by M. Hence $L(G) \neq \emptyset$ iff I has a solution. Since there is an effective construction for M and G, this shows that PCP $\rightsquigarrow$ ECSG and the proof is completed.

CONTEXT-FREE GRAMMARS

A *context-free* or *type 2* grammar (CFG) is a phrase structure grammar, $G = (N, T, P, S)$, where every production in P is of the form $A \to \beta, A \in N$, $\beta \in (N \cup T)^*$. A language generated by such a grammar is called a context-free or type 2 language (CFL). For example, the grammar, G_4, with the following productions is context-free.

$$S \to AB \mid aC$$
$$A \to aA \mid b \mid BB$$
$$B \to bSS \mid aB \mid \varepsilon$$
$$C \to ab$$

Now, since this grammar contains the production $B \to \varepsilon$, it is not context-sensitive. However, ε-*productions*, i.e. productions with ε on the right-hand side can be severely restricted. A grammar with no ε-productions is called ε-*free*. If a CFG, G, has ε-productions then we can construct an ε-free CFG, G', such that $L(G') = L(G) \backslash \{\varepsilon\}$. The construction is not difficult. If $G = (N, T, P, S)$ then $G' = (N, T, P, S)$ where P' is constructed from P according to the following two rules.

(1) Put all ε-free productions from P into P'.

(2) Find all the nonterminals $A \in N$ such that $A \overset{*}{\underset{G}{\Rightarrow}} \varepsilon$. Such non-terminals are said to be ε-*generating*. Then, for each production $p \in P$ with one or more ε-generating nonterminals appearing as substrings of the right hand side, add to P' any ε-free production which can be constructed from p by omitting one or more of these ε-generating nonterminals.

For our example, S, A and B are all ε-generating but C is not. The above two rules construct a context-free grammar with productions

$$S \to AB \mid aC \mid A \mid B$$
$$A \to aA \mid b \mid BB \mid a \mid B$$
$$B \to bSS \mid aB \mid b \mid bS \mid a$$
$$C \to ab$$

This CFG generates $L(G_4) \backslash \{\varepsilon\}$.

The construction we have described always produces from a CFG, $G = (N, T, P, S)$, an ε-free CFG, $G' = (N, T, P', S)$, generating $L(G) \backslash \{\varepsilon\}$ The proof of this is not difficult and relies on establishing the pact that for all $A \in N$ and $x \in T^+$, $A \overset{*}{\underset{G}{\Rightarrow}} x$ iff $A \overset{*}{\underset{G'}{\Rightarrow}} x$. If $\varepsilon \in L(G)$, G' is not equivalent to G. However, we can reintroduce ε and moreover, by introducing a new nonterminal S', we can arrange that the start symbol never appears as a substring of the right-hand side of any production. We set $G'' = (N \cup \{S'\}, T, P'', S')$ where $P'' = P' \cup \{S' \to \varepsilon, S' \to S\}$. For our example we have

$$S \underset{G_4}{\Rightarrow} AB \underset{G_4}{\Rightarrow} BBB \underset{G_4}{\overset{*}{\Rightarrow}} \varepsilon \text{ so } \varepsilon \in L(G_4). \text{ We thus construct } G_4'' \text{ with productions}$$

$$S' \to \varepsilon | S$$
$$S \to AB | aC | A | B$$
$$A \to aA | b | BB | a | B$$
$$B \to bSS | aB | b | bS | a$$
$$C \to ab$$

where S' is the new start symbol.

Given an arbitrary CFG, G, there is an algorithm to determine whether or not $\varepsilon \in L(G)$ (Exercise 4.13). If $\varepsilon \notin L(G)$ then G' constructed above is equivalent to G and if $\varepsilon \in L(G)$ then G'' is equivalent to G. In either case, the equivalent grammar so constructed conforms to our definition of context-sensitive grammar. We have thus established the following.

Theorem 4.13

Every context-free language is a context-sensitive language.

The converse of this theorem is not true. For example, $\{a^n b^n c^n | n \geq 1\}$, which we have already shown to be context-sensitive, is not context-free. The proof of this result is given in the companion text *A First Course in Formal Language Theory* (Rayward-Smith, 1983). Also in that text we show that the acceptors for CFLs are nondeterministic pushdown automata (NPDA). These machines can be viewed as restricted nondeterministic TMs equipped with one-way infinite tapes. On the first tape the input is written and the tape head on this tape is restricted to be a read only head which can never move left. The machine must not enter a final state until the leftmost blank on this tape is read. The second tape is used as a *stack*, i.e. if location k is the leftmost location containing a blank then all locations $> k$ also contain a blank. The tape head can scan location $k - 1$, replace the contents by a blank and move left (i.e. a *pop* operation) or it can scan location k and write there a nonblank symbol (i.e. a *push* operation). Any language accepted by a NPDA is necessarily context-free and, similarly, for every context-free language there is a NPDA which accepts it. If the machine must be deterministic, this is no longer the case. There are context-free languages which are not accepted by any deterministic pushdown automata.

Since we can construct a CSG from any CFG and the membership problem for CSGs is solvable, it follows that the membership problem for CFGs is also solvable. In fact, solving this problem efficiently is of great importance to computer scientists. The *syntax* (or grammatical structure) of a programming language is commonly defined in Backus–Naur Form (BNF) or in syntax charts both of which are notations equivalent to CFGs. To check whether a given program written in the language is constructed according to the defined syntax, we have to solve the membership problem. In practice, restrictions are often placed upon the grammar to ensure an efficient solution to this problem.

Let $G = (N, T, P, S)$ be any CFG and assume $L(G) \neq \emptyset$. From our discussion above, we can assume G is context-sensitive. For any $x \in T^+$ generating by G there is an associated derivation tree. We define the depth of a derivation tree to be equal to the length of the longest path from the root node, S, to a leaf node. Thus, for G_5 with productions

$$S \to AB$$
$$A \to aA \mid a$$
$$B \to bB \mid b$$

the derivation tree for $a^3 b^2 \in L(G_5)$ is given in Fig. 4.2 and has depth four.

If a derivation tree constructed using a CFG, $G = (N, T, P, S)$, has depth n

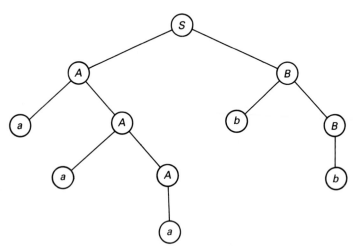

Fig. 4.2.

then there must exist a path with nodes labelled $A_1, A_2, \ldots, A_n$, a where $S = A_1, A_2, \ldots, A_n \in N$ and $a \in T$. If $n > \#(N)$, two or more of the nodes on this path must have the same label, say $A_i = A_j$ and $i < j$. We can construct a new derivation tree by replacing the tree rooted at A_i by the tree rooted at A_j. If we apply this argument repeatedly it follows that if there exists a derivation tree for $x' \in L(G)$ with depth $> \#(N)$ then there exists a derivation tree from some $x \in L(G)$ of depth $\leq \#(N)$. From this we conclude:

Theorem 4.14

The emptiness problem for CFGs is solvable, i.e., for any CGF, $G = (N, T, P, S)$, there is an algorithm to determine whether or not $L(G) = \varnothing$.

Proof: We assume that the CFG, G, is context-sensitive. Then, the algorithm first tests if $S \to \varepsilon$ is a production in P. If so $L(G) \neq \varnothing$ since $\varepsilon \in L(G)$. Otherwise, we construct all the possible derivation trees *but only to a depth* $\#(N)$. These are finite in number and none of them corresponds to a derivation of a terminal string iff $L(G) = \varnothing$.

A production $A \to \alpha$ in a CFG, $G = (N, T, P, S)$, is called *relevant* iff there exists a derivation of some $x \in L(G)$ which uses that production, i.e., iff $S \overset{*}{\Rightarrow} \alpha_1 A \alpha_2 \Rightarrow \alpha_1 \alpha \alpha_2 \overset{*}{\Rightarrow} x$ for some $x \in L(G)$. If a production in G is not relevant it is called *irrelevant* and we would like to be able to remove it. Now, for any $A \in N$, we can construct a new grammar $G_A = (N, T, P, A)$. If $L(G_A) = \varnothing$ then there is no possibility of generating a terminal string from A using productions in P. Thus from no sentential form of G containing A can we derive a terminal string. $L(G)$ will thus be unaffected if we remove from G all the productions with A on the left hand side or with A occurring on the right hand side. There may still be some irrelevant productions left in the grammar since there may be some $A \in N$ which can generate terminal strings but which can never appear in a sentential form. An argument similar to that used to prove theorem 4.14 can be used to show that, if A can occur in a sentential form, then there is a sentential form containing A that can be derived by a partial derivation tree of depth $< \#(N)$. (The tree is a *partial* derivation tree because its leaves are not terminals.) By generating all such trees, we can check if any $A \in N$ cannot appear in a sentential form. If this is the case then any production involving A can be removed as irrelevant.

Even though we can remove irrelevant productions from a CFG, and solve both the membership problem and the emptiness problem, there are still unsolvable problems associated with these grammars. For example,

The empty intersection problem for CFGs (EICFG)
INSTANCE: Two CFGs, G_1, G_2.
QUESTION: Does $L(G_1) \cap L(G_2) = \emptyset$?

Theorem 4.15

The Empty Intersection Problem for CFGs is unsolvable.

Proof. We show PCP $\rightarrow$ EICFG. If an instance, I, of PCP is given by $\underline{x} = (x_1, x_2, \ldots, x_n)$ and $\underline{y} = (y_1, y_2, \ldots, y_n)$, two n-tuples of strings in T^+, then we construct the corresponding instance of EICFG as follows. Let $\{s_1, s_2, \ldots, s_n\}$ be a set of n distinct symbols $\notin T$ and define $T' = T \cup \{s_1, s_2, \ldots, s_n\}$. Let $G_x = (\{S_x\}, T', P_x, S_x)$ and $G_y = (\{S_y\}, T', P_y, S_y)$ be two CFGs where P_x contains all the productions $S_x \rightarrow x_i S_x s_i$ and $S_x \rightarrow x_i s_i$, $i = 1, 2, \ldots, n$ and P_y contains all the productions $S_y \rightarrow y_i S_y s_i$ and $S_y \rightarrow y_i s_i$, $i = 1, 2, \ldots, n$. Then $L(G_x) = \{x_{i_1} x_{i_2} \ldots x_{i_m} s_{i_m} \ldots s_{i_2} s_{i_1} \mid m \geq 1\}$ and, similarly, $L(G_y) = \{y_{i_1} y_{i_2} \ldots y_{i_m} s_{i_m} \ldots s_{i_2} s_{i_1} \mid m \geq 1\}$. Hence, $L(G_x) \cap L(G_y) = \emptyset$ iff I has a solution. Since we have an effective construction of G_x and G_y from I, we have thus established the unsolvability of EICFG.

There are other unsolvable problems concerning CFGs. These include the following.

Totality problem for CFGs (TCFG)
INSTANCE: A CFG, $G = (N, T, P, S)$.
QUESTION: Does $L(G) = T^*$?

Equivalence problem for CFGs (ECFG)
INSTANCE: Two CFGs, G_1, G_2.
QUESTION: Does $L(G_1) = L(G_2)$?

Finite intersection problem for CFGs (FICFG)
INSTANCE: Two CFGs, G_1, G_2.
QUESTION: Is $L(G_1) \cap L(G_2)$ finite?

The proofs of these and other such results are to be found in Bar–Hillel, Perles & Shamir (1961) and Ginsburg & Rose (1963).

REGULAR GRAMMARS

A PSG $G = (N, T, P, S)$ is called a *regular grammar* provided:

(1)   if there exists an ε-production in G, then it is of the form $S \to \varepsilon$ and then S does not appear as a substring of the right-hand side of any other production in P;

(2)   all other productions are either of the form

$A \to a$ where $A \in N$, $a \in T$

or of the form

$A \to aB$ where $A, B \in N, a \in T$.

A language is called a *regular language* (or, sometimes, a *regular set*) iff it is generated by some regular grammar. Clearly, L is a regular language iff $L \backslash \{\varepsilon\}$ is generated by an ε-free regular grammar. Also, every regular grammar is necessarily context-free and hence every regular language is a CFL.

A simple example of a regular grammar is G_6 which has productions

$S \to aA \mid bB$
$A \to aA \mid a$
$B \to bB \mid b$

Then $L(G_6) = \{a^n \mid n > 1\} \cup \{b^n \mid n > 1\}$.

Any regular language can be accepted by a nondeterministic TM with a one-way infinite tape on which a read only head always moves right. The machine must enter a final state as soon as the leftmost blank is read and not before. Such machines are called *nondeterministic finite state automata* (NFSA).

The following theorem is established in Rayward-Smith (1983).

Theorem 4.16

The following definitions are equivalent:

(i) $L \subseteq T^*$ is generated by a regular grammar;

(ii) $L \subseteq T^*$ is accepted by a nondeterministic finite state automaton (NFSA);

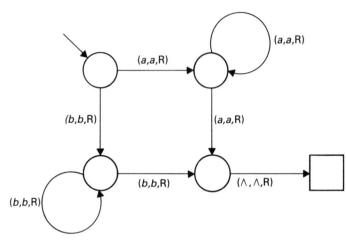

Fig. 4.3.

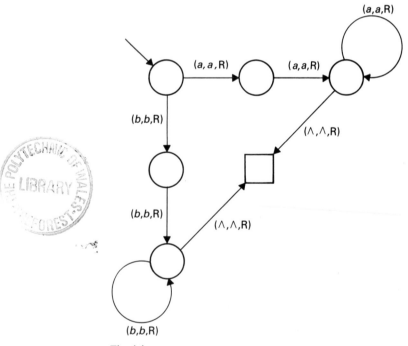

Fig. 4.4.

(iii) $L \subseteq T^*$ is accepted by a deterministic finite state automaton (DFSA).

For example, a NFSA accepting $L(G_6)$ is that of Fig. 4.3. Note, that in this example, every arc is labelled with a triple of the form (a, a, R) for some $a \in T \cup \{ \wedge \}$. This will always be the case for finite state automata since the tapehead is read only and must move right.

A DFSA equivalent to the NFSA of Fig. 4.3 in that it also accepts $L(G_6)$ is given in Fig. 4.4. Since by definition, regular grammars are always context-free, it follows that the membership, emptiness and finiteness problems for regular grammars are solvable. By constructing suitable finite state automata, it is also possible to show that the totality, equivalence, empty intersection and finite intersection problems are also solvable. The interested reader is referred to Hopcroft & Ullman (1969) for a proof of these results.

Regular grammars complete the Chomsky hierarchy of grammars and are thus sometimes known as type 3 grammars. We tabulate the hierarchy with the associated accepted and solvability of decision problems in Fig. 4.5.

		Type			
		0	1	2	3
	GRAMMAR	phrase structure	context-sensitive	context-free	regular
	LANGUAGE	recursively enumerable	context-sensitive	context-free	regular
	ACCEPTOR	Turing machine	linear bounded automaton	nondeterministic pushdown automaton	finite state automaton
	MEMBERSHIP	Unsolvable	Solvable	Solvable	Solvable
	EMPTINESS	Unsolvable	Unsolvable	Solvable	Solvable
	FINITENESS	Unsolvable	Unsolvable	Solvable	Solvable
	TOTALITY	Unsolvable	Unsolvable	Unsolvable	Solvable
PROBLEM SOLVABILITY	EQUIVALENCE	Unsolvable	Unsolvable	Unsolvable	Solvable
	EMPTY INTERSECTION	Unsolvable	Unsolvable	Unsolvable	Solvable
	FINITE INTERSECTION	Unsolvable	Unsolvable	Unsolvable	Solvable

Fig. 4.5. The Chomsky Hierarchy.

EXERCISES

1 Show that for any finite set, T, the set of TMs of the form $(Q, \Sigma, T, P, q_0, F)$ where $Q \subset \{q_i | i \geq 0\}$ and $\Sigma \subset T \cup \{s_i | i \geq 0\}$, is countably infinite. Show that every r.e. language is recognized by at least one of these TMs.

2 Show that $L = \{concat(x, rev\,x)) | x \in \{0,1\}^*\}$ is a recursive set by constructing a (deterministic) TM to calculate χ_L.

3 Prove theorem 4.7, i.e. that L is accepted by a (deterministic) TM iff L is r.e.

4 Show that if L is accepted by a deterministic one-way infinite TM then it can be accepted by such a machine that never prints a blank on its tape. [Hint: augment the auxiliary alphabet by a 'pseudo-blank' symbol.]

5 Show that the following problems are unsolvable.

Finiteness problem for PSGs
INSTANCE: A PSG, $G = (N, T, P, S)$.
QUESTION: Is $L(G)$ finite?

Totality problem for PSGs
INSTANCE: A PSG, $G = (N, T, P, S)$.
QUESTION: Is $L(G) = T^*$?

Equivalence problem for PSGs
INSTANCE: PSGs $G_1 = (N_1, T, P_1, S_1)$ and $G_2 = (N_2, T, P_2, S_2)$.
QUESTION: Is $L(G_1) = L(G_2)$?

6 Show that the *Totality problem for CSGs* is unsolvable.

7 Show that there are a countably infinite number of phrase structure grammars with $N \subset \{A_i | i \geq 0\}$, $S = A_0$ and $T = \{0,1\}$. Show that the number of these grammars which are CSGs is also countably infinite.

8 Prove that for any r.e. language there is a procedure for enumerating the strings of the language (hence the reason for calling such a language recursively enumerable). [Hint: use theorem 4.7.]

9 Show that we can set $k_1 = 1$ in the definition of linear-bounded automata without affecting the ability of such machines to recognize all the context-sensitive languages. What additional constraints can be imposed on k_2?

10 Show that the *Halting problem for linear-bounded automata* is solvable.

11 Show that the *Finiteness problem for CFGs* is solvable.

12 Prove formally that the construction of an ε-free CFG, G', from a CFG, G, which is given in the text does indeed satisfy $L(G') = L(G) \setminus \{\varepsilon\}$.

13 Show that it is solvable to determine for a given CFG, $G = (N,T,P,S)$, whether or not an arbitrary $A \in N$ is ε-generating. Hence deduce that there is an algorithm to determine whether or not $\varepsilon \in L(G)$.

14 Show that if L_1, L_2 are context-free languages then so are $L_1 \cup L_2$ and $L_1 L_2$. Construct an example to show that $L_1 \cap L_2$ is not necessarily context-free. [Hint: use the fact that $\{a^n b^n c^n | n \geq 1\}$ is not context-free.]

15 Show that $\{a^n b^n | n \geq 1\}$ is not a regular language but is context-free.

16 Construct a DFSA to accept $L = \{a,b\} \{aa,ba\} \{b\}^*$. Hence, or otherwise, construct a DFSA to accept $L^c = \{a,b\}^* \backslash L$.

Chapter 5

Recursive Functions

DEFINING FUNCTIONS

In general, a TM, $M = (Q, \Sigma, T, P, q_0, F)$, computes a partial function $f_M: T^* \to \Sigma^*$. In the previous chapter we have studied properties of the subset of T^* on which such an f_M is defined. In this chapter, we are going to study the functions themselves. We will be characterizing the class of functions which are Turing-computable (TM-computable) and examining properties thereof.

Because binary encoding is such a familiar concept to computer scientists, we will assume that both the arguments of our functions and their resulting values are given in binary form. Let $B = \{0, 1\}^*$ denote all the binary strings, then we are concerned with those n-ary functions, $B^n \to B$, $(n \geq 1)$ which are Turing-computable. We know from Chapter 2 that this does not include all functions on B, i.e. that there exist functions $B^n \to B$ which are not Turing-computable. In fact there are an uncountably infinite number of functions on B that are not computable (see Exercise 5.1).

We will start our discussion of computable functions by considering ways we can construct new computable functions from functions which we already know are computable.

Firstly, consider the m-ary function $h: B^m \to B$ and the m n-ary functions $g_1, g_2, \ldots, g_m: B^n \to B$. From these we can construct a new function, f, the *composition* of $h, g_1, g_2, \ldots, g_m$, which is also an n-ary function $B^n \to B$, defined by

$$f(x_1, x_2, \ldots, x_n) = h(g_1(x_1, x_2, \ldots, x_n), g_2(x_1, x_2, \ldots, x_n), \ldots,$$
$$g_m(x_1, x_2, \ldots, x_n)).$$

If for any n-tuple, $(x_1, x_2, \ldots, x_n)$, any value of $g_i(x_1, x_2, \ldots, x_n)$ is undefined,

$1 \leq i \leq m$, or h is undefined on arguments $g_1(x_1, x_2, \ldots, x_n)$, $g_2(x_1, x_2, \ldots, x_n), \ldots g_m(x_1, x_2, \ldots, x_n)$ then f is also undefined for that n-tuple.

Theorem 5.1

If $h: B^m \to B$ and $g_1, g_2, \ldots, g_m: B^n \to B$ are TM-computable functions, then so is the composition of $h, g_1, g_2, \ldots, g_m$.

Proof. Say the TM, M, computes h and TMs, $M_1, M_2, \ldots, M_m$, compute $g_1, g_2, \ldots, g_m$. Without loss of generality, we can assume that each of $M_1, M_2, \ldots, M_m$, takes its input of an n-tuple of elements of B using the same encoding—$e((x_1, x_2, \ldots, x_n))$. We now construct an $m+1$ tape TM, M', to compute the composition of $h, g_1, g_2, \ldots, g_m$. M' takes as input, $e((x_1, x_2, \ldots, x_n))$ and copies this to tapes 2, 3, $\ldots, m+1$. On tape i, $2 \leq i \leq m+1$, M' then simulates the action of TM, M_{i-1}. If all these machines halt, their outputs are copied onto tape 1, and suitably encoded for input to machine M. M' then simulates the action of M.

In Fig. 2.4, we showed that $cons0: B \to B$ is TM-computable. Similarly, one can show that $cons1: B \to B$ is TM-computable where

$$cons1(x) = 1x.$$

By theorem 5.1, we can now claim that functions such as

$$cons00(x) = cons0(cons0(x))$$
$$cons01(x) = cons0(cons1(x))$$

are also TM-countable.

Another function which is clearly TM-computable is $nil: B \to B$ defined by

$$nil(x) = \varepsilon \quad \text{for all } x \in B.$$

Then, the constant functions *zero* and *one* can be defined using composition by

$$zero(x) = cons0(nil(x)),$$
$$one(x) = cons1(nil(x))$$

and these too must be TM-computable.

When using composition to show a function is TM-computable, we do not, in practice, insist that each g_i in the construction is *n*-ary. By convention, we allow the use of functions $g_1, g_2 ..., g_n$ that are *k*-ary for any $1 \le k \le n$. Thus not all arguments $x_1, x_2, \ldots, x_n$ necessarily appear in the argument lists of all the functions $g_1, g_2, \ldots, g_m$. For example, we might have shown that *concat*: $B^2 \to B$ and *reverse*: $B \to B$ are both TM-computable. We might then deduce that the function

$$f_1(x, y) = concat(reverse(x), reverse(y))$$

is TM-computable since f_1 is constructed from *concat* and *reverse* by composition. This is really rather inaccurate because according to the definition of composition the innermost functions on the right-hand side of such an equation must involve all the arguments.

To be precise, we should have observed that the binary *projection functions*, δ_2^1 and δ_2^2, defined by

$$\delta_2^1(x, y) = x$$
$$\delta_2^2(x, y) = y$$

are both TM-computable. (The construction of the TM to compute such functions is obvious.) Hence, if *reverse* is TM-computable then by theorem 5.1, so is

$$reverse1(x, y) = reverse(\delta_2^1(x, y)) = reverse(x)$$
and $$reverse2(x, y) = reverse(\delta_2^2(x, y)) = reverse(y).$$

Hence, using theorem 5.1 again, we deduce that

$$f_1(x, y) = concat(reverse1(x, y), reverse2(x, y))$$
$$= concat(reverse(x), reverse(y))$$

is also TM-computable.

Now, in general, the *projection functions* $\delta_n^i: B^n \to B (1 \le i \le n)$ defined by

$$\delta_n^i(x_1, x_2, \ldots, x_n) = x_i$$

are easily shown to be TM-computable. By using projection functions in composition with known functions, we can enable unnecessary arguments to be dropped. Similarly, using projection functions, we can change the ordering of the arguments in an *n*-tuple. For example,

$$concat(x, y) = concat(\delta_2^2(x, y), \delta_2^1(x, y))$$
$$= concat(y, x)$$

We will not continue to include all the projections in our definitions merely to ensure that the format of such definitions exactly matches the specified format. Hence, we adopt the convention that in compositions of form

$$h(g_1(x_1,x_2,\ldots,x_n),g_2(x_1,x_2,\ldots,x_n),\ldots,g_m(x_1,x_2,\ldots,x_n))$$

not every argument $x_1,x_2,\ldots,x_n$ has to be used with each funcion g_i and moreover that these arguments do not have to occur in order. Thus, we would allow definitions such as

$$f_2(x,y)=concat(concat(y,x),reverse(x)).$$

Another way of constructing new functions from old is to use recursion. We have already seen in Chapter 1 how powerful this technique can be. We now need to formalize its use in defining functions on strings. As a first step, let us consider the format of the definition of a unary function $f:B\to B$ by recursion. Assuming h_1, $h_2:B^2\to B$ have already been defined, the definition of f in terms of h_1, h_2 will take the following form,

$$f(\varepsilon) = w(\text{either for some } w\in B \text{ or } w=\text{undefined})$$
$$f(0x)=h_1(x,f(x))$$
$$f(1x)=h_2(x,f(x))$$

It may be the case, however, that some of the arguments of h_1,h_2 will be missing and/or out of order.

A recursive definition of the identity function $iden:B\to B$ in terms of $cons0, cons1$ would be:

$$iden(\varepsilon) = \varepsilon$$
$$iden(0x)=cons0(x)$$
$$iden(1x)=cons1(x)$$

As a second example, the function $length:B\to B$ which computes, in unary form, the length of a string $\in B$ is defined recursively as follows.

$$length(\varepsilon) = \varepsilon$$
$$length(0x)=cons1(length(x))$$
$$length(1x)=cons1(length(x))$$

We now need to generalize the above method of defining functions to allow recursive definitions of n-ary functions for $n\geq 2$. Assuming g is an $(n-1)$-ary function $B^{n-1}\to B$ already defined and h_1,h_2 are $(n+1)$-ary functions, $B^{n+1}\to B$ already defined, then we can define f recursively in terms of g, h_1, h_2 as follows:

$$f(\varepsilon, x_2, \ldots, x_n) \quad = g(x_2, \ldots, x_n)$$
$$f(0x_1, x_2, \ldots, x_n) = h_1(x_1, x_2, \ldots, x_n, f(x_1, x_2, \ldots, x_n))$$
$$f(1x_1, x_2, \ldots, x_n) = h_2(x_1, x_2, \ldots, x_n, f(x_1, x_2, \ldots, x_n))$$

As before, we also allow, by definition, g to have arity $< n - 1$ and h_1, h_2 to have arities $< n + 1$ so some of the arguments of g, h_1, h_2 may be omitted. They also may appear out of order. Note that the correctness of a recursive definition of f can always be checked by using induction on the length of the first argument of f. For example, recursion can be used to define *concat* in terms of *iden, cons0* and *cons1*.

$$concat(\varepsilon, y) \quad = iden(y)$$
$$concat(0x, y) = cons0(concat(x, y))$$
$$concat(1x, y) = cons1(concat(x, y))$$

To prove $concat(x, y) = xy$ for all $x, y \in B$ we proceed by induction on the length of x. If $x = \varepsilon$, then $concat(\varepsilon, y) = iden(y) = y$. Let us assume $concat(x, y) = xy$ for all strings x of length $\leq n$. Now consider a string x of length $n + 1$, then $x = 0z$ or $x = 1z$ where $z = tail(x)$ is a string of length n. In the first case, $concat(x, y) = cons0(concat(z, y)) = cons0(zy)$, by induction hypothesis and $cons0(zy) = 0zy = xy$. Hence in this case $concat(x, y) = xy$. The case where $x = 1z$ is similar and from this we can deduce that $concat(x, y) = xy$ where x is a string of length $n + 1$. Hence this result holds for all $x, y \in B$ by induction.

In future examples of recursion in this chapter, the correctness proofs are not given but the reader should be able to produce them for himself.

To define *reverse* recursively, we first need to define $append0 : B \rightarrow B$ and $append1 : B \rightarrow B$ by

$$append0(x) = concat(x, zero(x))$$
and $$append1(x) = concat(x, one(x))$$

Then,

$$reverse(\varepsilon) \quad = \varepsilon$$
$$reverse(0x) = append0(reverse(x))$$
$$reverse(1x) = append1(reverse(x))$$

Another example is the *complement* function which given a string $x \in B$ replaces every 0 by 1 and every 1 by 0. Thus $complement(0010) = 1101$. A recursive definition is

$$complement(\varepsilon) \quad = \varepsilon$$
$$complement(0x) = cons1\,(complement(x))$$
$$complement(1x) = cons0(complement(x))$$

The importance of recursive definitions to us is given by the next result.

Theorem 5.2

If f is defined recursively in terms of TM-computable functions then f is TM-computable.

Proof. We outline the proof for the case where f is unary but the argument can easily be generalized to the case where f is n-ary for $n \geq 2$.

We assume f is defined in terms of TM-computable functions h_1, h_2 and takes the following form.

$$f(\varepsilon) \quad = w \ (w \text{ undefined or in } B)$$
$$f(0x) = h_1(x, f(x))$$
$$f(1x) = h_2(x, f(x))$$

The one-tape TMs which compute h_1, h_2 will be denoted by M_1, M_2. We do not assume that h_1, h_2 are necessarily defined using both arguments, $x, f(x)$.

The TM, M, to compute f has 3 tapes; the first is an input/output tape, the second is used to simulate a stack, and the third as a work tape. Say the string $z \in B$ is input to M. If $z = \varepsilon$ then if $w \in B$ the machine simply clears tape 1 and then writes w in locations $1, 2, \ldots, |w|$ of that tape; otherwise it enters an infinite loop. if $z \neq \varepsilon$ then either $z = 0x$ or $z = 1x$ for some $x \in B$. If $z = 0x$ and h_1 uses $f(x)$ as an argument then the string z followed by a separator symbol, $/$, is written in the leftmost nonempty locations > 0 of tape 2. However, if h_1 does not use $f(x)$ as an argument, the value of $f(z)$ can be calculated directly from x using M_1 on tape 3. Similarly, if $z = 1x$ and h_2 uses $f(x)$ as an argument we write $z/$ onto tape 2 but otherwise evaluate $f(z)$ on tape 3 using M_2. In either case, if we write $z/$ onto tape 2, the next step is to replace z on tape 1 by x and, if $x \neq \varepsilon$, to repeat the process.

Eventually, we reach one of the following situations.

Case 1. ε is on tape 1 and on tape 2 we have written $z/tail(z)/\ldots/$ $tail^{|z|-1}(z)/$. Now we enter the second phase of the computation. If $w \in B$

then we encode the pair (ε, w) to tape 3. We inspect the symbol to the right of the second righmost / on tape 2 to see if $tail^{|z|-1}(z)$ has a 0 as its first symbol. If so, we use M_1 to evaluate $f(tail^{|z|-1}(z))$ on tape 3; otherwise we use M_2. We then replace $f(tail^{|z|-1}(z))$ by an encoding of the pair $(tail^{|z|-1}(z), f(tail^{|z|-1}(z)))$ and delete the string $tail^{|z|-1}(z)/$ from tape 2. The process is then repeated to compute $f(tail^{|z|-2}(z))$, $f(tail^{|z|-3}(z))$, etc. If there is no infinite looping in the resulting simulations of M_1 or M_2 we eventually reach a situation where $f(z)$ is on tape 3 and tape 2 contains $z/$. At that stage, we copy $f(z)$ onto tape 1 and halt. If, however, w is undefined or there is infinite looping in the simulations of M_1 or M_2 then $f(z)$ is undefined and there is no resulting output.

Case 2. If tape 2 is empty then, providing $f(z)$ is defined, we must have its value on tape 3 and this can be simply copied to tape 1. Otherwise, for some $|z| > i \geq 1$, we have $y = tail^{|z|-i}(z)$ on tape 1, $z/tail(z)/\ldots/tail^{|z|-i-1}(z)/$ on tape 2 and $f(y)$ on tape 3. We now use the second phase of the computation process as described in Case 1. We encode $(y, f(y))$ to tape 3 and there evaluate $f(tail^{|z|-i-1}(z))$. Then, we proceed as before, to evaluate $f(tail^{|z|-i-2}(z)),\ldots,f(tail(z))$ and, finally, $f(z)$. Providing $f(z)$ is defined, no looping will have occurred and this value can then be copied to tape 1 and M can halt.

PRIMITIVE RECURSIVE FUNCTIONS AND PREDICATES

The primitive recursive functions on B are total functions $B^n \to B (n \geq 1)$ constructed according to the following rules.

(1) *Base functions.* The following are primitive recursive functions:
    (a) *nil*: $B \to B$ defined by

$$nil(x) = \varepsilon \quad \text{for all } x \in B;$$

    (b) *cons0* and *cons1*: $B \to B$ defined by

$$cons0(x) = 0x$$
and $cons1(x) = 1x$ for all $x \in B$;

    (c) the selector functions δ_n^i $(1 \leq i \leq n)$ where $\delta_n^i : B^n \to B$ is defined by

$$\delta_n^i(x_1, x_2, \ldots, x_n) = x_i.$$

(2) From known primitive recursive functions we can construct new functions using
    (a) *composition,*

(b) *primitive recursion*, i.e. recursive definitions of the form we have been discussing but not allowing the possibility of partial functions. This is achieved by simply insisting that a recursive definition of an *n*-ary function takes the form:
either (case $n = 1$)

$$f(\varepsilon) \quad = w$$
$$f(0x) = h_1(x, f(x))$$
$$f(1x) = h_2(x, f(x))$$

where $w \in B$ and h_1, h_2 are primitive recursive,
or (case $n > 1$)

$$f(\varepsilon, x_2, \ldots, x_n) \quad = g(x_2, \ldots, x_n)$$
$$f(0x_1, x_2, \ldots, x_n) = h_1(x_1, x_2, \ldots, x_n, f(x_1, x_2, \ldots, x_n))$$
$$f(1x_1, x_2, \ldots, x_n) = h_2(x_1, x_2, \ldots, x_n, f(x_1, x_2, \ldots, x_n))$$

where g, h_1, h_2 are primitive recursive. For both the above cases, we allow arguments of g, h_1, h_2 to be omitted and/or out of order.
(3)   No other functions except the base functions and those constructable according to the rules given in (2) are primitive recursive.

Since all the base functions are total and since both composition and primitive recursion preserve totality, it follows that all primitive recursive functions are total. Moreover, since the base functions are TM-computable, the following theorem follows from theorems 5.1 and 5.2.

Theorem 5.3

Every primitive recursive function is a TM-computable total function.

Previously, whenever we had to show a function was TM-computable, we either had to construct a specific TM to compute that function or revert to a 'hand-waving' argument. Now, we are in a much more satisfactory situation; if we can show a function is primitive recursive then we know that it must be TM-computable. We have already shown that the following functions are primitive recursive and hence TM-computable: *zero*, *one*, *iden*, *length*, *concat*, *reverse* and *complement*.

A further example of a primitive recursive function which we will use later is *condempty*. The expression *condempty* (x_1, x_2, x_3) delivers x_2 if $x_1 = \varepsilon$

and x_3 otherwise.

$$condempty(\varepsilon, x_2, x_3) \quad = iden(x_2)$$
$$condempty(0x_1, x_2, x_3) = iden(x_3)$$
$$condempty(1x_1, x_2, x_3) = iden(x_3)$$

Similarly we define $condzero(x_1, x_2, x_3)$ and $condone(x_1, x_2, x_3)$ in the obvious way.

$$condzero(\varepsilon, x_2, x_3) \quad = iden(x_3)$$
$$condzero(0x_1, x_2, x_3) = condempty(x_1, x_2, x_3)$$
$$condzero(1x_1, x_2, x_3) = iden(x_3)$$

and

$$condone(\varepsilon, x_2, x_3) \quad = iden(x_3)$$
$$condone(0x_1, x_2, x_3) = iden(x_3)$$
$$condone(1x_1, x_2, x_3) = condempty(x_1, x_2, x_3)$$

Other important primitive recursive functions which we have already met are *head, tail, foot* and *top*. The function *head* is defined using primitive recursion by

$$head(\varepsilon) \quad = \varepsilon$$
$$head(0x) = zero(x)$$
$$head(1x) = one(x),$$

Similarly, *tail* is defind by

$$tail(\varepsilon) \quad = \varepsilon$$
$$tail(0x) = iden(x)$$
$$tail(1x) = iden(x)$$

Defining *foot* and *top* by primitive recursion is left as an exercise for the reader (Exercise 5.4).

If a function $B^n \to B$ has codomain $\{0, 1\}$ (representing *false, true,* respectively) then we call this function an *n*-ary *predicate*. Primitive recursive predicates will play an important role in our discussion. Two predicates which we have already met are *zero* and *one* which are both unary. Another unary primitive recursive predicate is *null* defined by

$$null(x) = \begin{cases} 1 & \text{if } x = \varepsilon, \\ 0 & \text{otherwise.} \end{cases}$$

A primitive recursive definition of null is

$$null(\varepsilon) = 1$$
$$null(0x) = zero(x)$$
$$null(1x) = zero(x)$$

Then, the unary primitive recursive predicate $istrue(x)$, which tests if $x = 1$ or not, is defined by

$$istrue(\varepsilon) = 0$$
$$istrue(0x) = zero(x)$$
$$istrue(1x) = null(x)$$

Say $P(x_1, x_2, \ldots, x_n)$ is an n-ary predicate, then we can construct a new predicate $\sim P(x_1, x_2, \ldots, x_n)$ (the *negation* of P) from $P(x_1, x_2, \ldots, x_n)$ by defining

$$\sim P(x_1, x_2, \ldots, x_n) = \begin{cases} 1 & \text{if } P(x_1, x_2, \ldots, x_n) = 0, \\ 0 & \text{if } P(x_1, x_2, \ldots, x_n) = 1. \end{cases}$$

If $P(x_1, x_2, \ldots, x_n)$ is primitive recursive then so is $\sim P(x_1, x_2, \ldots, x_n)$ since

$$\sim P(x_1, x_2, \ldots, x_n) = condone(P(x_1, x_2, \ldots, x_n), zero(x_1), one(x_1)).$$

Also, if $P_1(x_1, x_2, \ldots, x_n)$ and $P_2(x_1, x_2, \ldots, x_n)$ are n-ary predicates then we can construct new predicates using the *connectives* $\wedge$ (and), $\vee$ (or) and $\Rightarrow$ (implies) as follows.

$$P_1(x_1, x_2, \ldots, x_n) \wedge P_2(x_1, x_2, \ldots, x_n) = \begin{cases} 1 & \text{if } P_1(x_1, x_2, \ldots, x_n) = 1 \\ & \text{and } P_2(x_1, x_2, \ldots, x_n) = 1, \\ 0 & \text{otherwise.} \end{cases}$$

$$P_1(x_1, x_2, \ldots, x_n) \vee P_2(x_1, x_2, \ldots, x_n) = \begin{cases} 1 & \text{if } P_1(x_1, x_2, \ldots, x_n) = 1 \\ & \text{or } P_2(x_1, x_2, \ldots, x_n) = 1, \\ 0 & \text{otherwise.} \end{cases}$$

$$P_1(x_1, x_2, \ldots, x_n) \Rightarrow P_2(x_1, x_2, \ldots, x_n) = \begin{cases} 1 & \text{if} \\ & \text{either } P_1(x_1, x_2, \ldots, x_n) = 0 \\ & \text{or} \\ & \text{both } P_1(x_1, x_2, \ldots, x_n) = 1 \\ & \text{and } P_2(x_1, x_2, \ldots, x_n) = 1, \\ 0 & \text{otherwise.} \end{cases}$$

If we define new predicates $(P_1 \wedge P_2)$, $(P_1 \vee P_2)$, $(P_1 \Rightarrow P_2)$ by

$$(P_1 \wedge P_2)(x_1, x_2, \ldots, x_n) = P_1(x_1, x_2, \ldots, x_n) \wedge P_2(x_1, x_2, \ldots, x_n),$$
$$(P_1 \vee P_2)(x_1, x_2, \ldots, x_n) = P_1(x_1, x_2, \ldots, x_n) \vee P_2(x_1, x_2, \ldots, x_n),$$
$$(P_1 \Rightarrow P_2)(x_1, x_2, \ldots, x_n) = P_1(x_1, x_2, \ldots, x_n) \Rightarrow P_2(x_1, x_2, \ldots, x_n)$$

then, providing P_1, P_2 are primitive recursive, so are $(P_1 \wedge P_2)$, $(P_1 \vee P_2)$ and $(P_1 \Rightarrow P_2)$. This follows since

$$(P_1 \wedge P_2)(x_1, x_2, \ldots, x_n) = condone(P_1(x_1, x_2, \ldots, x_n), P_2(x_1, x_2, \ldots, x_n),$$
$$zero(x_1)),$$
$$(P_1 \wedge P_2)(x_1, x_2, \ldots, x_n) = condone(P_1(x_1, x_2, \ldots, x_n), one(x_1),$$
$$P_2(x_1, x_2, \ldots, x_n)),$$
$$(P_1 \Rightarrow P_2)(x_1, x_2, \ldots, x_n) = condone(P_1(x_1, x_2, \ldots, x_n), P_2(x_1, x_2, \ldots, x_n),$$
$$one(x_1)).$$

Alternatively, to prove this third result, we could have observed that

$$(P_1 \Rightarrow P_2)(x_1, x_2, \ldots, x_n) = \sim P_1(x_1, x_2, \ldots, x_n) \vee P_2(x_1, x_2, \ldots, x_n).$$

In Chapter 2, we discussed some computable arithmetic operations using either the unary or the binary representation of natural numbers. We now define a predicate *unary(x)* which delivers 1 if $x \in B$ is a valid unary representation of a natural number and delivers 0 otherwise. This predicate is primitive recursive since

$$unary(\varepsilon) = 0$$
$$unary(0x) = zero(x)$$
$$unary(1x) = unary(x) \vee null(x)$$

If $unary(x) = 1$ then $\bar{x}$ will denote the integer represented by x in unary notation.

We will now consider defining functions to compute simple arithmetic operations using unary representations. To ensure the functions are total we use 0 for undefined. For example,

$$plus(x, y) = \begin{cases} 0 & \text{if } \sim unary(x) \vee \sim unary(y), \\ z & \text{otherwise, where } \bar{z} = \bar{x} + \bar{y}. \end{cases}$$

This is primitive recursive since

$$plus(x, y) = condone(unary(x) \wedge unary(y), concat(x, y), zero(x))$$

In exercise 5.5, the reader is asked to show that corresponding definitions of *minus, times* and *divide* are also primitive recursive. One arithmetic operation which will be particularly important is the function *powera(n)* which raises a number, *a*, to the power, *n*, to give a^n. For example, if we assume numbers are all represented in unary representation, we could define

$$power\,2(x) = \begin{cases} 0 & \text{if } \sim unary(x), \\ y & \text{otherwise, where } \bar{y} = 2^x. \end{cases}$$

This is primitive recursive since

$$power\,2(x) = condone(unary(x), upower\,2(x), zero(x))$$

where

$upower\,2(\varepsilon) = 1$
$upower\,2(0\,x) = zero(x)$ (or any other
                                          function—this case cannot arise)
$upower\,2(1\,x) = concat(upower\ 2(x), upower\,2(x))$

Corresponding to *unary* we have the predicate *binary* to check whether a string $x \in B$ is a valid binary representation of a natural number.

$binary(\varepsilon)\ \ = 0$
$binary(0\,x) = zero(x)$
$binary(1\,x) = one(x)$

Binary to unary conversion is achieved by the function *bintounary*: $B \to B$. If $x \in B$ is a valid binary representation then *bintounary(x)* delivers the corresponding unary representation; otherwise, it delivers 0.

$$bintounary(x) = condone(binary(x), bintounary\,1(x), zero(x))$$

where

$bintounary\,1(\varepsilon)\ \ = \varepsilon$
$bintounary\,1(0\,x) = bintounary\,1(x)$
$bintounary\,2(1\,x) = concat(upower\,2(length(x)), bintounary\,1(x))$

Showing the corresponding conversion, unary to binary, achieved by *unarytobin*, is primitive recursive is left as an exercise for the reader (Exercise 5.6). Then, if we have an *n*-ary arithmetic function, f_1, which assumes unary representation and have shown this to be primitive recursive, it follows that the corresponding function, f_2, which assumes binary representation, is also primitive recursive.

$$f_2(x_1,x_2,\ldots,x_n) = unarytobin(f_1(bintounary(x_1),\ bintounary\ (x_2),$$
$$\ldots,bintounary(x_n)))$$

Similarly, if we have an arithmetic function which assumes binary representation and have shown this to be primitive recursive, the corresponding function using unary representation is also primitive recursive.

If x,y are unary representations of $\bar{x},\bar{y}$ and $\bar{x} < \bar{y}$ then the primitive recursive predicate $lt(x,y)$ delivers 1; otherwise $lt(x,y)$ delivers 0.

$$lt(x,y) = condone(unary(x) \wedge unary(y), less(x,y), zero(x))$$

where

$$less(\varepsilon,y)\ \ = \sim null(y)$$
$$less(0x,y) = nil(x)\ \text{(or any other function—this case cannot arise)}$$
$$less(1x,y) = condempty(y,\ zero(x),\ less(x,tail(y)))$$

The natural lexicographic ordering of B, viz. $\varepsilon,0,1,00,01,\ldots$ has featured extensively in our work and will continue so to do. It is useful to develop some primitive recursive functions and predicates relating to this ordering. The *next* function which given $x \in B$ delivers the next string in the ordering is defined by

$$next(x) = reverse(prenext(reverse(x)))$$

where

$$prenext(\varepsilon)\ = 0$$
$$prenext(0x) = cons1(x)$$
$$prenext(1x) = cons0(prenext(x))$$

The predecessor function, *pred*, given an argument $x \in B$ delivers the string previous to x on the ordering. To ensure *pred* is total, we set $pred(\varepsilon) = \varepsilon$.

$$pred(x) = reverse(prepred(reverse(x)))$$

where

$$prepred(\varepsilon)\ \ = \varepsilon$$
$$prepred(0x) = condempty(x,nil(x),cons1(prepred(x)))$$
$$prepred(1x) = cons0(x)$$

If x is the ith string in the lexicographic ordering then $pos(x)$ delivers the unary representation of i.

$$pos(x) = concat(upower2(length(x)), bintounary1(x)))$$

Conversely, given $x \in B$, if $unary(x)$ then $lex(x)$ delivers the string y such that $pos(y) = x$; otherwise $lex(x)$ delivers ε.

$$lex(x) = condone(unary(x), lex2(x), nil(x))$$

where

$$
\begin{aligned}
lex2(\varepsilon) &= \varepsilon && \text{(or any other value)} \\
lex2(0x) &= nil(x) && \text{(or any other function)} \\
lex2(1x) &= condempty(x, nil(x), next(lex2(x)))
\end{aligned}
$$

We can now also prove the predicate $prev(x,y)$ defined by

$$prev(x,y) = \begin{cases} 1 & \text{if } x \text{ comes before } y \text{ in the} \\ & \qquad\qquad\qquad \text{lexicographic ordering,} \\ 0 & \text{otherwise} \end{cases}$$

is primitive recursive.

$$prev(x,y) = lt(pos(x), pos(y))$$

The equality predicate, $eq(x,y)$, which yields 1 if $x = y$ and 0 otherwise, is also primitive recursive since

$$eq(x,y) = \sim prev(x,y) \land \sim prev(y,x).$$

Another example of a primitive recursive predicate is *even* where $even(x) = 1$ iff x is a binary representation of an even number.

$$even(x) = binary(x) \land endsin0(x)$$

where

$$
\begin{aligned}
endsin0(\varepsilon) &= 0 \\
endsin0(0x) &= endsin0(x) \lor null(x) \\
endsin0(1x) &= endsin0(x)
\end{aligned}
$$

Then the function $odd(x)$ which equals 1 iff x is a binary representation of an odd number is similarly defined by

$$odd(x) = binary(x) \land endsin1(x)$$

where

$$
\begin{aligned}
endsin\,1(\varepsilon) &= 0\\
endsin\,1\,(0x) &= endsin\,1\,(x)\\
endsin\,1\,(1\,x) &= endsin\,1\,(x) \vee null(x)
\end{aligned}
$$

One can continue to construct more and more primitive recursive functions (and predicates). They are a very large and important class of functions but since they are all total they clearly do not encompass all the TM-computable functions. One might hope that they encompass all the total TM-computable functions but, unfortunately, that is not true either. In many ways, however, the primitive recursive functions do represent a most important subset of the total computable functions $B^n \to B$ since composition and primitive recursion are the primary ways of function construction. To construct a total function $B^n \to B$ which is TM-computable but not primitive recursive is not easy. The most famous such example is *Ackermann's function*, $Ack:B \to B$.

$$Ack(x) = a(x,x)$$

where

$$
a(x_1, x_2) = \begin{cases}
0x_2 & \text{if } x_1 = \varepsilon,\\
a(tail(x_1),0) & \text{if } x_1 \neq \varepsilon \text{ and } x_2 = \varepsilon,\\
a(tail(x_1), a(x_1, tail(x_2))) & \\
& \text{if } x_1 \neq \varepsilon \text{ and } x_2 \neq \varepsilon.
\end{cases}
$$

To prove that Ack is not primitive recursive one has to show that for every 1-ary primitive recursive function, g, there exists some $x \in B$ such that $|Ack(x)| > |g(x)|$. (See, for example, Hermes, 1965.)

PARTIAL RECURSIVE FUNCTIONS

Before we can define the class of partial recursive functions on B, we need to introduce yet another way of constructing new functions from old. This is called *unbounded minimization* (to be contrasted with bounded minimization, see Exercise 5.8).

If $P(x_1, x_2, \ldots, x_n)$ is an n-ary primitive recursive predicate ($n \geq 2$) then we construct an $(n-1)$-ary function, $f(x_1, x_2, \ldots, x_{n-1})$, from $P(x_1, x_2, \ldots, x_n)$ by unbounded minimization as follows. The value of $f(x_1, x_2, \ldots, x_{n-1})$ is defined to be the first y in the natural lexicographic ordering of B such that $P(x_1,x_2,\ldots,x_{n-1},y) = 1$. Of course, if there is no such y, then f will be undefined. When defining a function in this way we write

$$f(x_1,x_2,\ldots,x_{n-1}) = \mu y \cdot P(x_1,x_2,\ldots,x_{n-1},y)$$

and read $\mu y \cdot P(x_1,x_2,\ldots,x_{n-1},y)$ as 'the least y such that $P(x_1,x_2,\ldots,x_{n-1},y)$ is true'.

Theorem 5.4

If P is an n-ary primitive recursive predicate ($n \geq 2$) and f is an $(n-1)$-ary function defined by unbounded minimization then f is TM-computable.

Proof. Since P is primitive recursive we can assume that P is computed by a TM, M. Then the TM to compute f has three tapes. The first is used for input/output only and the second to generate B in the lexicographic ordering, $\varepsilon,0,1,00,01,\ldots$ As soon as a string y in this ordering is generated, we simulate on tape 3 the action of M with input $x_1,x_2,\ldots,x_n,y$ where $x_1,x_2,\ldots,x_n$ is copied from tape 1 and y is copied from tape 2. This simulation must always halt since P is a total computable function. If $P(x_1,x_2,\ldots,x_n,y)$ is computed to be 1, tape 1 is cleared, y is copied onto it and the process halts. Otherwise, we clear tape 3, generate the next string in the lexicographic ordering on tape 2 and continue the search.

We say a partial function $f:B^n \to B$ is a *partial predicate* if $f(x_1,x_2,\ldots,x_n)$ is either undefined or evaluates to 0 or 1. The above proof will not hold for TM-computable partial predicates since we cannot guarantee that the simulation on tape 3 will always halt. We may then find ourselves in a situation where $P(x_1,x_2,\ldots,x_n,y) = 1$ but for some y' preceding y, $P(x_1,x_2,\ldots,x_{n-1},y')$ is undefined. However, if this does not occur then our proof can be generalized. Thus if $P(x_1,x_2,\ldots,x_n)$ is a partial predicate ($n \geq 2$) we define

$$\mu y \cdot P(x_1,x_2,\ldots,x_{n-1},y) = \begin{cases} y' & \text{if } P(x_1,x_2,\ldots,x_{n-1},y') = 1 \\ & \text{and } P(x_1,x_2,\ldots,x_{n-1},y'') = 0 \\ & \text{for all predecessors } y'' \text{ of } y', \\ \text{undefined} & \text{otherwise.} \end{cases}$$

Then we have the result:

Theorem 5.5

If P is any n-ary predicate (total or partial) that is TM-computable and f is the $(n-1)$-ary function defined by $\mu y \cdot P(x_1, x_2, \ldots, x_{n-1}, y)$ then f is also TM-computable.

A simple example of a partial recursive function defined by unbounded minimization is the unary function *undef* which is always undefined.

$$undef(x) = \mu y \cdot zero(\delta_2^2(x, y)).$$

As before, the selector functions will normally be omitted from our definitions. Thus we allow ourselves to write

$$undef(x) = \mu y \cdot zero(y)$$

This function can also be defined using recursion since

$$undef(\varepsilon) \quad = \text{undefined}$$
$$undef(0x) = undef(x)$$
$$undef(1x) = undef(x)$$

This is not always the case, however. There are partial functions which can be defined using unbounded minimization which cannot be defined using just recursion and composition. However, one can restrict the use of minimization in any definition to just the one application and, moreover, can insist that this one application always involves a primitive recursive predicate (see Exercise 5.10).

We say a string $x \in B$ is a *palindrome* iff $x = reverse(x)$. If a palindrome has an even length then it can be written in the form $concat(y, reverse(y))$. The function *halfpalin* is then defined by

$$halfpalin(x) = \begin{cases} y & \text{if } x = concat(y, reverse(y)), \\ \text{undefined} & \text{otherwise.} \end{cases}$$

This function is partial recursive since

$$halfpalin(x) = \mu y \cdot P(x, y)$$

where P is the primitive recursive predicate defined by

$$P(x, y) = eq(x, concat(y, reverse(y))).$$

The class of *partial recursive functions* on B are functions $B^n \to B$ $(n \geq 1)$ constructed according the following rules.

(1) *Base functions.* The following are partial recursive functions:

(a) $nil:B \rightarrow B$ defined by

$$nil(x) = \varepsilon \quad \text{for all } x \in B;$$

(b) $cons0$ and $cons1:B \rightarrow B$ defined by

$$cons0(x) = 0x$$
$$\text{and} \quad cons1(x) = 1x \text{ for all } x \in B;$$

(c) the selector functions $\delta_n^i (1 \leq i \leq n)$ where $\delta_n^i:B^n \rightarrow B$ is defined by

$$\delta_n^i(x_1, x_2, \ldots, x_n) = x_i$$

(2) From known partial recursive functions and predicates we can construct new partial recursive functions using

(a) composition,

(b) recursion, and

(c) unbounded minimization.

When using recursion, we allow the definition of an n-ary function to take the form:

either (case $n = 1$)

$$f(\varepsilon) = w \text{ (either } w \in B \text{ or } w = \text{undefined)}$$
$$f(0x) = h_1(x, f(x))$$
$$f(1x) = h_2(x, f(x))$$

where h_1, h_2 are partial recursive.

or (case $n > 1$)

$$f(\varepsilon, x_2, \ldots, x_n) = g(x_2, \ldots, x_n)$$
$$f(0x_1, x_2, \ldots, x_n) = h_1(x_1, x_2, \ldots, x_n, f(x_1, x_2, \ldots, x_n))$$
$$f(1x_1, x_2, \ldots, x_n) = h_2(x_1, x_2, \ldots, x_n, f(x_1, x_2, \ldots, x_n))$$

where g, h_1, h_2 are partial recursive. For both the above cases, we allow arguments of g, h_1, h_2 to be omitted and/or out of order.

When using unbounded minimization, the predicate may be any partial recursive predicate although, as we have already observed, the class of functions would not be altered if we restricted this to allow just primitive recursive predicates.

(3) No other functions except the base functions and those constructable according to the rules given in (2) are partial recursive.

An immediate corollary of this definition and of theorems 5.1, 5.2 and 5.5 is the following result:

Theorem 5.6

(1)   Every partial recursive function on B is TM-computable.
(2)   Every primitive recursive function on B is partial recursive on B.

Of course, since partial recursive functions are not necessarily total, there are partial recursive functions that are not primitive recursive. One obvious example is *undef*: $B \rightarrow B$.

We are now in a position to present the major result of this chapter.

Theorem 5.7 (Kleene's theorem)

The partial recursive function on B are precisely the TM-computable functions on B.

Proof. Theorem 5.6(1) established the fact that every partial recursive function on B is TM-computable. We will outline the proof that every TM-computable function on B is partial recursive.

From theorem 2.6, we can assume that a TM, M, which computes a (possibly partial) function $B^n \rightarrow B$ only has $\{0, 1, \wedge\}$ as tape alphabet. Initially, the n-tuple $(x_1, x_2, \ldots, x_n) \in B^n$ is encoded as a binary string, z, say. We can assume that this encoding is itself partial recursive. We also can assume, without loss of generality, that the states of M are labelled $1, 2, \ldots, n$ where 1 is the start state and all states $\geq k$ for some $k \leq n$ are halt states. Finally, we can assume that the TM always moves left or right at each step and never stays scanning the same location.

Now, consider a configuration of M, $C = (q, i, \alpha, a, \beta)$, where $q \in \{1, 2, \ldots, n\}$, $i \in Z, \alpha, \beta \in B$ and $a \in \{\wedge, 0, 1\}$. We can encode such a configuration as an integer $\hat{C}$ using a Gödel numbering technique. For example, one possible encoding is

$$\hat{C} = \hat{q} \cdot \hat{i} \cdot \hat{\alpha} \cdot \hat{a} \cdot \hat{\beta},$$

where

$$\hat{q} = 2^q;$$
$$\hat{i} = \begin{cases} 3 \cdot 5^{i+1} & \text{if } i \geq 0, \\ 3^2 \cdot 5^{-i} & \text{if } i < 0; \end{cases}$$

$$\hat{\alpha} = \begin{cases} 7.11 & \text{if } \alpha = \varepsilon, \\ 7^2 \cdot 11^{n(\alpha)} & \text{if } head(x) = 1 \\ 7^3 \cdot 11^{n(\bar{\alpha})} & \text{if } head(\alpha) = 0, \end{cases}$$

and $n(\alpha)$ is the integer whose binary representation is α, $\bar{\alpha} = complement(\alpha)$ and $n(\bar{\alpha})$ its corresponding integer;

$$\hat{a} = \begin{cases} 13 & \text{if } a = \wedge, \\ 13^2 & \text{if } a = 0, \\ 13^3 & \text{if } a = 1; \end{cases}$$

and $\quad \hat{\beta} = \begin{cases} 17 & \text{if } \beta = \varepsilon, \\ 17^2 \cdot 19^{n(\beta)} & \text{if } head(\beta) = 1, \\ 17^3 \cdot 19^{n(\bar{\beta})} & \text{if } head(\beta) = 0. \end{cases}$

Thus an initial configuration $C_0 = (1,1,\varepsilon,0,101)$ would be encoded as $\hat{C}_0 = 2.3.5^2.7.11.13^2.17^2.19^5$. The advantage of using Gödel numbering technique is that from an encoding, $\hat{C}$, of C the components of C can be quickly and efficiently recovered using simple arithmetic operations. The binary equivalents of these simple operations are all primitive recursive functions. Now, for any positive integer, n, we denote the corresponding binary representation by $bin(n)$. Thus any configuration, C, can be represented by unique string $c = bin(\hat{C}) \in B$. It is then possible to show that the following functions are partial recursive.

$$first(x) = \begin{cases} bin(q) & \text{if } x = bin(\hat{C}) \text{ for some configuration} \\ & \quad C \text{ with first component equal to } q, \\ undefined & \text{otherwise} \end{cases}$$

$$second(x) = \begin{cases} bin(i) & \text{if } x = bin(\hat{C}) \text{ for some configuration} \\ & \quad C \text{ with second component equal to } i, \\ undefined & \text{otherwise.} \end{cases}$$

$$third(x) = \begin{cases} \alpha & \text{if } x = bin(\hat{C}) \text{ for some configuration} \\ & \quad C \text{ with third component equal to } \alpha, \\ undefined & \text{otherwise.} \end{cases}$$

$$fourth(x) = \begin{cases} a & \text{if } x = bin(\hat{C}) \text{ for some configuration} \\ & \quad C \text{ with fourth component equal to } a, \\ undefined & \text{otherwise.} \end{cases}$$

$$
\text{and} \quad \textit{fifth}(x) = \begin{cases} \beta & \text{if } x = bin(\hat{C}) \text{ for some configuration} \\ & \quad C \text{ with fifth component equal to } \beta, \\ \text{undefined} & \text{otherwise.} \end{cases}
$$

Now, consider a TM, $M = (\{1, 2, \ldots, n\},\ \{0, 1, \wedge\},\ \{0, 1\},\ P, 1, \{k, \ldots, n\})$. The function $P : \{1, 2, \ldots, k-1\} \times \{0, 1\} \to \{1, 2, \ldots, n\} \times \{0, 1\} \times \{L, R\}$ can be represented as three functions.

$$
\begin{aligned}
&\textit{nextstate} : \{1, 2, \ldots, k-1\} \times \{0, 1\} \to \{1, 2, \ldots, n\}, \\
&\textit{nextsym} : \{1, 2, \ldots, k-1\} \times \{0, 1\} \to \{0, 1\} \\
\text{and} \quad &\textit{move} : \{1, 2, \ldots, k-1\} \times \{0, 1\} \to \{L, R\}
\end{aligned}
$$

where $P(i, b) = (nextstate(i, b),\ nextsym(i, b),\ move(i, b))$, $i \in \{1, 2, \ldots, k-1\}$, $b \in \{0, 1\}$. By representing the integers $1, 2, \ldots, n$ using binary notation and using 0 for L and 1 for R, we can construct functions $B^2 \to B$ corresponding to *nextstate*, *nextsym* and *move*. These will be called *bnextstate*, *bnextsym* and *bmove* respectively. These three functions are all partial recursive since they can be defined case by case (see Exercise 5.9).

Now, we can define partial recursive functions $B \to B$ which given a binary representation of some digit $n \geq 0$, computes the binary representation of 2^n, 3^n, 5^n, 7^n, etc. These will be partial functions since they will be undefined if the input string starts with a 0. We will call these functions *bpower2*, *bpower3*, etc. The function $bmult : B^2 \to B$ is the multiplication function defined assuming binary representation.

Now, if $z \in B$ is input to our TM, M, then the initial configuration is

$$
C_0 = (1, 1, \varepsilon, \text{if } z = \varepsilon \text{ then } \wedge \text{ else } head(z), tail(z))
$$

This is encoded as $c_0 = bin(\hat{C}_0)$, and $c_0 = input(z)$ where *input* is the partial recursive function defined by

$$
input(z) = bmult(const(z), bmult(arg4(z), arg5(z)))
$$

where
(i) $const(z)$ is a constant function delivering the binary string for the integer encoding of the first three arguments $1, 1, \varepsilon$, of C_0, viz. the integer $2^1 . 3 . 5^2 . 7 . 11$,
(ii) $arg4(z) = bpower13(condempty(z, one(z), condzero(head(z), two(z),$
$$three(z))))$$

where *two*, *three* are constant functions delivering binary strings $10, 11$, respectively, and
(iii) $arg5(z) = condempty(tail(z), bpower17(one(z)),$

$condone\ (head(tail(z)),$
$\qquad bmult(bpower17\ two(z)),\ bpower\ 19(tail(z))),$
$\qquad bmult(bpower17\ (three(z)),\ bpower19\ (complement(tail(z)))))))$

The next step in the proof is to show that the *nextconfiguration* function is partial recursive. Given an encoding of a configuration, C_n, of M, *nextconfiguration* should compute the encoding of the next configuration, C_{n+1}, providing there is a possible move to M.
If $C_n = (q, i, \alpha, a, \beta)$ then

$$
C_{n+1} = \begin{cases}
(nextstate(q, a), i-1, top(\alpha), if\ \alpha = \varepsilon\ then\ \wedge\ else\ foot(\alpha), \\
\qquad concat(nextsymb(q, a),\ \beta)) \qquad\qquad if\ move(q, a) = L, \\
(nextstate(q, a), i+1, concat(\alpha, nextsymb(q, a)),\ if \\
\qquad \beta = \varepsilon\ then\ \wedge\ else\ head(\beta),\ tail(\beta)) \quad if\ move(q, a) = R, \\
undefined \qquad\qquad\qquad\qquad\qquad\qquad otherwise.
\end{cases}
$$

Now, if C_n is encoded as a binary string, $c_n = bin(\hat{C}_n)$, then binary strings representing its components, q, i, α, a, β, can be obtained by applying the partial recursive functions *first, second, third, fourth* and *fifth*. Thus, using the definition of C_{n+1}, we can see how to obtain the binary string $c_{n+1} = bin(\hat{C}_{n+1})$ from C_n by applying these functions in conjunction with *bnextstate*, *bnextsym* and *bmove*, the power functions, *bpower2*, *bpower3* etc., constant functions, *one*, *two* etc., conditional functions, *condempty*, *condzero*, *condone*, and *head*, *tail*, *top*, *foot*, and *concat*. The details are left to the reader—the work is not difficult but certainly cumbersome! We then obtain the partial function

$$
nextconfiguration(x) = \begin{cases}
undefined & \text{if x is not an encoding} \\
& \text{of a valid configuration} \\
& \text{of M or, even if it is,} \\
& \text{where there is no next move,} \\
\\
y & \text{where x is the encoding} \\
& \text{of a configuration C_n} \\
& \text{and the next move of} \\
& \text{M results in a configuration} \\
& \text{C_{n+1} with encoding, y.}
\end{cases}
$$

The function *constantk*: $B \rightarrow B$ is the constant function which given any binary string delivers the unary representation of k. If x is an encoding of a configuration, we can determine whether the machine is in a halt state or not by using the predicate

$$halt(x) = \sim lt(bintounary(first(x)), constantk(x)).$$

If $halt(x) = 1$ then x is an encoding of a final configuration and the resulting output is given by $output(x)$. Using the definition of *output* given in Chapter 2 together with *first, second* etc., it is not difficult to show that this function is also partial recursive.

Now, let $x, y \in B$, then we defined *machinemove* recursively by

$$machinemove(\varepsilon, y) \quad = y$$
$$machinemove(0x, y) = undef(y)$$
$$machinemove(1x, y) = nextconfiguration(machinemove(x, y))$$

Thus, if x is a unary string, *machinemove* (x, y) gives an encoding of the configuration of the machine M given an initial configuration y after $\bar{x}$ moves. If that number of moves is not possible or if y does not represent a possible configuration, $machinemove(x, y)$ is undefined.

We can now define the partial function $f_M : B^n \to B$ computed by M given input of z, an encoding of $(x_1, x_2, \ldots, x_m)$.

$$f_M(z) = output(machinemove(noofmoves(z), input(z)))$$

where

$$noofmoves(z) = \mu y \cdot condone(unary(y),$$
$$halt(machinemove(y, input(z))), \quad zero(y))$$

Hence f_M is a partial recursive function and the outline of this proof is completed. Note that there has only been one application of unbounded minimization.

Kleene's theorem gives us a way of proving that functions are Turing-computable. If we can provide a proof that a function is partial recursive then Turing computability follows. It is a powerful result which supports the importance attached to recursion by present day computer scientists.

The class of partial recursive functions was originally proposed as a formalization of the class of effectively computable functions. Kleene's theorem establishes that this assumption is simply another form of **Church's thesis**.

EXERCISES

1 Show that there are countably infinite computable total functions $B \to B$. Use a diagonalization argument to show that there are uncountably infinite total functions $B \to B$ and hence deduce that the number of noncomputable total functions $B \to B$ is also uncountably infinite.

2 Compute $Ack(011)$. Use an induction argument to prove that Ackermann's function is a total function $B \to B$.

3 Show that if g is a total function $B^{n+1} \to B$ and h_1, h_2 are total functions $B^{n+1} \to B(n \geq 1)$ then there is *precisely* one function $f: B^n \to B$ which satisfies

$$f(\varepsilon, x_2, \ldots, x_n) = g(x_2, \ldots, x_n)$$
$$f(0x_1, x_2, \ldots, x_n) = h_1(x_1, x_2, \ldots, x_n, f(x_1, x_2, \ldots, x_n))$$
$$f(1x_1, x_2, \ldots, x_n) = h_2(x_1, x_2, \ldots, x_n, f(x_1, x_2, \ldots, x_n))$$

Is this result also true for partial functions?

4 Show that the total functions *foot* and *top*: $B \to B$ defined in Chapter 1 are primitive recursive.

5 Define total functions which correspond to the arithmetic operations $-$, $\times$ and $\div$. Assume a unary encoding and show that these functions are all primitive recursive.

6 Show that *unarytobin*: $B \to B$ defined by

$$unarytobin(x) = \begin{cases} 0 & \text{if } x \text{ is not a unary string,} \\ y & \text{where } y \text{ is the binary representation} \end{cases}$$
$$\text{of } \bar{x}, \text{ otherwise}$$

is primitive recursive.

7 Show that if $P_1(x_1, x_2, \ldots, x_n)$ and $P_2(x_1, x_2, \ldots, x_n)$ are primitive recursive so is $(P_1 | P_2) (x_1, x_2, \ldots, x_n)$ where $(P_1 | P_2) (x_1, x_2, \ldots, x_n) = 0$ iff both $P_1(x_1, x_2, \ldots, x_n) = 1$ and $P_2(x_1, x_2, \ldots, x_n) = 1$. Show that $\sim P_1(x_1, x_2, \ldots, x_n)$ and $(P_1 \vee P_2)(x_1, x_2, \ldots, x_n)$ can both be defined purely in terms of the connective, $|$.

8 If P is an n-ary primitive recursive predicate then we can define an n-ary function $f (n \geq 1)$ by *bounded minimization* as follows. $f(x_1, x_2, \ldots, x_n, z)$ is the *first* word, y, in the lexicographic ordering of B such that $P(x_1, x_2, \ldots, x_n, y) = 1$ or $y = z$. Show that f is necessarily primitive recursive.

9 We say a function $f: B \to B$ is defined *case-by-case* if it is defined according to the following format.

$$f(x) = \begin{cases} b_1 & \text{if } x = a_1, \\ b_2 & \text{if } x = a_2, \\ \vdots & \vdots \\ b_{n-1} & \text{if } x = a_{n-1}, \\ b_n & \text{otherwise,} \end{cases}$$

for some distinct $a_1, a_2, \ldots, a_{n-1} \in B$ and any $b_1, b_2, \ldots, b_n \in B \cup \{\text{undefined}\}$. Show that any unary function $B \to B$ defined case-by-case is partial recursive. Extend the definition and result to case-by-case definitions of n-ary functions $B^n \to B (n > 1)$.

10 Show that if a function $f: B \to B$ is TM-computable then it can be defined as a partial recursive function where there is only one application of unbounded minimization and the predicate involved is primitive recursive. [Hint: use theorem 2.1 and the proof of theorem 5.7.] Hence, deduce that every primitive recursive function can be defined using at most one application of unbounded minimization where that application involves a primitive recursive predicate.

11 Show that the *nextconfiguration* and the *output* functions used in the proof of theorem 5.7 are indeed partial recursive.

12 Show that Ackermann's function is partial recursive.

Chapter 6

Complexity Theory

Ye gods! Annihilate but space and time

ALEXANDER POPE
The Art of Sinking in Poetry

ALGORITHM ANALYSIS

So far we have met two types of problem—those that are solvable and those, like the halting problem, that are unsolvable. Experience tells us that some solvable problems are much easier than others. For example, sorting a sequence of n integers is a relatively easy exercise, so is finding the minimal spanning tree of a graph. A hard problem will require a considerable amount of computer time and perhaps also a large amount of store before it can be solved. But, before we can classify a problem as hard, we will need to be sure that it is not simply that we are using a bad algorithm to solve it. We will want to be sure that even the best algorithm to solve such a problem uses a considerable amount of time and possibly also of space.

In this chapter, we will be formalizing some of these ideas and answering questions such as: When is a problem easy? When is one algorithm better than an other? When does a problem require considerable space? The branch of computability which addresses itself to these and similar problems is known as *complexity theory*. Most of the results we describe here have been formulated since 1970. Complexity theory is still a very active area of research with important repercussions throughout computing. We will survey some of the key concepts and, most importantly, develop and exploit the theory concerning NP-complete problems.

The time taken to solve a problem will almost always depend upon the 'size' of the particular instance being solved as well as the algorithm being used to find the solution. Size is often measured in a rather informal way; it provides some kind of measure of the amount of input required to describe the given instance. For example, consider the problem of multiplying two square integer matrices. If an instance of this problem comprised two $n \times n$ matrices, we could use n as a measure of the size. Alternatively, we could use n^2 or $2n^2$ as a size measure. If we use the usual algorithm to compute the product, we compute the (i, j)th entry in the solution to be the scalar product of the ith row of the first matrix and the jth column of the second matrix. To evaluate such a product (assuming no overflows) involves $2n$ reads, n multiplications, $n - 1$ additions and one write operation. So to evaluate the whole product matrix (assuming no overflows) would take $2n^3$ reads to memory, n^3 multiplications, $n^2(n - 1)$ additions and n^2 writes to memory. This is a measure of the amount of work (and hence, indirectly, of the time) required to multiply two $n \times n$ matrices using this algorithm.

In practice, when analysing algorithms (usually presented in some high level language) computer scientists do indeed count the number of primitive operations. These primitive operations include arithmetic and logical operations, file accesses and stores, reads and writes, etc. The *time complexity* of an algorithm, A, $time_A(n)$, is then expressed as a function of n, the size of the input. The value of $time_A(n)$ is usually defined to be the greatest number of primitive operations that could be performed by the algorithm given an input of size n. Thus $time_A(n)$ is a worst-case measure. Analysis is sometimes performed using average-case measures, but, in this introductory book, we will only be concerned with the easier task of analysing the performance of algorithms in the worst case.

Now, some primitive operations take more time than others and the precise time taken will be machine dependent. There are also many additional overheads in running any algorithm which we are ignoring. These include address calculations, bound checking for arrays, handling overflows, type checking, etc. Thus our definition of time complexity is rather crude and any constants that appear in our calculation will be unreliable. There is also another criticism that can be levelled at our definition. The time taken to solve small problems is usually dominated by some constant set-up costs and is not really so dependent upon the size of the problem or even of the algorithm being used. For all these reasons, results on time complexity of an algorithm are usually presented using 0-notation.

Say f, g are functions $Z^+ \to Z^+$, then we say that $f(n)$ is $0(g(n))$ [read: $f(n)$ is order $g(n)$] iff there exist positive constants c, N such that $f(n) \leq cg(n)$ for all $n \geq N$.

As an example, $3n^2 + 4n - 3$ is $0(n^2)$ since $3n^2 + 4n - 3 \leq 4n^2$ for all $n \geq 3$. In fact, any $a_2n^2 + a_1n + a_0$ where a_2, a_1, a_0 are constants is $0(n^2)$ since $a_2n^2 + a_1n + a_0 \leq (|a_2| + |a_1| + |a_0|)n^2$ for all $n \geq 1$. We do not imply from the definition that an $0(n^2)$ function includes a term in n^2. Any $0(n)$ function is also $0(n^2)$; similarly any $0(n\log n)$ function is $0(n^2)$.

The reverse of these statements is, however, not true.

Using the 0-notation, we would say the matrix multiplication algorithm described above is an $0(n^3)$ algorithm. For further examples of this type of analysis of algorithms, the reader is referred to either *The Design and Analysis of Computer Algorithms* (Aho, Hopcroft & Ullman, 1974) or to *Fundamentals of Computer Algorithms* (Horowitz & Sahni, 1978).

Say algorithms A, B solve a given problem, Π, and have time complexities $time_A$, $time_B$, respectively. We would then say that algorithm A is *better than* algorithm B for the solution of Π if

(1) $time_A$ is $0(time_B)$, but
(2) $time_B$ is not $0(time_A)$.

There are better algorithms for matrix multiplication than the one described above. For example, Strassen's algorithm (see Exercise 6.3) is $0(n^{2.81})$ but even this is known not to be the best.

The above definition of 'better than' might appear rather misleading. Say we had algorithms A, B such that

$$time_A(n) = \begin{cases} 1{,}000{,}000 & \text{for } n \leq 1{,}000{,}000, \\ n & \text{for } n > 1{,}000{,}000. \end{cases}$$

and

$$time_B(n) = \begin{cases} n & \text{for } n \leq 1{,}000{,}000, \\ n^2 & \text{for } n > 1{,}000{,}000. \end{cases}$$

then $time_A(n)$ is $0(time_B(n))$ since $time_A(n) \leq time_B(n)$ for all $n \geq 1{,}000{,}000$ but $time_B(n)$ is not $0(time_A(n))$. Hence, according to our definition, algorithm A is better than algorithm B. But, we may never use either algorithm for problems of size $> 1{,}000{,}000$. Hence, for all practical purposes, we would prefer algorithm B to algorithm A. In practice, such situations seem to rarely arise. The 0-notation and 'better than' definition do seem to provide a useful framework for algorithm analysis. Constants that appear in time complexity functions are usually relatively small and such functions relatively well behaved.

As well as 0-notation, Ω- and θ-notation are widely used in algorithm analysis. If f, g are functions $Z^+ \rightarrow Z^+$, then we say $f(n)$ is $\Omega(g(n))$ iff there exist positive constants c, N such that $f(n) \geq cg(n)$ for all $n \geq N$. For example, $3n^2 + 4n - 3$ is $\Omega(n^2)$ but it is also $\Omega(n)$ and $\Omega(n \log n)$. If we know that any algorithm to solve a problem Π must have a time complexity function which is $\Omega(g(n))$ for some $g(n)$ then we will know that any $0(g(n))$ algorithm to solve Π would be optimal in some sense. However, until we have found such an algorithm, we might not necessarily know such a one existed.

If f, g are functions $Z^+ \to Z^+$, we say $f(n)$ is $\theta(g(n))$ iff $f(n)$ is both $0(g(n))$ and $\Omega(g(n))$. Thus if f, g are polynomials and $f(n)$ is $\theta(g(n))$ then f, g must be of the same order but they need not be identical functions since the constants involved may differ.

We say an algorithm performs in *polynomial time* iff its time complexity function is $0(n^k)$ for some $k \geq 0$. In practice, if a problem is solvable by a polynomial time algorithm, one can usually find an algorithm with a time complexity function $0(n^k)$ where k is quite small (generally less than 5). Experts in algorithm design and analysis spend much time in searching for efficient algorithms to solve particular problems. There is, however, a whole class of problems for which they have been unable to find polynomial time algorithms. An algorithm which has time complexity function $\theta(c^n)$ for some $c > 1$ is called an *exponential time* algorithm. Any exponential time algorithm will not be a polynomial time algorithm and can perform really badly in the worst cases. For example, say algorithm A is used to solve a problem Π and for an instance of size n, it takes time 2^n. If Π could also be solved by an algorithm B and B takes time n^5, then it has been calculated that for a problem instance of size $n = 60$, if B solves the problem in one minute, A will take about 28,000 years!

For any reasonable size input, any algorithm which is not polynomial time is going to be potentially very time-consuming. We must remember, however, that we are doing a worst-case analysis. It may be that such an algorithm only takes an inordinate amount of time on a very few examples. In practice, it may work very well. The simplex algorithm used to solve linear programming problems is an example of an exponential time algorithm that works very well in practice. The simplex algorithm is thus usually used in preference to the so-called ellipsoid algorithm even though this is known to be a polynomial time algorithm.

If we have a problem, Π, and we have an algorithm which is not polynomial time, then we will usually continue searching for a better, polynomial time algorithm. What if we cannot find one? Maybe this is our fault but maybe it is a property of the problem Π—perhaps no such algorithm exists. We say a problem is *intractable* if there is no polynomial time algorithm for its solution but it is, nevertheless, solvable. There is every indication that there are classes of such problems and in the subsequent pages we will be developing a theory to support this claim.

Before embarking upon this theory, here is an example of a problem widely thought to be intractable since no one has been able to find a polynomial time algorithm to solve it. The theory we develop indicates that no one is likely to either! The problem is called the *travelling salesman problem* (TSP). Imagine n cities, $c_1, c_2, \ldots, c_n$ and a travelling salesman located at city c_1. For each pair of cities, c_i, c_j we are given the distance, d_{ij}, between them. The travelling salesman wishes to leave home, visit each of the cities $c_2, \ldots, c_n$, *once only*, and only then return home. He does not mind in which order he visits cities $c_2, \ldots, c_n$ but wants the total distance travelled to be as small as possible. The task then is to find this minimum cost tour. It is easy to design an algorithm to solve this problem given sufficient time—simply consider all $(n-1)!$ orderings of $c_2, \ldots, c_n$, evaluate the cost of the resulting tour starting and ending at c_1 and select the cheapest.

As in Chapter 3, we will be largely working with decision problems rather than optimization problems such as the travelling salesman problem. However, as we have previously observed, any optimization problem naturally gives rise to a corresponding decision problem. For the travelling salesman problem, we have the decision problem:

TSP
INSTANCE: A set $C = \{c_1, c_2, \ldots, c_n\}$ of n cities, for each pair, $c_i, c_j \in C$, a distance $d_{ij} \in Z^+$ and a bound $b \in Z^+$.
QUESTION: Can a travelling salesman located at city c_1, leave home, visit each of the cities in $\{c_2, c_3, \ldots, c_n\}$ once only and only then return home with a total distance travelled $\leq b$?

Now an algorithm is traditionally viewed as being deterministic, i.e. at each step of the algorithm, the next step is uniquely defined. We do not usually allow the construct *or* in our algorithm descriptions. However, if we had parallel processing facilities, then we might be able to use this. A statement

do A or do B

would be executed in parallel. One machine would explore A whilst the other would explore B. Parallelism thus provides a means of handling nondeterminism in algorithms. If we had unlimited parallelism (a rather silly concept!) then we would be able to solve TSP in polynomial time. Each machine would take one of the $(n-1)!$ orderings and cost it up. We would then look at the results and see if any had total cost $\leq b$. With only one machine, we would need to be able to 'guess' which of the $(n-1)!$

orderings to evaluate. If we guessed correctly and the answer was yes, we would solve the problem. We will see that the concept of a nondeterministic program proves important in the development of the theory we are going to describe.

THE CLASSES P AND NP

We will now formalize some of the above discussion using Turing machines as our computing devices. As in Chapter 3, we restrict our discussion to decision problems, i.e. problems with yes/no answers.

Consider a decision problem, Π, and an encoding, e, of instances, I, of Π, into strings of T^*. An algorithm which solves Π is then a TM, $M = (Q, \Sigma, T, P, q_0, F)$, which recognizes whether or not an input, $e(I)$, is or is not in the language $L_{\Pi, e} = \{e(I) | I \in Y_\Pi\}$.

We restrict our encoding, e, to be a sensible, concise encoding. By this we mean that (i) no encoding of any instance I should contain spurious 'padding symbols', (ii) any numbers or other such symbols occurring in I should be encoded in a binary notation (or octal, or decimal etc. but *not* unary) and (iii) that $e(I)$ can be uniquely and effectively decoded to I.

Say we have a deterministic TM, $M = (Q, \Sigma, T, P, q_0, F)$, and we input $x \in T^*$. We define the *time complexity function of a deterministic TM, M*, $time_M : Z^+ \to Z^+$ by

$$time_M(n) = \max\{m | \text{there is an } x \in T^n \text{ such that}$$
$$\text{computation of } M \text{ on input } x \text{ is of length } m\}.$$

Recall that the length of the computation of a deterministic TM on a given input is the number of configurations through which it passes before it halts. Thus the length of the computation corresponds exactly to the time taken by the TM. If M is an algorithm and hence halts for all inputs, $time_M(n)$ will be defined for all n. If this is not the case, M may loop infinitely for some x and then $time_M(|x|)$ is taken to be infinity.

If $time_M(n)$ is $0(n^k)$ for some $k \geq 0$, M is said to take *polynomial time*. A polynomial time deterministic TM must thus be an algorithm since it must halt for all inputs. We define the class of languages, P, by

$$P = \{L | \text{there is a polynomial time deterministic TM which accepts } L\}.$$

Thus every language in P is a recursive language (theorem 4.1). Although P is formally defined as a class of languages, we will also regard it as a class of decision problems. We will write $\Pi \in P$ iff there is some encoding e of Π such that $L_{\Pi,e} \in P$. P thus represents all the problems which can be solved by polynomial time deterministic algorithms.

Now, consider a nondeterministic TM, $M = (Q, \Sigma, T, P, q_0, F)$. We say that M solves the decision problem Π under encoding e iff $T(M) = L_{\Pi,e}$. Thus for each instance $I \in Y_\Pi$, if we input $e(I)$ to M, there is *some* sequence of possible moves which will enable M to halt and succeed. If we input $x \in T^*$ which is not an encoding of a yes-instance of Π, then no sequence of possible moves will enable M to halt and succeed.

Say M is a nondeterministic Turing machine (NDTM) which accepts $x \in T^*$. There is at least one computation sequence whereby M accepts x and possibly more. The time taken by M to accept x is the length of the least of these computation sequences. The time complexity function $time_M$ for a NDTM, M, depends only on the number of steps in accepting computations. If no inputs of length n are accepted by M, we put $time_M(n) = 1$, by convention. Thus the *time complexity function* for a $NDTM, M$, is defined by

$$
time_M(n) = \begin{cases} 1 & \text{if } T(M) \cap T^n = \varnothing, \\ \min\{m \mid \text{there is an } x \in T^n \\ \quad \text{such that the time taken by} \\ \quad M \text{ to accept } x \text{ is } m\} & \text{otherwise.} \end{cases}
$$

M is said to be a polynomial time NDTM iff $time_M(n)$ is $0(n^k)$ for some $k \geq 0$.

We can now define the class NP—these are the languages (and hence problems) accepted by NDTMs in polynomial time, i.e.

$$NP = \{L \mid \text{there is a polynomial time NDTM which accepts } L\}.$$

Thus every language in NP is an r.e. language. As with P, although NP is defined as a class of languages, it also corresponds to a class of decision problems. We say $\Pi \in NP$ iff there is some encoding e of Π such that $L_{\Pi,e} \in NP$. NP represents the problems that are solvable in polynomial time by a nondeterministic program.

From our discussion in Chapter 4 and above, it should be clear that $P \subseteq NP$. Also $P \neq NP$ would seem most likely—in fact, everyone thinks this result is true but nobody has to date been able to prove it. This is most unfortunate since the theory we are going to develop relies on this hypothesis. If ever it is proved that $P = NP$ then the reader should tear out these next few pages!

One decision problem that is in *NP* is TSP. Essentially, the non-deterministic part of our NDTM writes down a guessed tour of the cities for a given instance and the cost is then evaluated. If it is less than or equal to b then the answer is yes. If the NDTM makes the right moves (corresponding to a correct guess) it will solve the problem.

NP contains many problems like TSP which do not appear to be in *P*. In fact, we can show that if $P \neq NP$ then $TSP \notin P$. TSP is an example of an *NP*-complete problem. This is a class of problems lying in *NP* which are, in some sense, the most difficult of the problems in *NP*. The situation is summarized in Fig. 6.1.

Before defining *NP*-complete formally, we will investigate the class *NP* a little further. Let $M = (Q, \Sigma, T, P, q_0, F)$ be a NDTM recognizing a language $L \subseteq T^*$. If at some stage in the computation, M is in configuration $C = (q, i, \alpha, a, \beta)$ then, since $\#P(q, a)$ may be > 1, there may be several legitimate moves that can be made. A configuration resulting from C by making a legitimate move is called a *child* of C. We represent this situation graphically using a *configuration tree*. We construct the tree with the root node C_0, the initial configuration. This node is then joined to each child of C_0 and these in turn to their children, etc., as in Fig. 6.2. If a configuration in the tree has no children, it will be a leaf of the tree. Such a configuration is called an *accept configuration* iff it represents a situation where M is in a final state. Any path from the root node to an accept configuration represents a computation sequence accepting the original input. If we introduce a new state $q_y \notin Q$, set $P(q, a) = \{(q_y, a, 0)\}$ for all $q \in F$ and then redefine F as $\{q_y\}$, the NDTM, M will be in an accept configuration iff it is in state q_y. Such a state will be called the *accept state*. This observation proves the following.

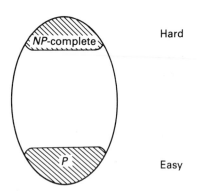

Fig. 6.1. The class *NP*.

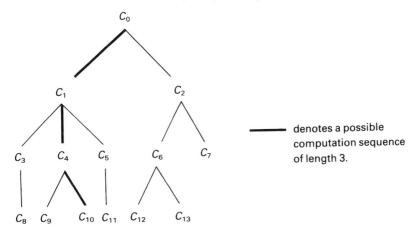

denotes a possible computation sequence of length 3.

Fig. 6.2. An example configuration tree.

Theorem 6.1

If L is accepted by a NDTM, M, then there exists a NDTM, M, with just one final state (known as the accept state) which also accepts L.

Note that if we input x to M' and it enters the accept state we know $x \in L$. However, if M' loops or reaches a *reject configuration*, i.e. one from which no move is possible but which is not an accept configuration, we cannot infer that $x \notin L$. We may just have explored the wrong path in the configuration tree.

Now, consider $x \in T^*$. If x is input to the NDTM, M, then the initial configuration is $C_0(x) = (q_0, 1, \varepsilon,$ if $x = \varepsilon$ then $\wedge$ else $head(x), tail(x))$. The string x is accepted by M iff there is a path in the configuration tree with root $C_0(x)$ from this root to some accept configuration. The length of such a path corresponds to the time taken by the computation. Thus M is a polynomial time NDTM accepting L iff there exists $k \geq 0$ such that for each $x \in L$, the shortest path in this tree from $C_0(x)$ to an accept configuration has length $l_M(x)$ where $l_M(x)$ is $0(|x|^k)$.

The maximum number of children of any configuration is given by $degree(m) = \max \{ \#P(q, a) | q \in Q,\ a \in \Sigma \}$, the *degree* of the NDTM, M. The first l levels of a configuration tree constructed for a degree $m(> 1)$ NDTM must necessarily have $\leq \sum_{k=0}^{l} m^k = (m^{l+1} - 1)/(m - 1)$ nodes.

Theorem 6.2

If L is accepted by a NDTM, M, then there exists a NDTM, M_2, of degree ≤ 2 which accepts L. Moreover, if M accepts L in polynomial time then so does M'.

Proof. Let $M = M_m = (Q, \Sigma, T, P, q_0, F)$, have degree $m > 2$. We first show how to construct a NDTM, $M_{m-1} = (Q', \Sigma, T, P', q_0, F)$, a degree $m-1$ NDTM which also accepts L.

Say there are just r distinct pairs $(q, a) \in Q \times \Sigma$ such that $\#P(q, a) = m$. Then, we introduce r new states $q'_1, q'_2, \ldots, q'_r$ and set $Q' = Q \cup \{q'_1, q'_2, \ldots, q'_r\}$. P' is defined to be equal to P except on the r pairs. If (q, a) is the ith of these pairs in some enumeration and $P(q, a) = \{(q_1, b_1, X_1), (q_2, b_2, X_2), \ldots (q_m, b_m, X_m)\}$ then we define

$$P'(q, a) = \{(q_1, b_1, X_1), (q'_i, a, 0)\}$$

and $\quad P'(q'_i, a) = \{(q_2, b_2, X_2), \ldots, (q_m, b_m, X_m)\}.$

Clearly $T(M_m) = T(M_{m-1})$ and M_{m-1} is of degree $m-1$. We can continue this process to get a sequence of NDTMs, $M_m, M_{m-1}, M_{m-2}, \ldots, M_2$ all of which accept L. Hence the first part of the theorem is established.

Say $M = M_m$ accepts x. Then in the configuration tree for M with root $C_0(x)$ there is a path of length $l_M(x)$. Say a node on this path has degree $k(1 < k \leq m)$ and represents a configuration C. The children of C are $C_1, C_2, \ldots, C_k$ (say). By the construction of M_2, the change of configuration C to one of its children is represented as in Fig. 6.3(b) for some permutation σ of $1, 2, \ldots, k$. Hence the path in the configuration tree for M_2 representing a change from C to any one of $C_1, C_2, \ldots, C_k$ is of length at most $k - 1 \leq m - 1$. So there is a path from the root node $C_0(x)$ to an accept node in the configuration tree for M_2 of length $l_{M_2}(x) \leq (m-1)l_M(x)$. Now if $l_M(x)$ is $0(|x|^k)$ so is $(m-1)l_M(x)$ and hence so is $l_{M_2}(x)$ and the second part of the theorem is thus established.

THE NP-COMPLETE CLASS

Say we had two problems Π_1, Π_2 and an algorithm A to solve Π_2. If each instance I of Π_1 could be easily transformed into some instance of Π_2 then we could use A to solve Π_1. For example, if we had an algorithm to solve TSP then we could also solve

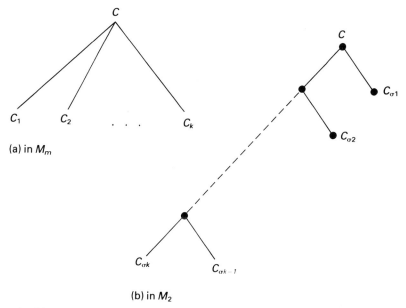

(a) in M_m

(b) in M_2

Fig. 6.3.

Hamiltonian circuit (HC)

INSTANCE: A graph G.

QUESTION: Does G contain a Hamiltonian circuit, i.e. a simple cycle connecting all its vertices?

We specify a function, f, which maps each instance of HC to a corresponding instance of TSP. The function f is simply defined. Suppose an instance of HC is specified by a graph G with vertex set V and edge set E, then the corresponding instance of TSP has $C = V$, and for any two cities $v_i, v_j \in C, d_{ij} = 1$ if v_i, v_j are connected in G and $d_{ij} = 2$ if they are not connected. The bound, b, is then set equal to $n = |V|$. Clearly, $I \in Y_{HC}$ iff $f(I) \in Y_{TSP}$.

Such an f is an example of a reduction. We have already met this idea in Chapter 3. Now, we are concerned with polynomial time and hence we want to restrict reductions to those reductions that can be performed in polynomial time. We say a problem Π_1 *polynomially reduces* or *transforms* to Π_2, written $\Pi_1 \propto \Pi_2$, iff there exists a function, $f: D_{\Pi_1} \to D_{\Pi_2}$, such that

(1)   for each $I \in D_{\Pi_1}$, $I \in Y_{\Pi_1}$ iff $f(I) \in Y_{\Pi_2}$, and

(2) f can be computed in polynomial time.

In a more formal, language-theoretic context, we say $L_1 \subseteq T_1^*$ polynomially transforms to $L_2 \subseteq T_2^*$, written $L_1 \propto L_2$, iff there exists a function $f:T_1^* \to T_2^*$ such that
(1)   for all $x \in T_1^*$, $x \in L_1$ iff $f(x) \in L_2$, and
(2)   there is a polynomial time deterministic TM that computes f.

Thus $\Pi_1 \propto \Pi_2$ iff there exist some (sensible, concise) encoding schemes e_1, e_2 such that $L_{\Pi_1,e_1} \propto L_{\Pi_2,e_2}$.

Theorem 6.3

$\propto$ is transitive.

Proof. We will work at the language level. Say $L_1 \propto L_2$ and $L_2 \propto L_3$. We have to show $L_1 \propto L_3$. If $L_1 \subseteq T_1^*$ and $L_2 \subseteq T_2^*$ then there exists a function $f:T_1^* \to T_2^*$ corresponding to the transformation $L_1 \propto L_2$. Say f is computed in polynomial time by TM, M_f. Similarly, corresponding to the transformation $L_2 \propto L_3$ where $L_2 \subseteq T_2^*$ and $L_3 \subseteq T_3^*$ there is a function $g:T_2^* \to T_3^*$ computed in polynomial time by a TM, M_g. We construct the TM, M, which simulates the action of M_f followed by the action of M_g. This deterministic TM will compute the function $g_0 f$ in polynomial time. Since $x \in L_1$ iff $f(x) \in L_2$ iff $g(f(x)) \in L_3, g_0 f$ defines the transformation $L_1 \propto L_3$.

Theorem 6.4

If $L_1 \propto L_2$ and $L_2 \in P$ then $L_1 \in P$.

Proof. Say $L_1 \subseteq T_1^*$ and $L_2 \subseteq T_2^*$ and $f:T_1^* \to T_2^*$ is the function corresponding to the transformation $L_1 \propto L_2$. Say M_f is a deterministic TM which computes f in polynomial time. $L_2 \in P$ so there exists a polynomial time TM, M_2, which accepts L_2. If M simulates the action of M_f followed by that of M_2 we will achieve a polynomial time deterministic TM which accepts L_1. Hence $L_1 \in P$.

We define two languages L_1, L_2 (and similarly two problems Π_1, Π_2) as being *polynomial equivalent* whenever $L_1 \propto L_2$ and $L_2 \propto L_1 (\Pi_1 \propto \Pi_2$ and $\Pi_2 \propto \Pi_1$). We know that $\propto$ is transitive from theorem 6.3, the identity function shows $\propto$ is reflexive and, by definition, polynomial equivalence is symmetric. Hence polynomial equivalence is an equivalence relation. One equivalence class is P (Exercise 6.4)—these correspond to the 'easiest' languages (problems) in NP. The 'hardest' languages (problems) in NP are the NP-complete problems.

A language L is *NP-complete* iff

(1) $L \in NP$, and
(2) for all $L' \in NP$, $L' \propto L$.

We say a problem Π is NP-complete iff for some sensible concise encoding e, $L_{\Pi,e}$ is NP-complete. Informally, Π is NP-complete iff $\Pi \in NP$ and for all $\Pi' \in NP$, $\Pi' \propto \Pi$.

We denote the class of NP-complete languages by NPC.

Theorem 6.5

(1) NPC is an equivalence class under polynomial equivalence.
(2) If $NPC \cap P \neq \varnothing$ then $NP = P$.

Proof.

(1) Say $L_1, L_2 \in NPC$, then by definition, $L_1, L_2 \in NP$. Since L_1 is NP-complete, $L_2 \propto L_1$ and since L_2 is NP-complete, $L_1 \propto L_2$. Hence L_1, L_2 are polynomially equivalent.
(2) Say $L \in NPC \cap P$. Since $L \in NPC$, for every $L' \in NP$, $L' \propto L$. But $L \in P$ and hence by theorem 6.4, every $L' \in P$. Hence $NP = P$.

Now, all the evidence is that $NP \neq P$ so it seems that no NP-complete problem is going to yield to a polynomial time algorithm. Moreover, if any NP-complete problem did yield to such an algorithm then so would every problem in NP. The first known NP-complete problem was the satisfiability of a set of clauses.

Consider a set of Boolean variables, $U = \{u_1, u_2, \ldots, u_n\}$. A *literal* from U is defined to be either one of these variables or the negation of some $u \in U$ (usually written $\bar{u}$). A *clause* over U is then a subset of the literals from U. Thus $\{u_2, \bar{u}_4, u_5\}$ is a clause over U comprising three literals. We say a clause is *satisfied* by an assignment of truth values to the Boolean variables if at least one of the literals of the clause evaluates to true. Thus $\{u_2, \bar{u}_4, u_5\}$ is satisfied by any assignment which assigns u_2 to be true or u_4 to be false or u_5 to be true. Now let C denote a set of clauses over U. We say C is *satisfiable* iff there exists some assignment of truth values to the Boolean variables U such that every clause in C is simultaneously satisfied. Thus $C = \{\{u_1, u_2, u_3\}, \{\bar{u}_2, \bar{u}_3\}, \{u_2, \bar{u}_3\}\}$ is satisfiable since every clause in C is satisfied by any of the following assignments.

u_1	T	T	F
u_2	T	F	T
u_3	F	F	F

set of clauses which is not satisfiable is $\{\{u_1, u_2\}, \{u_1, \bar{u}_2\}, \{\bar{u}_1\}\}$. The decision problem can be expressed as follows.

Satisfiability (SAT)
INSTANCE: A finite set, U, of Boolean variables and a finite set, C, of clauses over U.
QUESTION: Is there a satisfying truth assignment for C?

Cook (1971) established the following seminal result from which has grown a large number of important results.

Theorem 6.6 (Cook's theorem)

SAT is NP-complete.

Proof. To show SAT$\in NPC$, we have to show SAT$\in NP$ and that for all $\Pi' \in NP, \Pi' \propto$ SAT.

SAT$\in NP$ is fairly clear. If an instance, I, of SAT comprises n Boolean variables, the nondeterministic program which solves I simply guesses an assignment of truth values to these n Boolean variables and then checks if that assignment satisfies each of the clauses. If the clauses are unsatisfiable, no guess will find such a satisfying assignment.

To prove that for all $\Pi' \in NP, \Pi' \propto$ SAT at first appears a very difficult task. After all, we do not even know which problems are in NP! All we know is that for each such problem, Π', there must be a corresponding NDTM, M', which solves it in polynomial time. This must thus be our starting point. Let $M' = (Q, \Sigma, T, P, q_0, F)$ be a NDTM which accepts $L' = L_{\Pi', e'} \subseteq T^*$ for some suitable encoding, e'. We can assume that the time complexity function of this NDTM is $O(n^k)$ for some positive integer k. Moreover from theorem 6.2, we can assume m' is of degree 2.

Since $SAT \in NP$, we know that there is a polynomial time NDTM, M_{SAT}, which accepts $L = L_{SAT,e}$ for some sensible encoding, e. Working at the language level, we need to show that $L' \propto L$ and hence that, at the problem level, $\Pi' \propto SAT$. In fact for any such L', we shall show how to construct a function, $f_{L'}$, which maps strings in T^* to instances of SAT. These instances could then be encoded using e to get strings in L. Our function, $f_{L'}$, will satisfy $x \in L'$ iff $f_{L'}(x)$ has a satisfying truth assignment (and hence its encoding is in L). Thus, once we have established $f_{L'}$ and shown that it is computable in polynomial time, we will have established the existence of the desired polynomial transformation. We will now show how $f_{L'}(x)$ is defined in terms of the NDTM, M'.

If $x \in T^*$ is accepted by M', then since the time complexity function is $O(n^k)$, x must be accepted in time $\leq m = \max(c_1, c_2 |x|^k)$, for some constants c_1, c_2. Hence, the only part of the tape which need be used to test whether or not a given input $x \in T^*$ is accepted must lie between $-m+1$ and $m+1$. The configuration of the machine M' at any stage in the computation can be completely specified by giving the contents of these $2m + 1$ locations together with the current state and the position of the tape head. From theorem 6.1, we can assume M' has only one accept state and hence label the states, Q, as q_0 (the start state), q_1 (the accept state), $q_2, q_3, \ldots, q_a$ for some $a \geq 1$. The set, Σ, i.e. the symbols that can appear on the tape, are labelled $s_0 = \wedge, s_1, s_2, \ldots, s_b$ for some $b \geq |T| + 1$. Then, we define the following Boolean variables.

State-variables: for each $0 \leq i \leq m, 0 \leq k \leq a$, a variable $Q[i,k]$ which will be assigned true iff at time i, M' is in state q_k.

Head-variables: for each $0 \leq i \leq m, -m+1 \leq j \leq m+1$, a variable $H[i,j]$ which will be assigned true iff at time i, the tape head of M' is scanning location j.

Symbol-variables: for each $0 \leq i \leq m, -m+1 \leq j \leq m+1, 0 \leq k \leq b$, a variable $S[i,j,k]$ which will be assigned true iff at time i the symbol in location j is s_k.

Choice variables: for each $0 \leq k \leq a, 0 \leq l \leq b$ such that $\#P(q_k, s_l) = 2$ and for each $0 \leq i \leq m$ and $-m+1 \leq j \leq m+1$, two Boolean variables $P_1[i,j,k,l]$ and $P_2[i,j,k,l]$ which are used to indicate which of the two possible moves are selected.

These variables together comprise the set U of variables in the instance of

SAT which we are constructing from M' and a given $x \in T^*$. We now need to construct the clauses. These clauses are constructed from x in such a way that they are satisfiable if and only if there is an accepting computation of x by M'. Thus, the instance of SAT we construct is satisfiable iff $x \in L'$.

The clauses are constructed in various groups according to the following rules.

Unique state
At any time $0 \le i \le m$, the NDTM, M', must be in a unique state. The clauses.

$$\{Q[i,0], Q[i,1], \dots, Q[i,a]\} \quad \text{for each } 0 \le i \le m$$

ensure that the NDTM is in at least one state at every time. The clauses

$$\{\overline{Q[i,j]}, \overline{Q[i,j']}\}, \quad \text{for each } 0 \le i \le m \text{ and } 0 \le j < j' \le a$$

ensure that the state is unique.

Unique-head position
To ensure the tape head scans a unique location at every time, we have clauses

$$\{H[i, -m+1], H[i, -m+2], \dots, H[i, m+1]\} \quad \text{for each } 0 \le i \le m$$

and $\quad \{\overline{H[i,j]}, \overline{H[i,j']}\} \quad$ for each $0 \le i \le m$, $-m+1 \le j < j' \le m+1$.

Unique symbol
To ensure that each location has a unique symbol assigned to it at every time, we have clauses

$$\{S[i,j,0], S[i,j,1], \dots, S[i,j,b]\} \quad \text{for each } 0 \le i \le m$$
$$\text{and } -m+1 \le j \le m+1$$

and $\quad \{\overline{S[i,j,k]}, \overline{S[i,j,k']}\} \quad$ for each $0 \le i \le m$, $-m+1 \le j \le m+1$
$$\text{and } 0 \le k < k' \le b.$$

Initial configuration
At time $0, x \in T^*$ is written in location $1, 2, \dots, |x|$, all other locations contain blank, the tape head is scanning location 1 and the current state is q_0. This gives rise to the following clauses.

$$\{Q[0,0]\},$$
$$\{H[0,1]\},$$
$$\{S[0,1,i_1]\}, \{S[0,2,i_2]\}, \ldots, \{S[0,|x|,i_{|x|}]\} \text{ where } x = s_{i_1} s_{i_2} \ldots s_{i_{|x|}}$$
and $\{S[0,j,0]\}$ for $-m+1 \le j \le 0$ and $|x| < j \le m+1$.

Final accepting configuration

If $x \in L'$ then at a time $\le m$, the NDTM must have accepted x, so it will have entered state q_1. This is obtained by insisting that if $Q[i,1]$ is true then so is $Q[i+1,1]$. Then we must have $Q[m,1]$ being true. Hence we contruct clauses

$$\{\overline{Q[i,1]}, Q[i+1,1]\} \quad \text{for each } 0 \le i < m$$

and $\{Q[m,1]\}$.

Changing configuration

We now introduce a final group of clauses which ensure that the changes of configuration conform to the rules of M'. Say at time i, the tape head scans location j, is in state q_k and the symbol in location j is s_l. Then $H[i,j]$, $Q[i,k]$ and $S[i,j,l]$ must all be true.

If $P(q_k,s_l)$ is defined then we have two cases to consider.

Case 1. $\#P(q_k,s_l)=1$ so $P(q_k,s_l) = \{(q_{k'},s_{l'},X)\}$ for some $q_{k'} \in Q$, $s_{l'} \in \Sigma$ and $X \in \{L,0,R\}$. If $X=L$, then we will want $H[i+1,j-1]$, $Q[i+1,k']$ and $S[i+1,j,l']$ to be true. We thus introduce the clauses

$$\{\overline{H[i,j]}, \overline{Q[i,k]}, \overline{S[i,j,l]}, H[i+1,j-1]\},$$
$$\{\overline{H[i,j]}, \overline{Q[i,k]}, \overline{S[i,j,l]}, Q[i+1,k']\},$$
and $\{\overline{H[i,j]}, \overline{Q[i,k]}, \overline{S[i,j,l]}, S[i+1,j,l']\}.$

However, if $X=0$ we replace the first of these clauses by

$$\{\overline{H[i,j]}, \overline{Q[i,k]}, \overline{S[i,j,l]}, H[i+1,j]\},$$

and if $X=R$, by

$$\{\overline{H[i,j]}, \overline{Q[i,k]}, \overline{S[i,j,l]}, H[i+1,j+1]\},$$

the other two clauses being retained.

Case 2. $\#P(q_k,s_l)=2$ so $P(q_k,s_l) = \{(q_{k'},s_{l'},X), (q_{k''},s_{l''},Y)\}$ for some $q_{k'}, q_{k''} \in Q$, $s_{l'}, s_{l''} \in \Sigma$ and $X, Y \in \{L,0,R\}$. For these cases, we will need the two Boolean variables, $P_1[i,j,k,l]$ and $P_2[i,j,k,l]$. Then we introduce clauses

$$\{\overline{H[i,j]}, \overline{Q[i,k]}, \overline{S[i,j,l]}, P_1[i,j,k,l], P_2[i,j,k,l]\}$$

and $\{\overline{H[i,j]}, \overline{Q[i,k]}, \overline{S[i,j,l]}, \overline{P_1[i,j,k,l]}, \overline{P_2[i,j,k,l]}\}.$

These ensure that if $H[i,j]$, $Q[i,k]$ and $S[i,j,l]$ are true then precisely one of $P_1[i,j,k,l]$, $P_2[i,j,k,l]$ must be true. If $P_1[i,j,k,l]$ is true we are going to select $(q_{k'}, s_{l'}, X)$ as our move and if $P_2[i,j,k,l]$ is true we are going to select $(q_{k''}, s_{l''}, Y)$. To cover the change of state we introduce

$$\{\overline{P_1[i,j,k,l]}, Q[i+1,k']\}$$

and $\{\overline{P_2[i,j,k,l]}, Q[i+1,k'']\}$

The change of symbol is covered by introduced clauses

$$\{\overline{P_1[i,j,k,l]}, S[i+1,j,l']\}$$

and $\{\overline{P_2[i,j,k,l]}, S[i+1,j,l'']\},$

Finally the direction of move is covered by

$$\{\overline{P_1[i,j,k,l]}, H[i+1,j-1]\} \quad \text{if } X = \text{L},$$

or $\{\overline{P_1[i,j,k,l]}, H[i+1,j]\} \qquad \text{if } X = 0,$

or $\{\overline{P_1[i,j,k,l]}, H[i+1,j+1]\} \quad \text{if } X = \text{R},$

together with a corresponding clause

$$\{\overline{P_2[i,j,k,l]}, H[i+1,j-1]\} \quad \text{if } Y = \text{L},$$

or $\{\overline{P_2[i,j,k,l]}, H[i+1,j]\}, \qquad \text{if } Y = 0,$

or $\{\overline{P_2[i,j,k,l]}, H[i+1,j+1]\} \quad \text{if } Y = \text{R}.$

This completes case 2.

   The clauses constructed in the above two cases ensure that there are clauses representing the next move. We must also ensure that if the tape head is *not* scanning location j at time i then the symbol in location j does not change between time i and $i + 1$. To ensure this we introduce a clause

$$\{\overline{S[i,j,l]}, H[i,j], S[i+1,j,l]\}$$

for each $0 \le i < m$, $-m+1 \le j \le m+1$ and $0 \le l \le b$.

   This completes the construction of our clauses. If $x \in L'$, then there is an accepting computation of x on the machine M' which takes time $\le m$. This computation, given the interpretation of the Boolean variables which we have defined, imposes a truth assignment which satisfies all the clauses we have constructed. Moreover, the construction of the clauses has ensured that any satisfying truth assignment must correspond to an accepting computation of x on M. Hence $f_{L'}(x)$ (the set of clauses we have constructed from x) is satisfiable iff $x \in L'$. Moreover, if the reader counts the number of Boolean variables and also the clauses (Exercise 6.6) we have constructed, he will find that both are bounded by polynomials in $|x|$. (Remember, a and b are constants.) From this we can deduce that $f_{L'}(x)$ can be computed by a polynomial time algorithm. Hence, we have shown that for every $L' \in NP$, there exists a polynomial transformation from L' to SAT, e. Hence SAT is NP-complete. Note that in this proof, we did not have to know the precise nature of the NDTM accepting L'. All we had to know was that such a machine existed.

Having established the existence of one NP-complete problem, we can now use the following result to obtain many more.

Theorem 6.7

If L is NP-complete and $L_1 \in NP$ then $L \propto L_1$ implies L_1 is NP-complete.

Proof. For every $L' \in NP$, $L' \propto L$ by definition of NP-completeness. But $L \propto L_1$ and by theorem 6.3, $\propto$ is transitive. Hence for every $L' \in NP$, $L' \propto L_1$. Since $L_1 \in NP$, the result follows.

This gives us a strategy for developing a whole suite of NP-complete problems. Working at the problem level, we know SAT$\in NPC$. Now, we know that if we have established that $\Pi \in NPC$ and $\Pi_1 \in NP$ then if we can show $\Pi \propto \Pi_1$ it follows that $\Pi_1 \propto NPC$. Thus, in particular, if $\Pi_1 \in NP$ and SAT $\propto \Pi_1, \Pi_1$ must be NP-complete. SAT is the seed from which all our known NP-complete problems have grown. There are now several hundred such problems. A classic survey of those results known in 1978 is found in *Computers and Intractability: A Guide to the Theory of NP-Completeness* (Garey & Johnson, 1978). This has since been regularly undated by a series of articles in the *Journal of Algorithms*. In the next section, we give some examples of NP-complete problems together with the associated proofs. These illustrate the techniques that are used

in such proofs and the diversity of the problem class, NPC. Even accepting
$P \neq NP$, it should not be assumed that every problem in NP is either in
P or is NP-complete. In fact it has been shown that if $P \neq NP$, $NPI = NP\backslash(P \cup NPC)$ comprises an infinite collection of distinct equivalence
classes under polynomial equivalence (see Ladner, 1975). It is still true,
however, that the vast majority of practical problems that arise do indeed
lie in either P or NPC. The following two problems may perhaps lie in
NPI but this is just conjecture.

Graph isomorphism
INSTANCE: Two graphs, G_1 and G_2.
QUESTION: Is G_1 isomorphic to G_2?

Composite number
INSTANCE: Positive integer, k.
QUESTION: Are there integers $m, n > 1$ such that $k = mn$?

Under certain circumstances (e.g. the two graphs being planar), graph
isomorphism is solvable in polynomial time. There is, however, no known
polynomial time algorithm for the general case. Similarly, no one has been
able to prove the problem is NP-complete although *subgraph isomorphism*
(replace question by: Is G_1 isomorphic to a subgraph of G_2) is a known
NP-complete problem (see Exercise 6.11).

If we could design a deterministic algorithm to test a positive integer
for primality in polynomial time, then *composite number* would lie in P.
Such an algorithm for primality does not currently exist but a probabilistic
approach has proved remarkably good. M. Rabin's paper, 'Probabilistic
algorithms' (Traub, 1976), describes a probabilistic algorithm for primality
which works in polynomial time and which has a small chance of error
given any particular input. Probabilistic algorithms essentially randomly
choose which option in a choice of options to explore. In a probabilistic
algorithm, the majority of possible paths yield the correct answer.
Monte-Carlo algorithms always halt but there is a small chance of an
incorrect answer. *Las Vegas 'algorithms'* always yield the correct answer
but have a small chance of not halting. *Atlantic City 'algorithms'* may not
halt and, even if they do, may not produce the correct answer. The power
of probabilistic algorithms lies in this fact that they can be repeated so
that the probability of errors can be made very small indeed. A theoretical
approach to probabilistic algorithms is given in Gill (1977).

A SAMPLE OF FURTHER NP-COMPLETE PROBLEMS

Firstly, we consider a restriction of SAT where all the clauses comprise precisely three literals.

3-Satisfiability (3SAT)

INSTANCE: A set, U, of Boolean variables and a set, C, of clauses over U, where each $c \in C$ is such that $\#(c) = 3$, i.e. comprises three literals.
QUESTION: Is there a satisfying truth assignment for C?

Theorem 6.8

3SAT is NP-complete.

Proof. $3SAT \in NP$ since we can easily check a guessed assignment in polynomial time. We show that $3SAT \in NPC$ by exhibiting a polynomial transformation $SAT \propto 3SAT$.

Let $U = \{u_1, u_2, \ldots, u_n\}$ and $C = \{c_1, c_2, \ldots, c_m\}$ define an instance, I, of SAT. We will construct an instance $f(I)$ of 3SAT such that (i) $I \in Y_{SAT}$ iff $f(I) \in Y_{3SAT}$ and (ii) f is computable in polynomial time. To construct $f(I)$ we simply take each clause $c_i \in C$ and replace it by an equivalent collection of 3-literal clauses. To achieve this, we will need some additional Boolean variables; the Boolean variables used in the construction of clauses corresponding to c_i will lie in the set U_i'. U' then denotes all the additional Boolean variables introduced in this way.

Now, say $c_i \in C$ then we have four cases to consider.

Case 1. $\#(c_i) = 1$. So $c_i = \{x_1\}$ say.
Then $U_i' = \{u_i', u_i''\}$ where u_i', u_i'' are new Boolean variables.
We replace c_i by the four clauses

$$\{x_1, u_i', u_i''\}, \{x_1, u_i', \bar{u}_i''\}, \{x, \bar{u}_i', u_i''\}, \{x, \bar{u}_i', \bar{u}_i''\}.$$

Case 2. $\#(c_i) = 2$ so $c_i = \{x_1, x_2\}$ say.
Then $U_i' = \{u_i'\}$ where u_i' is a new Boolean variable.
We replace c_i by the two clauses

$$\{x_1, x_2, u_i'\}, \{x_1, x_2, \bar{u}_i'\}.$$

Case 3. $\#(c_i) = 3$ so this is left unchanged and $U_i' = \varnothing$.
Case 4. $\#(c_i) = k > 3$. So $c_i = \{x_1, x_2, \ldots, x_k\}$.
Then $U_i = \{u_i^j | 1 \leq j \leq k - 3\}$ are all new variables.

We replace c_i by the clauses

$$\{x_1, x_2, u_i^1\}$$
$$\{\bar{u}_i^1, x_3, u_i^2\}$$
$$\{\bar{u}_i^2, x_4, u_i^3\}$$
$$\vdots$$
$$\{\bar{u}_i^{k-3}, x_{k-1}, x_k\}.$$

Note that if $k > n$ then a clause in C with k literals must contain both u and $\bar{u}$ for some $u \in U$. The clause is thus trivially satisfied by any assignment of truth values and can be ignored. Hence, we can assume $\#(c_i) \le n$ for each $1 \le i \le m$ and thus both the number of new variables and clauses constructed above are bounded by polynomials in mn. Thus f is a polynomial transformation.

Say $t:U \to \{T, F\}$ is an assignment of truth values to the variables of U which satisfies each clause in C. We can extend t to obtain a truth assignment $t:U \cup U' \to \{T, F\}$ which satisfies all the constructed clauses. We first show how we can extend t to act on the variables in any set U_i'. If U_i' was constructed as in cases $1, 2, 3$ above, any extension of t will do since the clauses are already satisfied by t. If U_i' was constructed as in case 4, then we know that there must have been some $x_l, 1 \le l \le k$, such that $t(x_l) = T$. If $l = 1$ or 2 then we set $t(u_i^j) = F$ for $1 \le j \le k - 3$. If l is $k - 1$ or k then we set $t(u_i^j) = T$ for $1 \le j \le k - 3$. Otherwise we set $t(u_i^j) = T$ for $1 \le j \le l - 2$ and $t(u_i^j) = F$ for $l - 1 \le j \le k - 3$. We thus extend t to act on each of the sets $U_i', i = 1, 2, \ldots, m$ and hence find a truth assignment $t:U \cup U' \to \{T, F\}$ which satisfies all our constructed clauses. Hence $I \in Y_{SAT}$ implies $f(I) \in Y_{SAT}$. The converse is much easier to prove. For any truth assignment that satisfies all our constructed clauses the restriction to U can easily be shown to satisfy all the original clauses. Hence $I \in Y_{SAT}$ iff $f(I) \in Y_{SAT}$ and the proof is completed.

Although 3SAT is NP-complete, the corresponding 2SAT problem (i.e. each clause has just two literals) is solvable in polynomial time (Exercise 6.7). This is illustrative of a rather common phenomenon in this work. Often a problem involving triples is NP-complete but if we restrict this to just pairs, the problem lies in P. (Perhaps, that's why there are just two sexes!) To further support this observation, the following problem is known to be NP-complete. (The proof of this result and many others is given in the pioneering paper by R. M. Karp, 'Reducibility among combinatorial problems' [Miller & Thatcher, 1972].)

3-Dimensional matching (3DM)

INSTANCE: A set $M \subseteq X \times Y \times Z$ where X, Y, Z are disjoint sets each having n elements.

QUESTION: Does M contain a matching, i.e. a subset $M' \subseteq M$ such that $|M'| = n$ and no two elements of M' agree in any coordinate?

For example, if $X = \{x_1, x_2\}$, $Y = \{y_1, y_2\}$ and $Z = \{z_1, z_2\}$, then

$$\{(x_1, y_2, z_1),$$
$$(x_1, y_1, z_1),$$
$$(x_1, y_2, z_2),$$
$$(x_2, y_1, z_2)\}$$

contains a matching, viz. (x_1, y_2, z_1) and (x_2, y_1, z_2), but $\{(x_1, y_1, z_1), (x_1, y_2, z_1), (x_2, y_2, z_1)\}$ does not.

The corresponding *2-dimensional matching* lies in P (see Hopcroft & Karp, 1973).

We will devote the rest of this section to showing *Hamiltonian circuit* (HC) is NP-complete. We have already observed that HC $\propto$ TSP and that TSP$\in NP$. Hence a corollay of our result will be that TSP is also NP-complete. To show HC is in NPC we simply have to show HC$\in NP$ and then find an NP-complete problem Π such that $\Pi \propto$ HC. Any $\Pi \in NPC$ will do; theoretically, we know that if HC$\in NPC$, a transformation will always exist. The art of these proofs is to select a known NP-complete problem so that the proof is made as easy as possible. We will prove the result indirectly via a problem known as *vertex cover*.

Vertex cover (VC)

INSTANCE: A graph G with vertex set, V, and edges, E, and a positive integer $b \leq \#(V)$.

QUESTION: Is there a vertex cover of size b or less for G, i.e. is there a subset $V' \subseteq V$ such that $\#(V') \leq b$ and, for each edge $\textcircled{u}\text{———}^{e}\text{———}\textcircled{v}$ in V, at least one of u, v belongs to V'?

We will show 3SAT $\propto$ VC and VC $\propto$ HC. As the fund of known NP-complete problems grows, so proofs should become easier in the sense that one stands an increasingly good chance of finding a known $\Pi \in NPC$ which easily polynomially transforms to the problem under consideration. It is thus important to keep up with current developments and new results in this field. In this text we are simply giving a taste of the sort of proofs used and results obtained.

Theorem 6.9

VC is NP-complete.

Proof. VC$\in NP$ since we need only guess a subset of V of size b and check whether each edge in E has at least one of its vertices in the subset. This generation and checking can clearly be done in polynomial time.

To prove VC$\in NPC$ we exhibit a polynomial transformation 3SAT $\propto$ VC. Let I be an instance of 3SAT comprising the set $U = \{u_1, u_2, \dots, u_n\}$ of Boolean variables and the set $C = \{c_1, c_2, \dots, c_m\}$ of 3-literal clauses. From I, we must construct $f(I)$, comprising a graph G and a bound b, such that $f(I) \in Y_{VC}$, i.e. G has a vertex cover of size $\leq b$, iff $I \in Y_{SAT}$, i.e. I is satisfiable. Moreover, we must show that this construction can be undertaken in polynomial time.

For each $u_i \in U$, we construct two vertices $u_i, \bar{u}_i$ joined by a single edge, i.e. u_i——$\bar{u}_i$.

For each clause $c_j \in C$ we have three vertices c_{j1}, c_{j2}, c_{j3} connected in a triangle, as in Fig. 6.4. Now, if $c_j = \{x, y, z\}$ where x, y and z are literals, we join vertex c_{j1} to vertex x, vertex c_{j2} to vertex y and vertex c_{j3} to vertex z.

In this way, we construct a graph corresponding to I. For example, the graph corresponding to the instance of 3SAT comprising $U = \{u_1, u_2, u_3, u_4\}$ and $C = \{\{u_1, u_2, u_3\}, \{u_1, \bar{u}_2, \bar{u}_3\}, \{\bar{u}_2, \bar{u}_3, u_4\}\}$ is given in Fig. 6.5. The bound, b, is then set equal to $n + 2m$.

Now, suppose there exists a satisfying truth assignment $t: U \to \{T, F\}$ for I. Then we can select a vertex cover of G of size $n + 2m$ as follows. For each $u_i \in U$, select u_i if $t(u_i) = T$ and $\bar{u}_i$ if $t(u_i) = F$ (this gives n vertices). Then, for each $c_j \in C$, since t is a satisfying truth assignment one

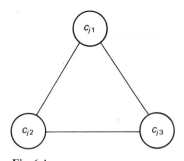

Fig. 6.4.

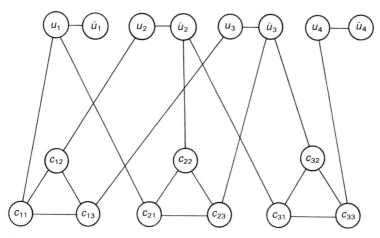

Fig. 6.5.

of the vertices c_{j1}, c_{j2}, c_{j3} must be connected to a selected vertex. So, we include in the cover the other two vertices and hence obtain a cover of size $n + 2m$. This shows $I \in Y_{SAT} \Rightarrow f(I) \in Y_{VC}$.

To prove the converse, consider any vertex cover of size $b \leq n + 2m$. Since there is an edge between u_i and $\bar{u}_i$ for each $u_i \in U$, this vertex cover must contain one of each of these pairs of vertices. Similarly, since c_{j1}, c_{j2}, c_{j3} are organized in a triangle, any cover must contain at least two of these vertices. This means any cover must contain $\geq n + 2m$ vertices so a vertex cover of size $\leq n + 2m$ must have exactly $n + 2m$ vertices. Moreover, this cover must include one vertex from each pair $u_i, \bar{u}_i$. We define a truth assignment by $t(u_i) = T$ if u_i is in the vertex cover and $t(u_i) = F$ otherwise. This assignment must satisfy each clause $c_j \in C$. Only two of the vertices c_{j1}, c_{j2}, c_{j3} appear in the cover and therefore for one of them, there must be an edge to a selected u_i or $\bar{u}_i$. Hence under t, each c_j is satisfied. Thus, $f(I) \in Y_{VC} \Rightarrow I \in Y_{SAT}$.

Having established that $I \in Y_{SAT}$ iff $f(I) \in Y_{VC}$, we only need to observe that the construction can obviously be computed in polynomial time for the proof of the result to be completed.

Theorem 6.10

HC (and hence TSP) is *NP*-complete.

Proof. $HC \in NP$ since a nondeterministic algorithm need only guess some ordering $v_{\sigma(1)}, v_{\sigma(2)}, \ldots, v_{\sigma(n)}$ of the n vertices of the given graph and then in polynomial time check if there is a cycle $v_{\sigma(1)}-v_{\sigma(2)}-\cdots-v_{\sigma(n)}-v_{\sigma(1)}$ in the graph.

To show HC∈NPC, we construct a polynomial transformation VC ∝ HC. Let an instance, I, of VC be given by a graph, G, with vertices, V, and edges, E, together with a bound $b \leq \#(V)$. We need to construct $f(I)$, an instance of HC, such that $I \in Y_{VC}$ iff $f(I) \in Y_{HC}$. This instance will be in the form of a graph, G', constructed from G as described below.

Firstly, we equip the graph G' with b vertices $w_1, w_2, \ldots, w_b$, which will be used to select b vertices from the vertex set V. Then, for each $e \in E$, there is a subgraph of G', G'_e, used to ensure that at least one of the two end vertices of e is among the selected b vertices. Say e is incident to $u, v \in V$, then G_e has 12 vertices labelled $(u^{(i)}e), (v^{(i)}, e)$ $1 \leq i \leq 6$ and connected with 14 edges as in Fig. 6.6. The vertices $(u^{(1)}, e)$, $(u^{(6)}, e)$, $(v^{(1)}, e)$, $(v^{(6)}, e)$ are called *corner*

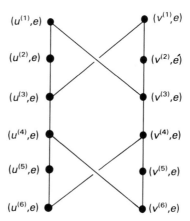

Fig. 6.6. G'_e, the subgraph of G' corresponding to edge e between u and v.

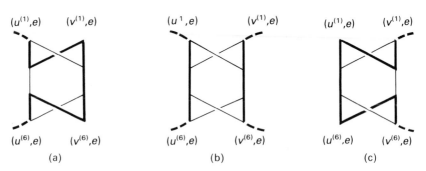

Fig. 6.7. Edges appearing in a Hamiltonian circuit.

vertices of the subgraph and these and only these will be connected to other parts of G'. Any Hamiltonian circuit of G' must then include one of the configurations shown in Fig. 6.7.

Now, for every $v \in V$, if d denotes *degree*(v), then there are d edges incident to v. let $e_{v[1]}, e_{v[2]}, \ldots, e_{v[d]}$ be some enumeration of these edges. We then connect the subgraphs corresponding to each of these edges by introducing edges $(v^{(6)}, e_{v[1]})$——$(v^{(1)}, e_{v[2]})$, $(v^{(6)}, e_{v[2]})$——$(v^{(1)}, e_{v[3]}), \ldots$, $(v^{(6)}, e_{v[d-1]})$——$(v^{(1)}, e_{v[d]})$. This set of edges is denoted by E'_v. Their inclusion ensures that for any $v \in V$, there exists in G' a single path through all the vertices labelled $(v^{(k)}, e)$ for $1 \leq k \leq 6$, $e \in E$.

The construction of G' is completed by joining the first and last vertices of each of these paths to every one of the vertices $w_1, w_2, \ldots, w_b$. In Fig. 6.9, we give a graph G' constructed in this way from the graph G of Fig. 6.8 and a value $b = 2$. G' can clearly be constructed from G in polynomial time. We claim that G' has a Hamiltonian circuit iff G has a vertex cover of size b.

Suppose V' is vertex cover of G with $\#(V') = b$. We can assume $\#(V') = b$ since additional vertices from V can be added to any cover and we will still have a cover. Let elements of V' be $v_{\lambda 1}, v_{\lambda 2}, \ldots, v_{\lambda b}$ and let $d_{\lambda i}$ denote the degree of $v_{\lambda i}$ in $G(1 \leq i \leq b)$. For each edge $e \in E$ connecting u and v, include in the circuit those edges of G'_e as described in Fig. 6.7(a), (b) or (c) according to whether $\{u, v\} \cap V'$ equals $\{u\}$, $\{u, v\}$ or $\{v\}$, respectively. We then include in the circuit, the edges $E'_{v_{\lambda 1}} \cup E'_{v_{\lambda 2}} \cup \cdots \cup E'_{v_{\lambda k}}$. Also include all edges between w_i and $(v^{(1)}_{\lambda i}, e_{v_{\lambda i}[1]})$, $1 \leq i \leq b$, between w_{i+1} and $(v^{(6)}_{\lambda i}, e_{v_{\lambda i}[d_{\lambda i}]})$, $1 \leq i < b$, and finally that edge between w_1 and $(v^{(6)}_{\lambda b}, e_{v_{\lambda b}[d_{\lambda b}]})$. It is not difficult to verify that these edges always constitute a Hamiltonian circuit. They are marked in Fig. 6.9 assuming the cover of size 2 comprises v_1, v_5.

Conversely, suppose G' has a Hamiltonian circuit. Consider a section of

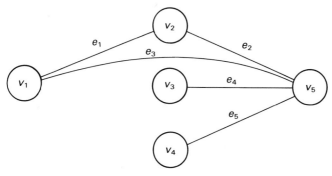

Fig. 6.8. The graph, G.

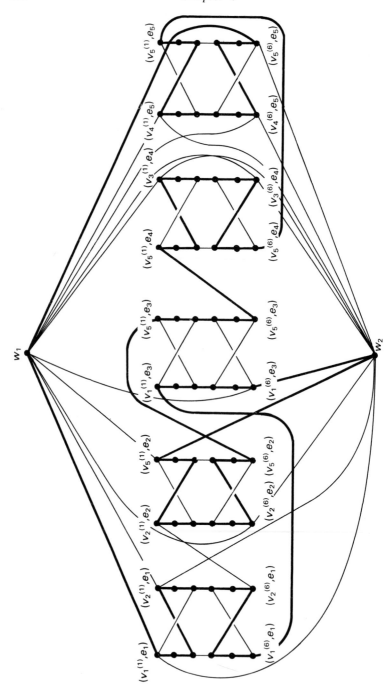

Fig. 6.9. The graph, G'.

this circuit beginning at w_i and ending at w_j for some $1 \leq i,j \leq b$ with no other such w-vertex appearing in this path. The first vertex on the path after w_i must be labelled $(v^{(1)}, e)$ or $(v^{(6)}, e)$ for some $v \in V$ and $e \in E$. Now, refer to Fig. 6.7 and the way we connected the subgraphs corresponding to edges. It must be that every vertex on the path until we reach w_j has a label with second component an edge incident to v. Now the Hamiltonian circuit can be broken down into b sections $w_{\mu 1}$ to $w_{\mu 2}$, $w_{\mu 2}$ to $w_{\mu 3}, \ldots, w_{\mu b}$ to $w_{\mu 1}$ for some ordering $\mu 1, \mu 2, \ldots, \mu b$ of the w-vertices. Each of these sections has no intermediate w-vertices and hence each section defines for us some $v \in V$. The b vertices defined by these b paths must together comprise a cover of V since every edge $e \in E$ will be incident to some $v \in V$. The proof of theorem 6.10 is thus completed.

Knowing that the decision problem TSP is NP-complete leads us to conclude that we will not be able to solve it in polynomial time unless $P = NP$. Since we are virtually sure $P \neq NP$, we can be equally sure that any algorithm for TSP will take more than polynomial time for some instances. The original optimization problem is not going to yield to a polynomial algorithm either. If it did then we could solve the decision problem simply by finding the shortest possible route and then checking if the distance travelled was less than or equal to our bound, b. To solve instances of the optimization problem which may arise in practice, some sort of heuristic programming is required. A heuristic is a 'rule of thumb' which intuitively should give a reasonable approximate solution. A crude heuristic for the travelling salesman problem is to always visit as next city the nearest unvisited city. We will call this heuristic the 'nearest neighbour' heuristic.

A heuristic designer will hope to produce a heuristic so that a solution to any instance of the problem under consideration can be found in polynomial time and will be within a certain small absolute or percentage error. Let a heuristic algorithm be denoted by H and the solution found for an instance, I, of some optimization problem, Π, be denoted by $H(I)$. Say the optimal solution of this instance is $\text{OPT}(I)$. For a minimization problem, one would hope to be able to prove a result of the form

$$H(I) \leq \alpha \text{OPT}(I) + \beta \qquad \text{where } \alpha, \beta \text{ are constants.}$$

A good heuristic would have α near 1 and β near 0. Now, if Π is the travelling salesman problem and NN is the nearest neighbour heuristic, it has been shown that, providing the triangle inequality holds, viz. $d_{ij} \leq d_{ik} + d_{kj}$ for all

$1 \leq i, j, k \leq n$ then

$$NN(I) \leq \tfrac{1}{2}(\lceil \log_2 n \rceil + 1)\, OPT(I)$$

where n is the number of cities. Moreover, for arbitrarily large values of n, there exist n-city instances for which

$$NN(I) > \tfrac{1}{3}(\log_2(n+1) + \tfrac{4}{3})\, OPT(I)$$

These results show how bad the nearest neighbour heuristic is!

The *performance ratio for a heuristic H applied to an instance I of a minimization problem*, Π, is defined by

$$R_H(I) = \frac{H(I)}{OPT(I)}$$

and the *absolute performance ratio*, r_H, for H on Π is

$$R_H = \inf\{r \geq 1 \,|\, R_H(I) \leq r \text{ for all instances } I \text{ of } \Pi\}.$$

The *asymptotic performance ratio*, R_H^∞ for H on Π is defined by

$$R_H^\infty = \inf\{r \geq 1 | \text{ for some } b \in Z^+, R_A(I) \leq r \text{ for all instances } I \text{ of } \Pi \\ \text{satisfying } OPT(I) \geq b\}.$$

Both the absolute and the asymptotic performance ratios are used in the analysis of the performance of heuristic algorithms. The nearer they are to 1, the better is the algorithm. The results above have shown $R_{NN} = R_{NN}^\infty = \infty$, which is a fierce indictment of that particular heuristic. There are, however, better heuristics than NN for the travelling salesman problem. Nevertheless, if the triangle inequality is not obeyed a good heuristic is not likely since it has been shown that if $P \neq NP$ then there is no heuristic algorithm H to solve the travelling salesman problem in polynomial time with asymptotic performance ratio $R_H^\infty < \infty$. This suggests that we might do better to concentrate on the design of algorithms which will perform satisfactorily on the majority of instances of the travelling salesman problem but with the knowledge that such algorithms may occasionally perform very badly.

For further general discussion on the design and analysis of heuristic algorithms the reader is referred to Chapter 12 of Horowitz & Sahni (1978). Results concerning the travelling salesman problem are collected in *The Travelling Salesman Problem* (*Lawler et al.*, 1984).

NUMBER PROBLEMS AND PSEUDO-POLYNOMIAL ALGORITHMS

In this next section of this chapter, we return once more to the restrictions on the encoding of instances of a problem. We were particularly careful to insist that the encoding of any numbers which occurred in a given instance was done in binary notation (or octal, decimal, etc. but *not* unary). Now, consider decision problems which have instances that are defined totally or in part by numbers which can range over all the integers. Such problems are known as *number problems*. For example, TSP is in this category since we have placed no restrictions on the distances between the cities. If $m \in Z$ is part of an instance I of a number problem, Π, then the restrictions we have placed on e ensure that the substring of $e(I)$ which encodes m will be of length $0(\log m)$.

We have formulated all our definitions in this chapter in terms of length$(e(I))$. Providing we adhere to the stated restrictions on encodings, it does not really matter which encoding we use since if e, e' are two such sensible, concise encodings, length$(e(I))$ and length $(e'(I))$ will be *polynomial related*, i.e. there will exist polynomials p, p' such that

$$\text{length}(e(I)) \leq p(\text{length}(e'(I)))$$
and $\quad \text{length}(e'(I)) \leq p'(\text{length}(e(I)))$

for any $I \in D_\Pi$. If length(I) denotes length$(e(I))$ for some such encoding, e, then we know that $\Pi \in P$ iff there is an algorithm which will find the solution of any $I \in D_\Pi$ with time complexity function $0(\text{length}^k(I))$ for some constant $k \geq 0$. However, if numbers are involved and we relax the constraint on encodings to allow unary encodings then this is no longer true. A number $m > 0$ represented in binary requires a string of length $\lfloor \log_2 m \rfloor + 1$ but in unary it requires a string of length m. The functions m and $\lfloor \log_2 m \rfloor$ are not polynomially related; a non-constant function which is polynomial in m will be exponential in $\lfloor \log_2 m \rfloor$.

Let Π be any decision problem and denote by max(I) the largest number occurring in any given instance I of Π. If I does not involve any number, set max(I) to 0. We formally define a *number problem* to be any decision problem Π such that there is *no* polynomial function, p, such that

$$\max(I) \leq p(\text{length}(I)) \text{ for all } I \in D_\Pi.$$

A pseudo-polynomial time algorithm for Π is an algorithm which solves Π and which has time complexity bounded above by a polynomial function of the two variables length(I) and max(I). Thus, all polynomial time algorithms are pseudo-polynomial time algorithms since such functions are bounded above by a polynomial function of just length(I). The converse would not seem to hold and thus it appears that we may be able to find pseudo-polynomial time algorithms to solve NP-complete problems. This is indeed the case; one commonly cited example is

Partition
INSTANCE: A   set $A = \{a_1, a_2, \ldots, a_n\}$ of n elements and a weight function $w: A \rightarrow Z^+$.
QUESTION: Can we partition A into two equally weighted subsets, i.e. is there $A' \subseteq A$ such that

$$\sum_{a \in A'} w(a) = \sum_{a \in A \setminus A'} w(a)?$$

The pseudo-polynomial algorithm to solve partition works as follows. Let sum $= \sum_{a \in A} w(a)$. If sum is not even, the answer is clearly no; otherwise, put $h = \text{sum}/2$. Then construct a matrix, M, of Boolean values, $M[i,j]$, $1 \le i \le n, 0 \le j \le h$ such that $M[i,j] = T$ iff there is a subset of $\{a_1, a_2, \ldots, a_i\}$ with weight exactly j. These values can be inserted into M row-by-row. Firstly, observe that $M[1,j] = T$ iff either $j = 0$ or $j = w(a_1)$. Then each subsequent row is computed using results from the previous row and the observation that for $1 < i \le n, 0 \le j \le h, M[i,j] = T$ iff either $M[i-1,j] = T$ or $j \ge w(a_i)$ and $M[i-1, j - w(a_i)] = T$. Once the entire matrix, M, has been filled in, the answer to the particular instance of *Partition* is yes iff $M[n,h] = T$. This algorithm can be easily shown to have a time complexity function which is polynomial in nh (Exercise 6.14). Since *Partition* is NP-complete, we would not, however, expect to find an algorithm to solve it with a time complexity function polynomial in $n\log_2 h$.

Given a decision problem, Π and a polynomial over the integers, p, we define Π_p to be the subproblem of Π comprising those instances, I, of Π that satisfy max(I) $\le p$(length(I)). Π_p is not then a number problem by definition. We say that a decision problem, Π, is NP-complete in the strong sense iff (i) $\Pi \in NP$ and (ii) there exists a polynomial p such that $\Pi_p \in NPC$.

Theorem 6.11

(1) Π is NP-complete and Π is not a number problem implies Π is NP-complete in the strong sense.

(2) Π is NP-complete in the strong sense implies Π is not solvable by a pseudo-polynomial algorithm unless $P = NP$.

Proof. (1)   follows immediately from the definitions.

(2) $\Pi \in NP$ and there exists a p such that $\Pi_p \in NPC$. We will show that if Π is solvable by a pseudo-polynomial time algorithm then $\Pi_p \in P$. Our algorithm considers any input x and checks if x encodes an instance I of Π such that $\max(I) \leq p(\text{length}(I))$. We can assume max and length can be calculated in polynomial time and hence this inequality can be checked in polynomial time. If the answer is yes we apply our pseudo-polynomial time algorithm for Π to I. Since $\max(I) \leq p(\text{length}(I))$, this pseudo-polynomial time algorithm will be polynomial in length(I). Hence $\Pi_p \in P$. But $\Pi_p \in NPC$. Hence the result.

An immediate corollary of this theorem is that *Partition* is not NP-complete in the strong sense. However, there are number problems in NPC which are NP-complete in the strong sense. One example in TSP. We proved TSP was NP-complete by describing a polynomial transformation HC $\propto$ TSP but the construction ensured that any instance of TSP so constructed only involved distances of only 1 or 2. This shows that a restriction of TSP to the case where distances are ≤ 2 is still an NP-complete problem and hence TSP is NP-complete in the strong sense.

COMPLEMENTARY PROBLEMS

If Π is some decision problem then its question part will have the general format: 'given an instance, I, is some condition, B, true for I?' The *complement* of the problem Π, usually denoted by Π^c, is identical to Π except that the question asked is whether the condition, B, is false for I. Thus Π^c has domain D_Π and $Y_{\Pi^c} = D_\Pi \backslash Y_\Pi$. As an example, the complement of

Composite number
INSTANCE: Positive integer, k.
QUESTION: Are there integers $m, n > 1$ such that $k = mn$?

is

Prime
INSTANCE: Positive integer, k.
QUESTION: Are there no integers $m, n > 1$ such that $k = mn$, i.e. is k prime?

Now, if $\Pi \in P$ then clearly $\Pi^c \in P$. Given the DTM, M, which solves Π we can easily obtain a DTM, M^c, to solve Π^c (see Exercise 6.15). Thus M accepts x iff M^c rejects x. The construction described in the exercise works because M is deterministic and thus halts on all inputs. This proof cannot be generalized to apply to nondeterministic algorithms.

If we define co-$P = \{\Pi^c | \Pi \in P\}$ or, at the language level, co-$P = \{T^* \backslash L | L$ is a language over T and $L \in P\}$ then we have established

Theorem 6.12

co-$P = P$.

Now, let us consider an NP-complete problem, say TSP. The complement of TSP is TSP^c.

TSP^c

INSTANCE: A set $C = \{c_1, c_2, \ldots, c_n\}$ of n cities, for each pair c_i, $c_j \in C$, a distance $d_{ij} \in Z^+$ and a bound $b \in Z^+$.

QUESTION: Is it impossible for a travelling salesman located at city c_1 to visit all cities in $\{c_2, \ldots, c_n\}$ once only and then return home with a total distance travelled $\leq b$, i.e. do *all* such tours costs $> b$?

There appears no easy way to give a yes answer to TSP^c even with 'inspired' guesses. Essentially, we must examine all the tours or, at least, a large proportion of them before we can be sure they all cost $> b$. It appears that TSP^c is not likely to be solvable in polynomial time even on a nondeterministic Turing machine.

Thus, if we define co-$NP = \{\Pi^c | \Pi \in NP\}$ or, at the language level, co-$NP = \{T^* \backslash L | L$ is a language over T and $L \in NP\}$ then, from our discussion, we might conjecture that $NP \neq$ co-NP. We have previously conjectured that $NP \neq P$ and based a whole theory upon it. This new conjecture is, in some senses, an even stronger conjecture since it is impossible to have $NP \neq$ co-NP and $P = NP$; such a situation would lead to an immediate contradition of theorem 6.12. It might, however, be the case that $P \neq NP$ even though $NP =$ co-NP but this is not considered to be at all likely.

If we defined co-NPC in the obvious way, then the following theorem

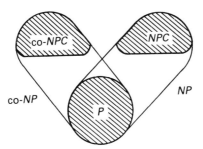

Fig. 6.10.

establishes some important properties. These are illustrated in Fig. 6.10 where we assume $P \neq NP$ and $NP \neq$ co-NP both hold.

Theorem 6.13

(1) $P \subseteq (NP \cap \text{co-}NP)$.
(2) $NP \neq$ co-NP implies both $NPC \subseteq (NP \backslash \text{co-}NP)$ and co-$NPC \subseteq (\text{co-}NP \backslash NP)$.

Proof.
(1) $P \subseteq NP$ and $P = \text{co-}P \subseteq \text{co-}NP$ so the result follows.
(2) We will prove $NPC \subseteq (NP \backslash \text{co-}NP)$; the second part of the result then follows by symmetry. Now, $NPC \subseteq NP$ by definition so we have to show that there is no problem in NPC which lies in co-NP. Let us assume there is some such problem, Π, say, and seek a contradiction. Let Π_1 be any problem in NP then, since $\Pi \in NPC$, $\Pi_1 \propto \Pi$. It is then easy to establish that $\Pi_1^c \propto \Pi^c$. Now, since $\Pi \in$ co-NP, $\Pi^c \in NP$ and since $\Pi_1^c \propto \Pi^c$, we must have $\Pi_1^c \in NP$. Hence we have shown that co-$NP \subseteq NP$. Hence $NP = \text{co-}(\text{co-}NP) \subseteq \text{co-}NP$ and thus $NP = \text{co-}NP$—the contradiction we sought.

We have noted that *Composite number* lies in NP and we have suggested this problem as a likely example of a problem lying in $NPI = NP \backslash (NPC \cup P)$. The complement of *Composite number*, viz. *Prime*, can also be shown to lie in NP and this supports our suspicion that *Composite number* is not in NPC—if it were then we would have a proof that $NP = \text{co-}NP$. It may, of course, still be the case that *Composite number* lies in P; research continues to either prove or disprove this. Since various encryption

schemes are based upon prime factorization, there is considerable interest
in the result.

THE POLYNOMIAL HIERARCHY

Let Π' be a decision problem and suppose that we have written a routine
to solve it. A user of this routine simply inputs an instance $I \in D_{\Pi'}$ and
the routine delivers the answer 1 to 0 according to whether $I \in Y_{\Pi'}$ or
not. The user need have no interest in how our routine works as long as
it always produces the correct answer. Now, let us assume that running
this routine on any particular instance will only cost the user a single time
unit irrespective of how difficult Π' is and how much time is actually
required by our routine to solve the given instance. We will then call our
routine an *oracle*.

A problem Π is said to be *NP-easy* if it can be solved in polynomial
time by a deterministic algorithm which has access to an oracle which
solves some problem in NP. Clearly, any problem in NP must also be
NP-easy—we just equip ourselves with an oracle to solve the problem in
question. Also, if $\Pi \in NP$, an oracle to solve Π can obviously be used to
design a trivial algorithm to solve Π^c and hence any problem in co-NP is
also NP-easy.

If X is any class of problems, we define

$$P^X = \{\Pi | \Pi \text{ can be solved in polynomial time by a deterministic}$$
$$\text{algorithm given access to an oracle which solves}$$
$$\text{some problem } \Pi' \in X\}.$$

Then the NP-easy problems are precisely those in P^{NP}. We have shown
$P^{NP} \supseteq NP \cup \text{co-}NP$ and provided $NP \neq \text{co-}NP$, this containment is known
to be strict.

Following the definition of P^X, an obvious next step is the definition of
NP^X,

$$NP^X = \{\Pi | \Pi \text{ can be solved in polynomial time by a non-}$$
$$\text{deterministic algorithm given access to an oracle which}$$
$$\text{solves some problem } \Pi' \in X\}.$$

Then we have $NP^{NP} \supseteq P^{NP} \supseteq NP \cup \text{co-}NP$ as illustrated in Fig. 6.11. We
have already explained that the second of these containments is likely to be
strict and there is good reason to believe that this is also true of the first.

The NP-easy problems are so-called because in some sense they are

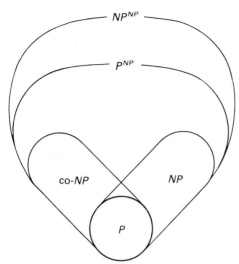

Fig. 6.11.

no harder than any problem in NP. Not to be confused is the concept of an NP-*hard* problem. A problem Π is NP-*hard* if there exists some NP-complete problem Π' which could be solved by a polynomial time deterministic algorithm provided it is equipped with an oracle to solve Π. An immediate consequence of this definition is that a decision problem cannot be NP-hard and lie in P unless $P = NP$. An example of a problem that is NP-hard but does not appear to be NP-easy is

Minimum equivalent expression (MEE)
INSTANCE: A well-formed Boolean expression, E, involving literals on a finite set of variables, constants, T (true) and F (false), and logical connectives $\wedge$ (and), $\vee$ (or), $\sim$ (not) and $\Rightarrow$ (implies) together with $k \in Z^+$.
QUESTION: Is there a well-formed Boolean expression, E', that contains $\leq k$ occurrences of literals such that E' is logically equivalent to E?

Showing that MEE is NP-hard is left as an exercise (Exercise 6.16).
   Although no one has been able to show MEE is in P^{NP} and it is now widely believed not to be in P^{NP}, it is, nevertheless, in NP^{NP}. We show this by equipping the oracle with a routine to solve SAT. The non-deterministic algorithm to solve MEE will then guess an expression E' involving $\leq k$ occurrences of literals and then use the oracle to check

whether $\sim ((E \Rightarrow E') \wedge (E' \Rightarrow E))$ is satisfiable. If not, the given instance must lie in Y_{MEE}.

The hierarchy described in Fig. 6.9 has been generalized to obtain an infinite hierarchy as follows.

$$\Sigma_0^p = \Pi_0^p = \Delta_0^p = P$$

and for all $k \geq 0$,

$$\Delta_{k+1}^p = P^{\Sigma_k^p},$$
$$\Sigma_{k+1}^p = NP^{\Sigma_k^p},$$

and $\quad \Pi_{k+1}^p = \text{co-}\Sigma_{k+1}^p.$

Thus:

$$\Delta_1^p = P^P = P, \ \Sigma_1^p = NP^P = NP, \ \Pi_1^p = \text{co-}NP,$$
$$\Delta_2^p = P^{NP}, \quad \Sigma_2^p = NP^{NP}, \quad \Pi_2^p = \text{co-}NP^{NP}, \text{etc.}$$

For any k, one can show that $\Delta_k^p \subseteq \Pi_k^p \cap \Sigma_k^p$ and $\Pi_k^p \cup \Sigma_k^p \subseteq \Delta_{k+1}^p$ as described in Fig. 6.12. This whole hierarchy of complexity classes is known as the *polynomial hierarchy*. The set $PH = \bigcup_{k=1}^{\infty} \Sigma_k^p$ represents all the problems in this hierarchy. Further details concerning this hierarchy are described by Stockmeyer (1976). In the previously cited text (Garey & Johnson, 1978), the notion of an oracle Turing machine is introduced and the ideas we have discussed here are further formalized and expanded upon.

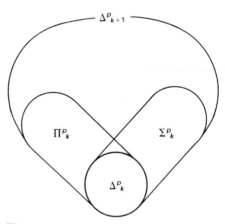

Fig. 6.12.

SPACE CONSTRAINTS

So far, throughout this chapter we have been exclusively concerned with time constraints. However, computer memory is also an important constraint and limitations on memory can, in practice, be very restrictive. The amount of computer memory required to run an algorithm is referred to as its *space requirement*. For a TM, the space requirement is thus simply the number of distinct locations visited by the tape head. An important observation is that since the number of distinct locations visited cannot exceed the amount of time spent on the computation, it must be that any problem solvable in polynomial time must also be solvable in polynomial space. Hence, if we define

$PSPACE = \{L|$there is a polynomially space bounded
DTM which halts on all inputs and accepts $L\}$

or, in terms of problems,

$PSPACE = \{\Pi|\Pi$ is a decision problem which can be solved by a
polynomially space bounded DTM which halts for all inputs$\}$

then we have $P \subseteq PSPACE$. From the proof of theorem 4.8, it follows that $NP \subseteq PSPACE$. Also, co-$NP \subseteq PSPACE$ and, in fact, the whole polynomial hierarchy $PH \subseteq PSPACE$. $PSPACE$ is thus a large class of problems.

Although all problems solvable in polynomial time can be solved in polynomial space, it is not known whether there are problems solvable in polynomial space which are not solvable in polynomial time. Such a conjecture seems very plausible; certainly, if $P \neq NP$ or even if $P \neq PH$, it would follow that $P \neq PSPACE$.

As with NP, we can identify a class of problems in $PSPACE$ which can be regarded as the most difficult. Keeping to the language formulation, we say L is $PSPACE$-complete iff $L \in PSPACE$ and for all $L' \in PSPACE$, $L' \propto L$. Then it follows that if L is $PSPACE$-complete then $L \in P$ iff $P = PSPACE$. These definitions are then extended to apply to problems in the obvious way. Even if $P = NP$, it may be the case that $P \neq PSPACE$ and hence showing a problem to be $PSPACE$-complete is a stronger indication of intractability than showing it to be NP-complete. However, NP-complete problems appear to be the ones that most commonly arise in practice and hence the reason for the emphasis in this book.

The core $PSPACE$-complete problem which plays a role similar to that of SAT for the NP-complete problems is

Quantified Boolean formula (QBF)

INSTANCE: A well-formed quantified Boolean formula

$$F = (Q_1 x_1)(Q_2 x_2)\ldots(Q_n x_n)E$$

where E is a Boolean expression over the variables $x_1, x_2, \ldots, x_n$ and each Q_i is either the existential quantifier ($\exists$) or the universal quantifier ($\forall$).

QUESTION: Is F true?

Having defined *PSPACE*, the reader may next be expecting a definition of *NPSPACE*—the class of languages recognized by nondeterministic TMs using polynomial space. However, this proves a fruitless exercise since it has been shown that $PSPACE = NPSPACE$. Instead of seeking complexity classes larger than *PSPACE*, we will restrict space even more and produce a smaller complexity class.

We can envisage our DTM as having two tapes—a read-only input tape and a read/write work tape on which the final output will be found. When measuring space used it would seem reasonable to only measure that used on the work tape. Certainly, if we are to consider space restrictions which are sublinear (i.e.$\Omega(n)$ but not $0(n)$) then, since the input requires n locations, this is the only realistic way we can proceed. Recent research has focussed on the class

$$DLOGSPACE = \{L \mid L \text{ can be recognized by a DTM program.}$$
$$\text{with work space bounded by } \lceil \log_2 n + 1 \rceil \text{ where}$$
$$n \text{ is the length of the input string}\}.$$

It is relatively easy to show $DLOGSPACE \subseteq P$ but it is not known whether or not this containment is strict. One can show that it is impossible to have both $P = DLOGSPACE$ and $P = PSPACE$ and it is conjectured that neither of these are true. Thus, we suspect that there are problems in P which require more than logarithmic work space for their solution.

Let L_1, L_2 be languages over alphabets T_1, T_2. We define a *log-space transformation* from L_1 to L_2 to be a function $f: T_1^* \to T_2^*$ such that
(1) $x \in L_1$ iff $f(x) \in L_2$; and
(2) f can be computed by a DTM with work space bounded by $\lceil \log_2 |x| + 1 \rceil$ for any input string $x \in T_1^*$. If such a log-space transformation exists from L_1 to L_2 we write $L_1 \propto_{\text{LOG}} L_2$.

It can then be show that $\propto_{\text{LOG}}$ is transitive and that if $L_1 \propto_{\text{LOG}} L_2$ and $L_2 \in DLOGSPACE$ then $L_1 \in DLOGSPACE$. We thus define a language $L \in P$ to be *log-space complete for P* iff for all $L' \in P$, $L' \propto_{\text{LOG}} L$. Then, if

L is log-space complete for P it follows that $L \in DLOGSPACE$ iff $DLOGSPACE = P$. This class of problem is receiving considerable attention currently; it has been conjectured that problems which are log-space complete for P are likely to be problems whose solution will not be achieved significantly more quickly by the introduction of parallelism. This conjecture has been called the *Parallel computation hypothesis*.

SUMMARY

Our final view of the world of complexity classes is summarized in Fig. 6.13. There are many complexity classes which have been proposed and researched which are outside the scope of this text. However, we have discussed all the most important classes and, in particular, those which correspond to relevant real-world problems. In this way, we have been able to apply some interesting theory to practical problems.

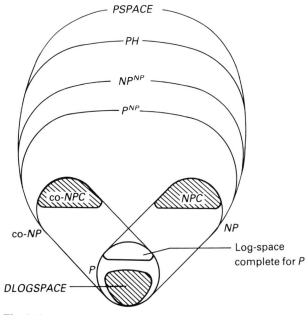

Fig. 6.13.

EXERCISES

1   Show that
    (a) 2^n is $O(n!)$;

(b) $\log_2 n$ is $\theta(\log_k n)$ for any $k \geq 2$;

(c) $f(n)$ is $\theta(g(n))$ implies $g(n)$ is $\theta(f(n))$.

2   Find a solution to the travelling salesman problem defined by the labelled graph in Fig. 6.14. Did you have to consider all 4! possible circuits? Assuming A is the home base, would NN have necessarily given you the correct solution? How bad a result could you have got using this algorithm on this example?

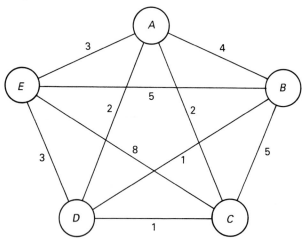

Fig. 6.14.

3   Let A, B be two $n \times n$ matrices where $n = 2^k$. Imagine that A, B are each partitioned into four submatrices of dimension $n/2 \times n/2$ as below

$$A = \begin{bmatrix} A_{11} & A_{12} \\ A_{21} & A_{22} \end{bmatrix} \qquad B = \begin{bmatrix} B_{11} & B_{12} \\ B_{21} & B_{22} \end{bmatrix}$$

If the product matrix $C = AB$ is similarly partitioned, express $C_{11}, C_{12}, C_{21}, C_{22}$ in terms of

$$\begin{aligned}
P &= (A_{11} + A_{22})(B_{11} + B_{22}) \\
Q &= (A_{21} + A_{22})B_{11} \\
R &= A_{11}(B_{12} - B_{22}) \\
S &= A_{22}(B_{21} - B_{11}) \\
T &= (A_{11} + A_{12})B_{22} \\
U &= (A_{21} - A_{11})(B_{11} + B_{12}) \\
V &= (A_{12} - A_{22})(B_{21} + B_{22})
\end{aligned}$$

The values P, Q, R, S, T, U, V can be computed using 7 matrix multiplications and 10 matrix additions/subtractions. How many additional additions/subtractions are required to compute $C_{11}, C_{12}, C_{21}, C_{22}$, from these values? Let $T(n)$ denote the overall computing time required to multiply the two $n \times n$ matrices. Deduce the recurrence relation

$$T(n) = \begin{cases} b & n \le 2, \\ 7T(n/2) + an^2 & n > 2, \end{cases}$$

where a, b are constants. Hence deduce an $0(n^{\log_2 7})$ algorithm to multiply two $n \times n$ matrices. (This algorithm is known as Strassen's algorithm.)

4 Show that P is an equivalence class under polynomial equivalence. [Hint: solve the problem in the transformation.]

5 Show that if M is a degree $m(> 1)$ NDTM which accepts L then there exists a degree 2 NDTM, M', accepting L such that for all $x \in L$, $l_{M'}(x)$ is $0((\log m)l_M(x))$.

6 How many Boolean variables and how many clauses are constructed in the proof of Cook's theorem?

7 (a) Describe a polynomial time algorithm to solve 2SAT. [Hint: if $\{A, B\}$ and $\{\bar{B}, C\}$ are satisfiable then so is $\{A, C\}$.]

(b) Show that kSAT ($k \ge 4$) is NP-complete.

8 Consider the following problem:

Exact cover by 3 sets (X3C)

INSTANCE: Set X with $|X| = 3q$ and a collection C of 3-element subsets of X.

QUESTION: Does C contain an exact cover for X, i.e. a subcollection C' of C such that every element of X occurs in one member of C'?

(a) Construct an instance, $I \in Y_{X3C}$, and an instance $I' \notin Y_{X3C}$.

(b) Show that X3C $\in NP$.

(c) By exhibiting a polynomial transformation 3DM $\propto$ X3C, prove X3C is NP-complete.

9 Let G be a graph with vertices, V, and edges, E. Let $c: E \to Z^+$ be a cost function defined on the edges of G. Let $V' \subseteq V$. Consider the problem of computing the least cost subgraph of G which is connected and includes all the vertices, V' (and possibly some others). This problem is known as the Steiner tree problem in graphs.

(a) Show that the solution must necessarily be a tree.

(b) Show that if $V' = V$ or if $\#(V') = 2$, the problem is solvable in polynomial time.

(c) Let $\#(V) = n$ and $\#(V') = m$. If $2 < m < n$, show that the problem can be solved using 2^{n-m} applications of the minimum spanning tree algorithm.

(d) Describe the decision problem associated with the Steiner tree problem in graphs. Show that problem to be NP-complete. [Hint: construct a polynomial transformation from X3C.]

10 Let G be a graph with vertex set, V, and edges, E. A *clique* in a graph G is a subset, $V' \subseteq V$ such that every two vertices in V' are joined by an edge of the graph. The *complement* of G has vertices V and an edge $ⓤ————ⓥ$ iff u, v are not connected in G. Show that V' is a clique in the complement of G iff $V \backslash V'$ is a vertex cover for G. Hence deduce that the following is an NP-complete problem.

Clique
INSTANCE: A graph G and a positive integer b.
QUESTION: Does G contain a clique comprising $\geq b$ vertices?

11 Show that we are unlikely to be able to find a polynomial time algorithm to solve *subgraph isomorphism*, i.e. the problem of finding one given graph a subgraph isomorphic to another given graph. [Hint: look at question 10.]

12 Show that the following problem is NP-complete.

Multiprocessor scheduling
INSTANCE: A finite set J of jobs and a length, $l(j) \in Z^+$ for each job $j \in J$, a number $n \in Z^+$ of processors and a deadline $d \in Z^+$.
QUESTION: Is there a partition $J = J_1 \cup J_2 \cup \ldots \cup J_n$ of J into n disjoint sets such that

$$\max \left\{ \sum_{j \in J_i} l(j) \mid 1 \leq i \leq m \right\} \leq d?$$

13 A Hamiltonian path in a graph is a path which visits each vertex of the graph just once. By modifying the proof of theorem 6.10, show that the problem of knowing whether or not a graph has a Hamiltonian path is NP-complete.

14 Consider the partition problem comprising 8 elements $a_1, a_2, \ldots, a_8$ with weights $2, 3, 4, 5, 5, 6, 7, 8$. Use the pseudo-polynomial time algorithm described in the text to test whether or not a partition exists. Show that the algorithm is an $0(nh)$ algorithm where n is the number of elements and $h = \Sigma a_i/2$.

15 Show that if $L \in P$ then there exists a DTM, M, which accepts L and which has a unique accept state (i.e. final state) and a unique reject state (i.e. a state in which the machine halts and fails). Hence show that $L \in P$ iff $L^c \in P$. Explain why your construction will not work for $L \in NP$.

16 Show that a DTM equipped with an oracle to solve MEE can be used to solve SAT in polynomial time. Hence, deduce that MEE is an NP-hard problem.

17 Show that every NP-easy problem lies in $P^{\{SAT\}}$.

18 Show that $NP \subseteq PSPACE$. [Hint: look at theorem 4.8.]

Appendix

The Turing Machine Simulator

The Pascal program given below can be used to simulate the action of a Turing machine, $M = (Q, \Sigma, T, P, q_0, F)$, the only significant restriction being that the amount of tape used must be limited. Without loss of generality, we assume that the states, Q, are the integers $1, 2, \ldots, n$ for some $n \geq 1$ and that the final states, F, are those states in the range $m, m + 1, \ldots, n$ for some $1 \leq m \leq n$. The symbols which comprise the tape alphabet, Σ, may be of length ≥ 1 but, in the simulator, each such symbol must have the same length. To achieve this, we may need to pad out some symbols with spaces. Thus, for example, if $\Sigma = \{0, 01, 02\}$, the maximum length of any symbol in Σ is two so we would use character arrays of length two, viz. ' 0', '01', '02'.

A TM program is input to the simulator in two stages. Firstly, the following constants used in the simulator must be correctly initialized.

NmbrOfStates: the number of states in Q, it then being assumed that the states are the integers in the range 1.. NmbrOfStates.

StartState: the integer representing the start state.

FirstHaltState: the least integer representing a final state, it then being assumed that every state in the range FirstHaltState..NmbrOfStates is a final state.

NmbrOfSymbols: the number of distinct tape symbols in Σ.

MaxSymSize: the maximum length of any symbol in Σ, it then being assumed that each symbol in Σ has that same length.

Blank: the symbol used to represent the blank symbol (which must, of course, be of length MaxSymSize).

Tracing: a Boolean variable set to TRUE if the programmer wishes the output to detail each configuration of the TM; otherwise, set to FALSE.

TapeLimit: a bound on the size of the tape. The tape is limited to locations $-$ TapeLimit.. TapeLimit.

Secondly, the TM program, P, is represented by the file, TupleFile. If $P(q, a) = (q', a', X)$, $q, q' \in Q$, $a, a' \in \Sigma$, $X \in \{L, R, 0\}$ then we have an entry in the file of the form given in Fig. A.1, where

168

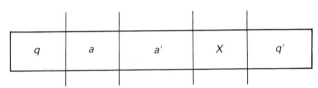

Fig. A.1.

q, q' are of type STATETYPE = 1.. NmbrOfStates,

a, a' are of type SYMBOLTYPE = **PACKED ARRAY**

[1.. MaxSymSize] of CHAR,

and X is of type MOVE = CHAR.

Note that the simulator does not require any ordering of these entries nor does it need to know Σ in advance. By scanning TupleFile, the exact nature of Σ can be determined automatically.

Having fully described the TM, M, to the simulator, the programmer must specify the input to the TM using the file TMTape. TMTape is a file of SYMBOLTYPE and each such symbol must comprise exactly MaxSymSize characters. The program is written in VAX-11 Pascal version 2.0.

```
PROGRAM TuringMachine (TMTape, TupleFile, OUTPUT);

CONST
    Dummy Entry        = -1;
    BlankCode          = 0;
    NmbrOfStates       = 27;
    StartState         = 1;
    FirstHaltState     = 26;
    NmbrOfSymbols      = 5;
    MaxSymSize         = 1;
    Blank              = "∧";
    Tracing            = TRUE;
    TapeLimit          = 1000;
```

These constants should be set according to instructions.
Values shown here were used for a simulation of the binary to unary converter (Fig. 2.9).

```
TYPE
    SYMBOLTYPE         = PACKED ARRAY [1.. MaxSymSize] OF
                         CHAR;
    MOVETYPE           = (L, R, 0);
```

```
STATETYPE              = 1 .. NmbrOfStates;
SYMCODE                = 0 .. NmbrOfSymbols;
ACTION                 = RECORD
                              WriteSymbol  : SYMCODE;
                              Move         : MOVETYPE;
                              NewState     : INTEGER
                         END;
RAW5TUPLE              = RECORD
                              CurrentState : STATETYPE;
                              ReadSymbol   : SYMBOLTYPE;
                              WriteSymbol  : SYMBOLTYPE;
                              Move         : CHAR;
                              NewState     : STATETYPE
                         END;
TAPEINDEX              = − TapeLimit .. TapeLimit;

VAR
    Alphabet                  : ARRAY [SYMCODE] OF SYMBOLTYPE;
    Transition,
    ReqdAction                : ACTION;
    TransitionTable           : ARRAY [STATETYPE, SYMCODE]
                                OF ACTION;
    Tape                      : ARRAY [TAPEINDEX] OF SYMCODE;
    Symbol                    : SYMBOLTYPE;
    RawTuple                  : RAW5TUPLE;
    FuncDefined,
    TapeFull,
    FinalTape                 : BOOLEAN;
    SymbolsKnown,
    Reading                   : SYMCODE;
    State                     : STATETYPE;
    SymbolNmbr                : SYMCODE;
    TapeHead,
    RightMost, LeftMost       : TAPEINDEX;
    TMTape                    : FILE OF SYMBOLTYPE;
    TupleFile                 : FILE OF RAW5TUPLE;
```

FUNCTION FindSymCode (SearchSym : SYMBOLTYPE) : SYMCODE;
(*This returns the integer encoding for the given symbol. If the symbol has*)

(*not yet been inserted into the symbol table then it is put at the end and*)
(*this new position returned.   *)
VAR
    Found : BOOLEAN;
    SymNum : SYMCODE;

BEGIN
Found := FALSE;
SymNum := 0;
WHILE (SymNum <= SymbolsKnown) AND NOT Found DO
    IF Alphabet [SymNum] = SearchSym THEN
        Found := TRUE
    ELSE
        SymNum := SymNum + 1;
IF SymNum > SymbolsKnown THEN
    BEGIN
    Alphabet [SymNum] := SearchSym;
    SymbolsKnown := SymbolsKnown + 1
    END;
FindSymCode := SymNum
END;

PROCEDURE DisplayResult;
(* This prints the non-black characters on the tape; all of them if it is a trace,*)
(* but those from position 1 upwards if it is the final tape (i.e. the output*)
(* computed).   *)

VAR
    Ptr, LeftPtr, RightPtr : TAPEINDEX;

BEGIN
IF Tracing AND NOT FinalTape THEN
    BEGIN
    LeftPtr := LeftMost;
    WHILE (LeftPtr <= 0) AND (Tape [LeftPtr] = BlankCode) DO
        LeftPtr := LeftPtr + 1;
    WRITELN ('New state = ', State : 0, 'Tape Head at ', TapeHead : 0);
    WRITELN ('TAPE IS: ')
    END

```
ELSE
    BEGIN
    LeftPtr:= 1;
    WRITELN ('OUTPUT COMPUTED IS:')
    END;
RightPtr:= RightMost;
WHILE (RightPtr > = 1) AND (Tape [RightPtr] = BlankCode) DO
    RightPtr:= RightPtr - 1;
FOR Ptr := LeftPtr TO RightPtr DO
    WRITELN (' Position', Ptr:2,'      ', Alphabet [Tape[Ptr]]);
WRITELN; WRITELN
END;


PROCEDURE GetAction;
(* This finds the next state to go to and the symbol to write.*)

    BEGIN
    IF TransitionTable [State, Reading].Newstate < > DummyEntry THEN
      ReqdAction:= TransitionTable [State, Reading]
    ELSE
      FuncDefined:= FALSE
    END;

BEGIN
(*Initialization*)
FOR State:= 1 TO NmbrOfStates DO
    FOR SymbolNmbr:= 0 TO NmbrOfSymbols DO
    TransitionTable [State, SymbolNmbr]. NewState:= DummyEntry;
FOR TapeHead:= - TapeLimit TO TapeLimit DO
    Tape [TapeHead]:= BlankCode;
FOR SymbolNmbr:= 0 TO NmbrOfSymbols DO
    Alphabet [SymbolNmbr]:= Blank;
WRITELN ('Start state is', StartState:0);
WRITELN ('Halt states are > = state number', FirstHaltState:0);

(*Read the tape*)
RESET (TMTape);
WRITELN ('THE INITIAL TAPE CONTAINS:');
SymbolsKnown:= 0;
```

```
TapeHead := 1;
WHILE NOT EOF (TMTape) DO
    BEGIN
    READ (TMTape, Symbol);
    WRITELN ('Position', TapeHead:0,'     ', Symbol);
    Tape [TapeHead] := FindSymCode (Symbol);
    TapeHead := TapeHead + 1;
    END;
RightMost := TapeHead;


(* Read the tuples. *)
RESET (TupleFile);
WRITELN ('The Turing Machine program is:');
WHILE NOT EOF (TupleFile) DO
    BEGIN
    READ (TupleFile, RawTuple);
    WITH RawTuple DO
        WRITELN (CurrentState, ReadSymbol, WriteSymbol, Move,
        NewState);
    State := RawTuple.CurrentState;
    Reading := FindSymCode (RawTuple.ReadSymbol);
    WITH ReqdAction DO
          BEGIN
          WriteSymbol := FindSymCode (RawTuple.WriteSymbol);
          CASE RawTuple.Move OF
              'R'  : Move   := R;
              'L'  : Move   := L;
              'O'  : Move   := O
              END;
          NewState := RawTuple.NewState
          END;
TransitionTable [State, Reading] := ReqdAction
END;


(* Run the TM program. *)
TapeHead := 1; LeftMost := 1;
State := StartState; Reading := Tape [1];
FuncDefined := TRUE; TapeFull := FALSE; FinalTape := FALSE;
GetAction;
```

```
WHILE FuncDefined AND NOT TapeFull Do
    WITH ReqdAction DO
        BEGIN
        State := NewState;
        Tape [TapeHead] := WriteSymbol;
        CASE Move OF
          L : BEGIN
            TapeHead := TapeHead − 1;
            IF TapeHead < LeftMost THEN
                LeftMost := TapeHead
            END;
          R : BEGIN
            TapeHead := TapeHead + 1;
            IF TapeHead > RightMost THEN
                RightMost := TapeHead
            END;
          0 :
          END;
        IF TracingTHEN
          DisplayResult;
        IF ABS (TapeHead) <= TapeLimit THEN
          BEGIN
          Reading := Tape [TapeHead];
          GetAction
          END
        ELSE
          TapeFull := TRUE
        END;
IF TapeFull THEN
    WRITELN ('Tape limit reached.')
ELSE
    IF State < FirstHaltState THEN
        WRITELN ('Turing Machine halts and fails.')
    ELSE
        BEGIN
        FinalTape := TRUE;
        DisplayResult
        END
END.
```

Bibliography

Including suggested texts for further reading

Aho, A. V., Hopcroft, J. E. & Ullman, J. D. (1974) *The Design and Analysis of Computer Algorithms.* Addison–Wesley, Reading, Massachusetts.

Aho, A. V. & Ullman, J. D. (1977) *Principles of Compiler Design.* Addison–Wesley, Reading, Massachusetts.

Bar-Hillel, Y., Perles, M. & Shamir, E. (1961) On formal properties of simple phrase structure grammars. *Zeitschrift für Phonetik, Sprachwissenschaft und Kommunikationsforschung,* **14**, 143–172.

Beckman, F. S. (1980) *Mathematical Foundations of Programming.* Addison–Wesley, Reading, Massachusetts.

Bell, J. & Machover, M. (1977) *A Course in Mathematical Logic.* North Holland, Amsterdam.

Bird, R. (1976) *Programs and Machines.* J. Wiley, New York.

Boolos, & Jeffrey, R. (1974) *Computability and Logic.* Cambridge University Press, Cambridge.

Brainerd, W. S. & Landweber, L. H. (1974) *Theory of Computation.* J. Wiley, New York.

Chomsky, N. (1956) Three models for the description of language. *PGIT,* **2**, 113–124.

Chomsky, N. (1959) On certain formal properties of grammars. *Information and Control,* **2**, 137–167.

Church, A. (1936a) An unsolvable problem of elementary number theory. *American Journal of Mathematics,* **58**, 345–363. (Reprinted in Davis, 1965.)

Church, A. (1936b) A note on the Entscheidungsproblem. *Journal of Symbolic Logic,* **1**, 40–41, 101–102. (Reprinted in Davis, 1965.)

Church, A. (1956) *Introduction to Mathematical Logic.* Princeton University Press, Princeton.

Cook, S. (1971) The complexity of theorem proving procedures. *Proceedings of the Third Annual ACM Symposium on the Theory of Computing,* 151–158.

Cutland, N. J. (1980) *Computability: An Introduction to Recursive Function Theory.* Cambridge University Press, Cambridge.

Davis, M. (1958) *Computability and Unsolvability.* McGraw-Hill, New York.

Davis, M., ed. (1965) *The Undecidable.* Raven Press, New York.

Dowsing, R. D., Rayward-Smith, V. J. & Walter, C. D. (1985) *A First Course in Formal Logic and its Applications in Computer Science.* Blackwell Scientific Publications, Oxford.

Even, S. (1979) *Graph Algorithms.* Computer Science Press, Potomac, Maryland.

Fischer, P. C. (1963) On computability by certain classes of restricted Turing machines. *Proceedings of the Fourth Annual Symposium on Switching Circuit Theory and Logical Design,* 23–32. Chicago.

Fischer, P. C. (1965) Multitape and infinite state automata—a survey. *Communication of ACM,* **8**, 799–805.

Fischer, P. C. (1966) Turing machines with restricted memory access. *Information and Control*, **9**, 364–379.

Garey, M. R. & Johnson, D. S. (1979) *Computers and Intractability: A Guide to the Theory of NP-Completeness.* W. H. Freeman, San Francisco.

Gill, J. T. (1977) Computational complexity of probabilistic Turing machines. *SIAM Journal of Computing*, **6**, 675–695.

Ginsburg, S. (1966) *The Mathematical Theory of Context-free Languages.* McGraw-Hill, New York.

Ginsburg, S. & Rose, G. F. (1963) Some recursively unsolvable problems in ALGOL-like languages. *Journal of ACM*, **10**, 29–47.

Gödel, K. (1931) On formally undecidable propositions of Principia Mathematica and related systems, I. *Monatshefte für Mathematik und Physik*, **38**, 173–198. (Reprinted in translation in Davis, 1965.)

Harary, F. (1969) *Graph Theory.* Addison–Wesley, Reading, Massachusetts.

Hartmanis, J. (1967) Context-free languages and Turing machine computations. *Proceedings of Symposia in Applied Mathematics*, **19**, American Mathematical Society, Providence, Rhode Island.

Hartmanis, J. (1978) *Feasible Computations and Provable Complexity Properties.* SIAM, Philadelphia.

Hartmanis, J., Lewis, P. M. & Stearns, R. E. (1965) Hierarchies of memory limited computations. *IEEE* Conference Record on Switching Circuit Theory and Logical Design, 179–190. Ann Arbor, Michigan.

Hermes, H. (1965) *Enumerability, Decidability, Computability.* Springer-Verlag, New York.

Hopcroft, J. E. & Karp, R. M. (1973) An $n^{5/2}$ algorithm for maximum matchings in bipartitle graphs. *SIAM* Journal of Computing, **2**, 225–231.

Hopcroft, J. E. & Ullman, J. D. (1968) Decidable and undecidable questions about automata. *Journal of ACM*, **15**, 317–324.

Hopcroft, J. E. & Ullman, J. D. (1969) *Formal Languages and their Relation to Automata.* Addison–Wesley, Reading, Massachusetts.

Hopcroft, J. E. & Ullman, J. D. (1979) *Introduction to Automata Theory, Languages, and Computation.* Addison–Wesley, Reading, Massachusetts.

Horowitz, E. & Sahni, S. (1978) *Fundamentals of Computer Algorithms.* Computer Science Press, Potomac, Maryland.

Karp, R. M. (1972) Reducibility among combinatorial problems. In *Complexity of Computer Computations* (eds R. E. Miller and J. W. Thatcher), pp. 85–104.

Kleene, S. C. (1936) General recursive functions of natural numbers. *Mathematische Annalen*, **112**, 727–742. (Reprinted in Davis, 1965.)

Kleene, S. C. (1952) *Introduction to Metamathematics.* D. Van Nostrand, New York.

Kowalski, R. (1979) *Logic for Problem Solving.* North Holland, Amsterdam.

Kruskal, J. B. (1956) On the shortest spanning subtree of a graph and the travelling salesman problem. *Proceedings of the American Mathematical Society*, **7**, 48–50.

Kuroda, S. Y. (1964) Classes of languages and linear-bounded automata. *Information and Control*, **7**, 207–223.

Ladner, R. E. (1975) On the structure of polynomial time reducibility. *Journal of ACM*, **22**, 155–171.

Landweber, P. S. (1963) Three theorems on phrase structure grammars of type 1. *Information and Control*, **6**, 131–136.

Landweber, P. S. (1964) Decision problems of phrase structure grammars. *PGEC*, **13**, 354–362.

Lawler, E., Lenstra, J. K., Rinnooy Kan, A. H. G. & Shmoys, D. B. (1984) *The Travelling Salesman Problem* (in press).

Lewis, H. R. & Papadimitriou, C. H. (1981) *Elements of the Theory of Computation.* Prentice-Hall, Englewood Cliffs, NJ.

Manna, Z. (1974) *Mathematical Theory of Computation*, McGraw-Hill, New York.

McKeown, G. P. & Rayward-Smith, V. J. (1982) *Mathematics for Computing.* Macmillan Press, London.

McNaughton, R. (1982) *Elementary Computability, Formal Languages and Automata.* Prentice-Hall, Englewood Cliffs, NJ.

Miller, R. E. & Thatcher, J. W., eds (1972) *Complexity of Computer Computations.* Plenum Press, New York.

Minsky, M. L. (1967) *Computation: Finite and Infinite Machines.* Prentice-Hall, Englewood Cliffs, NJ.

Péter, R. (1967) *Recursive Functions.* Academic Press, New York.

Post, E. (1936) Finite combinatory processes. Formulation I. *Journal of Symbolic Logic*, **1**, 103–105. (Reprinted in Davis, 1965.)

Post, E. (1946) A variant of a recursively unsolvable problem. *Bulletin of the American Mathematical Society*, **52**, 264–268.

Rabin, M. O. (1963) Probabilistic automata. *Information and Control*, **6**, 230–245.

Rabin, M. O. & Scott, D. (1959) Finite automata and their decision problems. *IBM Journal of Research and Development*, **3**, 114–125.

Rayward-Smith, V. J. (1983) *A First Course in Formal Language Theory.* Blackwell Scientific Publications, Oxford.

Schutzenberger, M. P. (1963) On context-free languages and pushdown automata. *Information and Control*, **3**, 372–375.

Shepherdson, J. C. & Sturgis, H. E. (1963) Computability of recursive functions. *Journal of ACM*, **10**, 217–255.

Stockmeyer, L. J. (1976) The polynomial time hierarchy. *Theoretical Computer Science*, **3**, 1–22.

Strassen, V. (1969) Gaussian elimination is not optimal. *Numerische Mathematik*, **13**, 354–356.

Traub, J. F., ed. (1976) *Algorithms and Complexity: New Directions and Recent Results.* Academic Press, New York.

Turing, A. M. (1936) On computable numbers with an application to the Entscheidungsproblem. *Proceedings of the London Mathematical Society* (Series 2), **42**, 230–265. (Reprinted in Davis, 1965.)

Index